THE HAUNTED SMILE

ALSO BY LAWRENCE J. EPSTEIN

A Treasury of Jewish Anecdotes

A Treasury of Jewish Inspirational Stories

LAWRENCE J. EPSTEIN

THE HAUNTED SMILE

THE STORY OF
JEWISH COMEDIANS
IN AMERICA

PublicAffairs · NEW YORK

BOOK DESIGN BY JENNY DOSSIN

Library of Congress Cataloging-in-Publication data
Epstein, Lawrence J. (Lawrence Jeffrey)
The haunted smile: the story of Jewish comedians in America / Lawrence J. Epstein.
p. cm.
Includes bibliographical references and index.
ISBN 1-891620-71-1
1. Jewish comedians—United States—History.
2. Jewish wit and humor—History and criticism.
3. American wit and humor—History and criticism. I. Title.
PN3035.E67 2001
792.7'028'089924—dc21
2001031869

FIRST EDITION
1 3 5 7 9 10 8 6 4 2

This book was written in memory of my mother

LILLIAN SCHEINERT EPSTEIN

whose kindness, wisdom, love, and laughter echo across time.

CONTENTS

INTRODUCTION: The World of Jewish Comedians   *ix*

I

THE GOLDEN DOOR
AND THE VELVET CURTAIN
1890–1930

1. The Land of Hope and Tears: Comedians and
   Immigrant America   3
2. Curtain Up and Curtain Down: The Age of Vaudeville   21

II

THE YEARS OF FEAR
1930–1950

3. Theater of the Mind: Radio's Finest Hour   55
4. Laughing in the Dark: Films   79
5. The Jewish Alps: The Rise of the Borscht Belt   104

Contents

III

THE YEARS OF ACCEPTANCE
1950–1965

6. The Magic Box: The American Television Revolution   129
7. "Is There Any Group I Haven't Offended?": The
   Changing World of Stand-up Comedy   155

IV

THE YEARS OF TRIUMPH
1965–PRESENT

8. "I Need the Eggs": Jewish Comic Filmmakers   195
9. Masters of Their Domain: Comedy All Over the Place   220
10. Kosher at Last: Jewish Women Comedians   253
11. The Cost of Victory: The Psychological and Social
    World of American Jewish Comedians   270
12. Not the Last Laugh: The Future of Jewish Comedians
    in America   278

APPENDIX: Schlemiels and Nudnicks: The Sources
and Nature of Jewish Humor   287

REFERENCES   309

ACKNOWLEDGMENTS   331

INDEX   343

THE WORLD OF

JEWISH COMEDIANS

Jerry Seinfeld was standing in front of a live audience. "I grew up in Massapequa on Long Island," he began. Pausing for a second with the comic timing he had perfected, he then explained. "It's an old Indian word meaning 'by the mall.'" When the laughter died down, he continued, "My folks just moved to Florida this past year. They didn't want to move to Florida, but they're in their sixties and that's the law."

The audience loved his jokes, but it wasn't always so easy for Seinfeld. In his early twenties, on the same day he graduated college, he made his first stand-up comedy appearance at New York's Catch a Rising Star. It was open-mike night, and the young comedian had his chance. He walked up to the microphone and froze.

He managed to blurt out the subjects of his would-be jokes but not the jokes themselves. He stood there saying words: "The beach. Driving. Shopping. Parents." Unable to continue, he left the stage.

Seinfeld's story, as all American television viewers know, had a happy ending. That is so, in part, because Seinfeld had enormous talent, incredible determination, and a desire for perfection. His comedic talents simply wouldn't be denied.

But Jerry Seinfeld also had another weapon: the rich wealth of the tradition of Jewish comedy. Seinfeld was his generation's follow-up to Jack Benny, the Marx Brothers, George Burns, and literally hundreds of others.

This embarrassingly rich crop of American Jewish comedians defies common sense. In 1979, for example, *Time* estimated that whereas Jews made up only 3 percent of the American population, fully 80 percent of professional comedians were Jewish.

The story of Jewish comedians in America is one of triumph and success. But their stage smile is tinged with a sadness. It is haunted by the Jewish past, by the deep strains in American Jewish life—the desire to be accepted and the concern for a culture disappearing—by the centuries of Jewish life too frequently interrupted by hate, and by the knowledge that too often for Jewish audiences a laugh masked a shudder. The comedians' story in America includes bitter encounters with anti-Semitism and the lures of an attractive culture along the way. The jokes these comedians told, their gags, and their nervous patter need to be set alongside the obstacles they overcame.

However haunted the smile might be, though, ultimately it was a smile that won America's heart. Jewish comedians have achieved unprecedented acceptance. George Burns, Milton Berle, Fanny Brice and their contemporary heirs—Woody Allen, Joan Rivers, and Jerry Seinfeld—stand at the very center of American humor.

Not only are their individual achievements etched in our collective cultural consciousness, but as a group these comedians occupy a crucial place in contemporary American culture as well.

They were all extraordinary entertainers, providing an endless parade of gags, an unstoppable flow of jokes, and a unique slant on life and on society. They provided audiences with a diversion from the strains of family, work, and community life as well as the struggles of participating in the human condition. The comedians offered audiences consolation through laughter in times of distress. They played a game of wit, allowing audience members to laugh at language, at unexpected turns of logic, at improbable situations. They bound the diverse members of the American community to one another; Americans who could laugh together didn't fight. Finally, the comedians gave their audiences a weapon, characteristically satire, to confront life's unfairness.

Beyond being extremely talented entertainers, however, Jewish comedians have fulfilled a special mission in American life, serving as the most important mediators between Jews and American culture. They exemplified two great themes of American Jewish life: assimilation and the search for an American Jewish identity. The comedians gave Jews strategies to survive entering and adapting to American culture and reduced anxiety about that adaptation. They gained for Jews acceptance from an alien Gentile culture and did so in a way that was not threatening to middle America. They had power and control over an audience when such authority wasn't yet available to Jews in the wider society and, by doing so, illustrated that other Jews could also eventually achieve such authority. They also provided a cultural identity for the many nonreligious American Jews. And above all, they made Jews proud.

But the Jewish comedians did more than just bring the American community to the Jewish one. They brought the Jewish community to the wider American culture, ultimately completely transforming the very nature of American comedy.

The attractions of Jewish comedy for the wider American audience are more elusive than for the Jews themselves. Still, even as the comedians used their humor to separate Jew from Gentile, even as the nebbishes, schlemiels, kibitzers, and gonifs of Jewish humor found their way into American homes and hearts, even as Jewish antic and chaotic routines strangled reason, American audiences loved the humor. Traveling far from the homey folksiness of a Mark Twain or a Will Rogers, American humor gathered in its Jewish influences and changed completely.

The major reasons for this embrace of Jewish humor involved the changes in American society itself. Searching for a way to deal with the emerging anxieties of the modern age, America turned to the Jews, the masters of handling history's troubles. Jewish humor, so useful in helping generations of anxious Jews, was called to action to serve the similar needs of the wider American community. An immigrant generation found in the Jews a people repeatedly practiced in starting over again in a new place while feeling marginal and scared. A depression generation saw in the Jews a people who had stared poverty in the face for two thousand years and survived, families and pride intact. After World War II, the United States confronted a seemingly invincible Soviet threat, a threat that included the ever present possibility of nuclear annihilation. The United States eventually grew into a society marked by generational, racial, and gender conflicts. It became a society divided by an unpopular war in Vietnam. Americans felt increasingly confused by divorce, the physical and emotional separation of families, a political structure they increasingly believed corrupt, a changing racial mix, the radical change in the role of women in the society, drugs, a transformed sexual ethic, and much else.

Such a society understandably had profound anxieties. At the same time, though, the transformations were to some extent deeply wanted. Forbidden words and ideas could finally be expressed. Taboo but long-sought actions could be undertaken.

American society turned to the Jews to use humor in order to deal with its own anxieties and to vindicate its desires. Jewish comedians could draw on a tradition of dealing with anxiety-ridden lives, of mastering close family and communal ties in the face of those troubles, and of exploring the widest ranges of language to express their deepest feelings.

In each generation, Jewish comedians were able to find in Jewish tradition, culture, and history a way to express the feelings of the wider American culture in which they lived. They drew on their heritage in ways they themselves didn't always understand. As they used that heritage to find ways to express truths about America, they transformed American culture, making Jews and Jewishness acceptable, even enviable.

Jewish comedians had several valuable assets to aid them in this effort. They had an expansive linguistic tradition that prized and rewarded quick thinking and a quicker tongue. The Yiddish cultural tradition they inherited nurtured both self-mockery and the mockery of the powerful. As history's most famous outsiders, the Jews had developed a survival instinct, an alertness bred from a fear that was almost always justified, an early warning system of the feelings of the majority culture. This instinct could often help them see where a society was going before it went there. In America, this survival instinct was not so much needed to predict, forestall, or prepare for organized acts of hatred against Jews as it was used to heighten Jewish sensitivities to majority-group anxieties.

Jewish comedians could sense majority anxieties early and transform them into humor, giving these anxieties a shape and a name as well as a way to cope. In America such insights would allow

Jewish comedians to identify and meet the audience's deepest emotional needs.

Only in America could Jewish comedians—indeed, Jews in general—have succeeded as they did. After all, as *New York Times* columnist Frank Rich has suggested, the very basis of American history was that insecure immigrants came to settle the land. Jews, the most insecure, the most common of immigrants, could understandably serve as a symbol for Americans as they could for no other people.

Had Jews come earlier in large numbers, they might have been fully assimilated, but they mostly entered with large numbers of other immigrants and just when mass media developed. They were in America when vaudeville, radio, motion pictures, and television were being introduced. This lucky coincidence, combined with their enormous talents, gave them a chance to enter and transform these fields.

Of course, Jewish comedians still operated within the larger comic tradition of America. Focusing specifically on Jewish comedians is not to suggest that they were funnier or better than Gentile comedians or that the extraordinary contributions by comedians who were not Jewish should be ignored or demeaned.

It is also important to stress that there were often enormous differences among Jewish comedians themselves. Some lived and breathed their Jewish heritage; others had an ongoing conflict with their Jewish identity. Some included a lot of Jewish material in their comedy, whereas others were careful to avoid Jewish content. Some used the techniques of Jewish humor and applied them to American culture, and others drew on American comic traditions. Although the differences among these comics are significant, the comedians nonetheless shared characteristics that made them part of a wider, equally diverse American Jewish community.

Seeing these comedians as particularly Jewish provides a distinct way to understand their humor, to recognize some of their comedy ancestors, and to see their place in entertainment history.

It is also helpful to understand the inherited background of Jewish comedy and the peculiar nature and language of Jewish humor in order to grasp the full contribution made by these comedians. For example, the comedians created types. One of the most famous Jewish comic types is the schlemiel, a clumsy, maladjusted, hard-luck loser. Sometimes, as in the classic schlemiels created by Woody Allen, this poor character is also profoundly neurotic. His one-liners comically reflect negative emotions ("When we played softball, I'd steal second, then feel guilty and go back") or a sense of being trapped by unfeeling institutions ("I went to a school for emotionally disturbed teachers").

With his small, thin frame, his dark glasses and sad face, Allen was a standing sight gag. His distinctive New York voice added to the effect as he told his audience the story. He'd been hunting and shot a moose, he confided to them. His story grows wilder as the seemingly dead moose awakens on the fender of the car. Allen, seeing the live moose, hatches a plan to get rid of it. He realizes that friends are having a costume party. He decides to go, pawning off the moose as his friends the Solomons. The moose goes to the party and is doing well until the prizes are finally handed out for the best costume and the Berkowitzes, who are a Jewish couple dressed as a moose, win. The real moose is understandably furious at this slight and locks horns with the well-costumed Berkowitzes. Allen then presumably walks in to find the couple unconscious. Figuring this is his chance, Allen then tells of scooping up the moose to dump him back in the woods. As it turns out, though, it is not the real moose he's gotten, but the Berkowitzes. The poor couple wakes up in the woods the next morning, only to be shot, stuffed, and eventually mounted at the New York Athletic Club. Allen concludes by noting the irony because the club is restricted.

Acceptance, disguise, discrimination, and fear—all could be found in Allen's humor, but so could a sort of wild, sometimes naive optimism. One typical scene is from the film *Play It Again, Sam*. Allen's character, Allan Felix, is newly separated from his wife. He goes to an art museum to find an attractive woman standing in front of a Jackson Pollock painting. Felix approaches her and asks what she thinks of the work. Her voice is flat as she responds: "It restates the negativeness of the universe. The hideous lonely emptiness of existence. Nothingness. The predicament of Man forced to live in a barren, Godless eternity like a tiny flame flickering in an immense void with nothing but waste, horror, and degradation forming a useless, bleak straitjacket in a black, absurd cosmos." Absorbing but ignoring this, Felix then asks, "What are you doing Saturday night?" The woman responds, "Committing suicide." Felix barely pauses. "What about Friday night?" he asks.

Allen's neurotic character, living in a death-drenched, frightening world, finds moments of solace through love and comedy. His comic ancestors, the Marx Brothers, collectively formed a different comic type, the free soul who doesn't so much criticize all social mores as mock and ignore them. The Marx Brothers created confusion wherever they went, playfully chased money and young women, and used an incredible range of comic tools—from Groucho's enormous mustache and endless wisecracking to Chico's ethnic accent and malapropisms to Harpo's pantomime in fright wig, bicycle horn, and large overcoat—to draw laughter. They created characters who were uncontrolled and unrestrained by rules of language, manners, or society's ways.

Groucho's lines are particularly pointed. Talking to a character played by Margaret Dumont in *Animal Crackers*, Groucho says, "You've got beauty, style, money. You've got money, haven't you? If not we'll stop right now." In *Duck Soup*, he says to her, "They're fighting for your honor. Which is more than you ever did."

Some Jewish comedians adopted comic types with the very characteristics of anti-Semitic stereotypes and ended up challenging and overcoming the stereotypes with humor. Jack Benny, though not specifically playing a Jewish character, went out of his way to stress his character's stinginess. For example, Benny used to say that instead of bringing a date flowers he'd bring her seeds. He was once invited to throw out the first ball at a World Series game and delighted the crowd by putting the ball in his pocket and sitting down.

Of course, Jews developed many other comic types: the fool (Ed Wynn and Rodney Dangerfield), the social critic (Lenny Bruce and Mort Sahl), and the observer (Jerry Seinfeld). All these types played off central aspects of Jewish humor and, in the end, played the same roles in society.

The pangs of recognition honed by Seinfeld, the neuroses of Allen, and the chaos of the Marx Brothers reflected the ages in which these comedians lived and the tastes of their audience. But ultimately they came from the same sources: Yiddish culture and the emotions and experiences associated with being an immigrant.

Yiddish entered American comedy through individual expressions rather than as a complete language. The words chosen by comedians were sometimes vulgar, whereas other words were selected because the sound of the word itself was funny, so that audiences identified Yiddish as inherently comic. Of course, Yiddish was more than just a particular vocabulary. Its words were spoken with what became known as Jewish rhythm. This rhythm was frequently characterized by answering one question with another, framing a rhetorical question and then answering it, talking in a singsong cadence that emerged from the method students used to study the Talmud together, and using a syntax dependent on inverting words in a sentence.

Jackie Mason is among the most famous Jewish comedians who

still employs a virtually undiluted Jewish rhythm. In one routine about psychiatry Mason mocks the analyst's attempt to have him search for his real self. Mason wonders, "What if I find the real me, and I find that he's even worse than I am? I don't make enough for myself—I need a partner?" The psychiatrist then asks for a payment of seventy-five dollars. This sets Jackie off again; he says to the analyst, "What if you're the real me? Then you owe me seventy-five dollars." The defeated psychiatrist finally says, "If you promise never to come back, we'll call it even."

Jewish humor did not just emerge from a particular language, of course. Jewish culture is by its nature extraordinarily verbal. Words form the center of study, of prayer, and of entertainment. The emphasis on language and on the argumentative patterns of Talmudic reasoning provided Jews with a style of thinking.

Jewish theology also contributed. Jews were permitted, even encouraged, to question. There is no prescribed set of beliefs a Jew must follow. It is a common tradition, for example, to question God's ways not only to denounce evil in the world but also to search for truth. Truth is of the highest value in the Jewish tradition. If God is allowed to be challenged, then it is understandable, and even expected, that less powerful forms of authority (parents, bosses, societies) can also be questioned. Such a challenge to authority is a hallmark of Jewish humor. Jewish comedians were notable in their willingness to test their audiences' sense of which subjects and words were acceptable.

Of course, many people ascribe the particular pathos of Jewish humor to the suffering the Jews underwent and the marginal existence they led in various countries. It is a common understanding that humor appealed to Jews in Eastern Europe as a form of therapy, a way to manage the stresses of daily life. That life was routinely lived in poverty and separateness and was sometimes cruelly punctuated by violence and death. Such an existence engendered humor, this explanation goes, as an outlet, a way of releasing the tensions.

Comedy did have certain unique virtues in this respect. It provided Jews with acknowledgment, acceptance, approval, and applause, all experiences that Jews rarely felt when confronting Gentile cultures. Comedy therefore played a psychological, even political, role in helping the Jews deal with majority cultures.

The stresses of immigrant life played a similar role in shaping especially the first generation of American Jewish comedians in the early years of the twentieth century. As the children of immigrants, they were neither insiders, privy to power or easy passage through American life, nor outsiders, living in a foreign country dreaming of America as the Golden Land. This precarious identity provided a particular perspective, a skepticism about life in general, a distrust of institutions, and a palpable anxiety that sometimes found its way into humor.

Although there had been Jewish comedians before the immigrant generation, the story of Jewish comedians as a national treasure can most usefully begin with those who made their names in vaudeville and burlesque: George Burns, Milton Berle, Jack Benny, Sophie Tucker, Fanny Brice, Ed Wynn, Bert Lahr, and many others.

These comedians developed "tags," characteristics that audiences could use to define them. Milton Berle, for instance, became well known for stealing jokes from other comedians. One of his lines was about seeing another comic at work: "He was so funny I almost dropped my pad and pencil." Berle had started his career early. While still under ten, he cut out a piece of fur from a hand warmer his mother owned and pasted the fur under his nose. He then entered a Charlie Chaplin imitation contest, twisted his lips, walked with a swaying motion—and won.

Fanny Brice deliberately affected a Yiddish accent even though she could neither read nor speak Yiddish.

George Burns, having gone through a succession of partners (including a trained seal), ultimately found in Gracie Allen his perfect partner. Playing off Gracie's sweet silliness, Burns became a consummate straight man, using his cigar for dramatic pause and his bemused face and gravelly voice for setups and observations.

These early Jewish comedians did not always have an easy time. Ed Wynn's father disowned him when Wynn entered show business. Jack Benny turned to comedy after failing at music. But one principal asset that many of them did have was a Jewish mother who was a great, positive influence on their lives. Sadie Berle, Milton's mother, used to hire people to sit in the audience and laugh at his jokes She once hired Henny Youngman, then an aspiring comedian, and paid him fifty cents to laugh at Berle's act. Youngman later commented that he thought the act was so good he would have done it for forty cents.

Minnie Marx, mother of the Marx Brothers, was the one who decided that the five brothers should be in show business. They began as a musical act, and it was only when the audience in Nacogdoches, Texas, left the theater to watch a wild mule that comedy entered their routine. Furious at the audience, Groucho began to insult them when they returned. The audience thought the insults were part of the act and laughed uproariously.

Sadie Berle and Minnie Marx were emblematic of a generation of Jewish women who were not performers but who took their drive, their intelligence, their unbreakable will, and their determination to succeed in show business, and transferred that dynamic energy to the careers of their children, especially their sons.

The early comedians also had to deal with questions of assimilation: How much should they, could they, separate themselves from their Jewish heritage? Jewish comedians became the shock troops of American Jewish assimilation, gaining acceptance decades before the wider Jewish community did. Many of these comedians embraced both Gentile values and Gentile women with great fervor. Others struggled to define their own relationship to the more traditional organized Jewish community. Jewish comedians therefore became among the first to reflect, although in an exaggerated way, the tortured relationship American Jews sometimes had with their religion and its culture.

Jewish comedians frequently stood outside the community. They were tougher than Jewish humorists such as Sam Levenson who told heartwarming stories about loving families coping with adversity. Jewish comics were harsher in their evaluation of life and the Jewish religion and community. Lenny Bruce, the harshest of the comics, would compare Christian and Jewish ideas about God: "Christians are lucky because your God, the Christian God, is all over. . . . He saves you . . . He's been in three films . . . The Jewish God—where is the Jewish God? He's on a little box nailed to the doorjamb. In a mezuzah. I told my super, 'Don't paint God.'"

Many comedians, most notably Jackie Mason, stood someplace in between, making fun of Jews and simultaneously standing with them. Mason masterfully lampoons his people while embracing them. "Every Jew loves food. What do you think Jews talk about for breakfast? Where to eat lunch. At lunch, where should we have dinner? Where should we have coffee? . . . You never see a Jew in a bar except if he gets lost looking for a piece of cake."

But it wasn't all laughs. Samuel Janus, a psychologist looking for a common comedic psyche, spent ten years interviewing seventy-six Jewish comedians, including George Burns, Milton Berle, Sid Caesar, and many others. In 1979, he told a meeting of the American Psychological Association that Jewish humor emerged from depression and intense alienation from the culture. "Comedy," he argued, "is a defense mechanism to ward off the aggression and hostility of others." These comedians, it turned out, were very unhappy people.

Little did the Jewish comedians before the 1960s know it, but American audiences would ultimately joyfully accept overtly Jewish types, language, and humor, and Jewish comedy would reconfigure the very shape of American humor.

Jerry Seinfeld, then, was not alone on that stage at Catch a Rising Star. Like the Jews themselves, he wouldn't quit. The world saying no became just an incentive to go on. Seinfeld became a great success in America, but in the tradition of his people, he continues to search for what to make of that success.

The story of the ultimate triumph of Jewish comedians can best begin by going back to the turn of the twentieth century, back to a time when Jews in large numbers were arriving in the Golden Land, and when those Jews were about to make their explosive entrance onto the American comedic stage.

I

THE GOLDEN DOOR
AND THE VELVET CURTAIN

1890–1930

1

THE LAND OF
HOPE AND TEARS

COMEDIANS AND IMMIGRANT AMERICA

M eyer Kubelsky's father had to struggle for nearly ten years before saving enough money to send his son to the Golden Land, the one place where hope still breathed, where Jews, through hard work and cheerful optimism, could survive, the land where even the Cossacks could not ride their horses. Meyer's father, a wine merchant, had followed the rules and gotten a passport for his son. Then, with the frightening control the authorities so arbitrarily exercised over Jewish lives, a government official told the family that despite the passport Meyer would not be allowed to leave. Distraught, the father concocted a desperate plan. He knew a man who delivered empty bottles to the Kubelsky wine shop and tavern. The man, seeking to help the young Kubelsky and to make a profit, agreed to the plan: Meyer would be smuggled out of Lithuania, hiding under a shipment of the bottles.

The escape was successful. Meyer made his way to Hamburg, a principal departure point for ships to America, and in 1889 he landed in New York Harbor. Ellis Island had not yet been designated as the entry point for new immigrants, so Meyer entered the country through Castle Garden. He remained in New York for just a few days before setting out across the country to Chicago, where some of his landsmen had already settled and where he would eventually marry and become the father of a son named Benjamin, later known as Jack Benny.

Such stories were not unique. Although most accounts of Jewish immigration to America begin at the New World's gateway, typically New York, in fact the effort to reach such debarkation points as Hamburg was often the most dangerous part of the entire journey. Sophie Tucker, for example, was born on the road from Russia across Poland. Her mother and young brother were traveling in a large wagon when Sophie's mother tapped the driver on the shoulder to let him know that the baby inside her had decided to enter the world. The driver promptly let the expectant mother and the two-year-old boy named Philip off the wagon— and then drove away. Luckily, there was a house nearby, and the mother and son got there in time for Sophie to be born. Sophie Tucker's mother was seventeen years old.

Marrying so young was common. Another young man living in Eastern Europe named Louis Birnbaum was sixteen when he married Dorothy Bluth, fourteen. Two years and two children later, the couple decided that their future lay in the faraway land that all young Jewish people were talking about. After a two-week journey, they arrived in New York, where they would eventually have twelve children, the most famous of whom grew up to be George Burns.

Many immigrants traveled alone and, like Meyer Kubelsky, would meet other immigrants in America and get married. Sam Marx, for instance, emigrated from Alsace wearing a green topcoat and a black stovepipe hat. Minnie Schoenberg came to America at fifteen from Dornum, Germany, where her father was a magician and her mother a harpist. Sam married her when Minnie was eighteen, and together they raised the most brilliant, riotous, hilarious brother act in American history, sons who would define comedy for their generation and beyond.

Most of the comedians who became famous at the beginning of the twentieth century had ancestors who left Russia or Poland and ventured across hostile land only to make a dangerous ocean crossing and to disembark poverty stricken onto the shores of their dreamland. They joined the German Jewish immigrants who had come earlier in the nineteenth century and the Sephardic Jews who had come even earlier.

Some of these comedians' ancestors had come earlier as well. George Jessel's grandfather, Edward Aaron Jessel, entered America in 1835, immediately joined in the gold rush, and eventually became an auctioneer in Chicago. Jessel's father was a playwright who then traveled the country selling what he could.

Also, not all immigrants were poor. Milton Berle's father and the rest of the Berlinger family came from Wamp, Germany, and were well off. The first Uncle Miltie (Milton Berle's actual uncle for whom he was named) would rise to become the vice president of the Ex-Lax Corporation. The Berlingers were deeply proud of their German Jewish heritage and, like some others in that community, believed that the East European Jews were beneath them. Berle's mother's family came from Poland and was poor. His father's family was so upset at the match that they disowned him.

These families of the great comedians were part of a historic movement of the Jewish people. Between 1880 and 1920, 2 million

Jews from Eastern Europe came to the United States. One-third of East European Jews left their homeland, with 80 percent coming to knock on America's Golden Door.

They came for a variety of reasons. They were mostly poor, of course, and they saw in America a chance to pick up the gold that surely lay untouched on every street. Jews were persecuted as well. The sad legacy of the hatred of the Jews had its own poignant nineteenth-century chapters.

Still, up until the last two decades of the century, Jews prayed and adapted; they rarely left their Russian villages. Despite the crushing poverty, most Jews accepted their condition as a seemingly permanent element of Jewish existence.

The generally optimistic spirit of the age buoyed the Jews and allowed them to perceive continuing Russian hatred of the Jews as a historical anachronism doomed to oblivion by what they sensed would be the inevitably humanizing effects of a spreading European enlightenment. In time, the Jews generally believed, czarist Russia would evolve into a democracy that would grant them civil and religious rights. They saw no urgent need to leave their homes when the light of reason streaming across Europe was headed their way.

These hopes evaporated immediately after the assassination of Czar Alexander II of Russia in 1881. Although Jews were not involved in the attack, the new czar, Alexander III, blamed them. The czar had a fanatic hater of Jews as a teacher, Konstantin Pobedonostev, who wielded immense power in the government. Together they developed a neatly symmetrical solution to what Pobedonostev termed Russia's Jewish problem: one-third of the Jews would emigrate, one-third would be converted to Russian Orthodoxy, and one-third would starve to death. At the time, Russian Jews constituted half the Jews in the world.

In April 1881, the first organized attack against the Jews prompted by the assassination began. Although pogroms had occurred earlier in Russian history, this new fury was coordinated and supported by the government, and had clear political and economic goals. About thirty more attacks took place just in April. They continued into May and then resumed in July and August. Over time, the increasingly violent pogroms were characterized by the murders of individuals or whole families, numerous sexual assaults, the looting of property, and the burning of houses and land.

The Russian government, arguing that the peasants had to be protected from the purported economic domination by Jews, began passing laws (known as the "May Laws") that forbade the Jews from returning to their hometowns and that severely restricted their access to a high school education.

The military draft was another factor sending Jews out of the land. The May Laws and hatred of the Jews did not prevent the czar from continuing the practice of conscripting Jewish boys. At the age of eight, they were drafted as cantonists, or military trainees. They continued with that training for ten years at which time they were drafted into the army. The young Jews were obligated to serve in the army for twenty-five years. They were not, of course, allowed to follow Jewish customs during their service; religious Jews were forcibly fed pork products. Every Russian town had a quota to fill. As the *New York Evening Post* wryly commented in 1905 about Jews being conscripted to fight in the Russo-Japanese War: "Russia, while denying her Jewish subjects all civil rights, does not object to sending them to Manchuria to stop Japanese bullets."

The increasingly tenuous lives that the Jews of Russia led became simply intolerable. These realities prompted especially young Jews to conclude that their parents' hopes for a democratic Russia were dangerous delusions. The young unblinkingly looked at the lives they were going to lead and realized that escape to

America, however wrenching the departure, however uncertain the prospects, provided the best hope for a place where their dreams and their futures would not be crushed.

So, more and more, the younger generation of Jews left Eastern Europe. The trip itself was made affordable even for the poverty-stricken masses of Jews by the increasing use of steamships, which could make the journey across the Atlantic in eight to fourteen days depending on the weather, rather than the previous one to three months. The steamships journeyed to America to collect freight to take back to Europe and saw in potential immigrants a way to make extra money by filling their empty ships on the way west. Most Jews found it possible to save the thirty-four dollars it cost to go from Hamburg to New York. Of course, the steamship companies tried to make the voyage appear attractive. The advertising posters showed parties on board the ships as potential immigrants headed toward the land of liberty.

For its part, America needed the immigrants. Six hundred thousand Civil War deaths had left a huge shortage of workers for decades to come. This happened at the same time as the American gears of capitalism shifted forcefully into forward. Of course, America had tremendous natural resources. These, combined with the effects of the Industrial Revolution in providing new machinery, completely altered the economic landscape. Still, people were needed to do the work. Between 1865 and 1900, the population of the United States doubled in large part because of immigration and despite the losses from the Civil War. Manufactured goods increased sevenfold. This led to a quadrupling of America's national wealth. America desperately needed more healthy workers if the boom was to continue.

Almost all of the Jewish immigrants were, indeed, healthy. This was not only a tribute to their hygienic habits and their kosher diets, but also reflected the simple economic fact that steamship lines would not accept as passengers anyone in obvious bad health. The companies were held responsible not only for returning the ill back to Europe but were charged one hundred dollars by immigration authorities for each of those passengers as well. Indeed, on the ships themselves, the baggage was fumigated and antiseptic baths were given. Passengers stayed in seaport hotels for about four days, and then, thirty-six hours before departure, they were deloused again and put in quarantine on a clean side of the hotel.

The ships had three classes of passengers: first class, second class, and steerage—the unhappy alternative most Jews were forced to choose because of their economic straits. Steerage (named for where the steering mechanisms for the ship had once been placed) was on the lower deck. A thousand people were packed onto the deck for the voyage. People wore their clothes the entire trip, slept when they could and where they had been placed, felt most forcefully the rocking of the boat during storms, and had to endure a pervasive stench that inevitably accompanied the overcrowding.

For those immigrants who came to New York, the first stop was actually the Hudson or East River Pier. First- and second-class passengers were examined on board and allowed to enter. Steerage passengers were sent on a ferry or barge to Ellis Island to be examined. Sometimes, of course, hours were spent on the boat even before being sent to Ellis Island.

When the immigrants finally were off the ferry or barge and, for the first time in weeks, felt the land beneath their tired feet, some bent down and kissed the ground.

As they came onto Ellis Island, landing cards pinned to their clothing, they went in groups of thirty to the front door and into the baggage room. From the baggage room, the immigrants went up the staircase to the second floor. There was a line inspection, with officials searching for immigrants who had any difficulty breathing or made odd facial expressions (indicating mental prob-lems). Blue chalk marks were put on the lapel of immigrants who required further scrutiny. An *X* chalk mark indicated a mental ill-ness was suspected. If the *X* was circled, the inspector believed that the immigrant showed definite signs of such an illness.

Of course, for immigrants this health inspection was both odd and profoundly embarrassing. Many of the Jews had never been to a doctor. Their religion and cultural upbringing made them very uneasy about exposing even part of themselves in a large room filled with strangers.

Those who passed the health inspection went to the Registry Hall, a hot and crowded place where immigrants sat on benches waiting for their names to be called. The average wait was five hours. The hall was divided into sections based on the country of origin. The immigrant was eventually called up to see the official, who used the manifest lists with their twenty-nine questions to grill the immigrant. Could the immigrant read? Write?

The trickiest question of all involved work. Immigrants were asked if they had jobs waiting. It might be assumed that a positive answer to this question would help the immigrant. In fact, those immigrants who had jobs waiting were sent back; they were seen as taking jobs from Americans. Young, single women without sponsors were detained until social workers could find someone to sponsor them.

After the Registry Hall, immigrants descended the stairs (dubbed by them the "stairs of separation") and went either to the detention room or to the "kissing post," so-called because they could see the people—often their families—who were coming to meet them. They then went to the service center where, for exam-ple, they could exchange money, and, finally, they left Ellis Island—the place the immigrants dubbed the Isle of Hope, the Isle of Tears—and walked through the Golden Door to America.

Most Jewish immigrants to America went first to New York City. Some, like Henny Youngman's father, headed to the Lower East Side and the Mills Hotel, which charged twenty-five cents a night and was popular with the new immigrants who didn't have waiting families. Others became boarders with families. Soon the Lower East Side became a teeming symbol of immigrant Jewish life.

In 1880, there were 80,000 Jews living in New York. By 1910, that number had swelled to 1,250,000. By one estimate, a typical block consisted of 2,781 people—and no bathtubs. George Burns, for example, lived at 259 Rivington Street with a coal-burning stove in the kitchen used for both cooking and heating. The three bathrooms for the building were three flights down the stairs and out into the yard. The family lit the apartment by gaslight, and when the gas ran out they had to put a quarter in the meter. Baths were a special problem in the household. On Thursdays, Burns's mother would boil water and pour it into her washtub. The girls would jump into the washtub first, one at a time, moving quickly, and then the boys rushed in, each in turn, hoping the water would still be hot when they got there. No one dared hope the water would still be clean.

Eddie Cantor's mother died a few months before his second birthday, his father either died or disappeared soon after, and his grandmother Esther Kantrowitz raised the young boy. The poor woman took her grandson and moved to a basement apartment at 47 Henry Street. The apartment had three rooms, a living room, kitchen, and bedroom. They rarely had money. Once, when Cantor needed to see a dentist but couldn't afford to go, he earned money by going down to the docks and bringing new immigrants to boardinghouses. The renters paid Cantor a small commission, and soon he got his teeth fixed.

Cantor's strongest memory was the heat in the summer. As in

all tenements, gas jets and steam boilers supplemented the sun's heat. It could be unbearable; for example, in just eight days in 1896, 420 New Yorkers died from the heat. Tenement dwellers had other worries as well, particularly fires caused by the heat and the smoking of cigarettes.

A typical tenement building had six or seven stories, usually with four apartments on each floor. Most front apartments had four rooms, whereas rear apartments had 325 square feet partitioned into three rooms. The back apartments were not desirable because of the foul smell coming from the shared privies in the backyard. One room in each apartment faced the street or other tenements, presumably to let in sunlight. The other rooms were so dark that a law was passed in 1901 requiring every room to have a window, whether or not the window faced the outdoors. Children frequently slept on orange crates or thick rugs. The ten- to twenty-dollar monthly rent could most commonly be paid only if a family took in boarders who slept on cots or folded beds, in a situation sadly reminiscent of their lives in steerage. Many women used the front room for piecework, sewing clothing, rolling cigars, gluing labels on cigar boxes, making artificial flowers, or other similar jobs.

The streets, too, were crowded. On Friday mornings in the market on Hester Street, a double row of pushcarts filled the area. People, struggling to prepare for the Sabbath—"Shabbes" in Yiddish—pushed and wiggled, looking for the perfect piece of fruit to eat. Fish was particularly popular for Shabbes dinner. Old men with beards behind the pushcarts screamed in Yiddish: *"Gutes frucht! Metziehs!"* meaning "Good fruit! Bargains!" Often they would interject English. "Three pennies for the whole lot" became *"Drei* pennies *die* whole lot."

Deprived for so long of the certainty that there would be food for the next meal, Jews embraced the abundance of food in the

Golden Land. Mothers, especially, urged their children to eat. Food was a living symbol of the Jewish drive for survival. A chicken on Shabbes meant a successful life. The aroma of a Shabbes meal sustained many with its rich assurances and its heady promises of even greater success.

These streets overflowed with boisterous merchants and were raucous with the teeming collective rhythms of immigrant life. The children played stickball when they could and looked for free ways to entertain one another. Eddie Cantor's first audience was made up of all the kids in his neighborhood. Cantor dated a young woman named Kitty Brookman when she was fourteen or fifteen. Although the romance didn't blossom, Kitty never quite got out of the comedy business. After marrying someone else, she later gave birth to a boy who grew up to be Mel Brooks.

The difficult life they led might have crushed others, but the Jews and other immigrants were survivors. They were mostly young and optimistic. They dwelled in the house of possibility. Their sense of adventure—exemplified in their willingness to leave Eastern Europe and journey to a new life—carried them through tough times. Additionally, the Jews had a healthy tradition of helping one another. *Landsmanshaften*, or mutual aid societies for people from the same city or town, sprang up, providing much- needed health insurance and for such matters as burials. The *landsmanshaften* supplemented the more fundamental unit of immigrant Jewish life: the family. For Jews the family meant not just the immediate or even extended family, but ultimately included the entire community. A sense of communal obligation encompassed all those within the immigrant Jewish world. When families were in trouble—when, for instance, a husband died or abandoned the family—others came to provide support.

Family in this broader sense was assumed by Jews to be part of life. Jews might (and did) complain about a spouse's habits, a child's truancy and bad manners, a parent's refusal to learn English, or an aunt or uncle's meddling. Sometimes they even did this in public, in the Bintel Brief column of the most famous of the Yiddish dailies, the *Forverts* (the *Jewish Daily Forward*). Letters were printed in the column, and then an editor would respond to them. The plaintive, despairing tone of many of the missives reflects the troubled communal substructure that betrays any attempt to romanticize immigrant life. But, despite the annoyances engendered by such a life, the assumption that, however meddlesome, a family was always there, a last resort in times of trouble, was ultimately comforting. Such an assumption would give Jewish comedians a tremendous psychological resource, not to mention generations of material.

There was also a strong religious life in the neighborhood. In 1905, the Lower East Side housed 350 congregations in synagogues and storefronts. An exciting Jewish cultural flowering was also taking place there. There were Yiddish newspapers (four dailies before World War I), books, and theater. Yiddish plays were filled with adoration of the "*Yiddische* mama," the Jewish mother. Almost every play had a wedding and a happy ending. This sentimental communal experience was vital in reassuring the Jews that their arduous trip across the Atlantic had not deprived them of their heritage.

In a way, the Yiddish theater was a counterpoint to vaudeville, which was more American. It is no accident that Burns, Berle, Benny, Cantor, Jessel, Brice, and the other comedians of that age did not go to the Yiddish theater, for they sought a larger stage. The great Yiddish stars, with rare exceptions, never achieved fame outside the Jewish community. Even at this point, there was a struggle within the American Jewish soul about whether they should embrace their tradition or their new land.

There were other attempts at community in the new country as well. Immigrant Jewish workers frequently joined together for common cause, attempting to organize unions. The 1909 strike by teenage women shirtwaist workers and the 1910 strike of sixty thousand largely male cloak makers provided huge victories for the workers and gave great strength to the International Ladies Garment Workers Union, which had been established in 1902.

Of course, not all Jews lived on the Lower East Side. The Marx Brothers grew up in Yorkville, a German neighborhood, and lived at 179 East Ninety-third Street. Bert Lahr lived at First Avenue and Eighty-fourth Street. Phil Silvers was born at 417 Pennsylvania Avenue in Brooklyn in 1911. His kitchen included an iron bathtub covered by a wooden plank that was used for ironing. As children, Milton Berle and George Jessel lived next door to each other at 68 and 66 West 118th Street in Harlem until the Berlinger family (Milton's mother changed the name for her son because she didn't think "Berlinger" would fit on a marquee) was evicted. Jack Benny grew up in Waukegan, Illinois, living over a butcher shop. Sophie Tucker was raised in Hartford and Ed Wynn in Philadelphia.

The young and poor found their escapes where they could. In the Lower East Side, the candy store became a social center, especially for an immigrant boy. "The candy store," the *New York Tribune* reported, "serves as a clubhouse where he can meet old friends and make new ones, as well as a haven of refuge and a safe retreat from the persecution of the corner policeman."

This last statement was no exaggeration. Many of the immigrant children were young thieves. George Burns always claimed that he took his name from the Burns Brothers coal yard. He and his brother would steal the coal, and neighbors would shout, "There go the Burns brothers." (This story may, of course, be apocryphal. George Burns enjoyed exaggerating the truth and bragged about it. His name could simply be a shortened form of his real name—Birnbaum—or even an attempt to "pass" as Irish.) He also claimed that he had gone to the Automat with a sister's hairpin, stood by the beef stew, and after someone bought the stew, Burns slipped in the hairpin, preventing the door from closing. He either stole the next stew for his own meal or sold it to another customer. Phil Silvers stole from pushcarts and sold stolen pipe. Fanny Brice stole gum from her mother's store and then began shoplifting until she was caught. Eddie Cantor stole from pushcarts. At thirteen, he stole a purse. Bert Lahr stole from local stores and resold the goods at an open market on Saturday mornings (the Sabbath to observant Jews). He once stole a pumpkin from a police officer. The cop knocked on the Lahrheim door only minutes after the theft. Young Irving Lahrheim had not turned out to be a very good thief; the pumpkin was sitting on the fire escape. Groucho Marx didn't exactly steal. His mother would give him six cents for a loaf of bread. He knew day-old bread cost only a nickel, so he'd buy that and keep the penny, sometimes earning a nickel a week, which was exactly his allowance. His mother always knew what he was doing; she let him continue because she thought it showed initiative.

These childish acts, born of a simple desire to eat and an environment that—indirectly, at least—encouraged such behavior, nevertheless had an effect. All of the comedians stopped stealing at a very young age. But the antiauthoritarian nature of such thievery helped make them feel apart not only from the rules of society but also from their own Jewish culture and sometimes, even, their families. It was a sort of assertion and transgression that would in subtle ways influence the Jewish comic voice.

Beyond frequent petty thievery, the emerging comedians also shared an active distaste for school. Unlike so many young Jews, who saw in education the gateway to all the splendors the new land had to offer, the young comedians found school either difficult or useless, or, more commonly, both. These young comedians were bright but spent a lot of time fantasizing about money and pleasure rather than reading books and learning. They were unable or unwilling to do regular work like their peers.

Jack Benny skipped school to play his violin in a theater when there were matinees. He quit school when he was thirteen. Bert Lahr did poorly in school and always felt trapped in a classroom. Fanny Brice was a truant and, unsurprisingly, had low grades. Henny Youngman never made it through high school. George Burns quit in the fifth grade. George Jessel managed all of eight months in school. Harpo Marx was thrown out of school in the second grade—literally. Two raucous classmates would take the poor young boy by his belt and shoulder and toss him out of the window on the first floor. One day he simply decided not to return.

Nor did the young comedians find much comfort in Jewish life. Jack Benny had a powerful memory of one Yom Kippur. He had joined his Orthodox father in the synagogue but walked out in the middle. His father hit him in the face with a prayer book. That night, Meyer Kubelsky tried, in his way, to apologize by saying that it was considered a great blessing to be hit with the prayer book on Yom Kippur.

Phil Silvers once refused to recite his lessons in Hebrew school, and the teacher slapped his palm with a ruler. Silvers then pushed the teacher back into a chair. When the teacher unbuckled his strap, Silvers ran away and never returned.

Groucho Marx's only memories of his bar mitzvah involved the fountain pen he received that, when it dripped, made unusual designs on his shirt. Henny Youngman didn't even have a bar mitzvah ceremony until sixty years after the normal age. Milton Berle had his bar mitzvah ceremony at Mount Zion Temple at 119th Street. The synagogue was strategically located because Berle was then appearing in a show and was scheduled to perform right after the ceremony. While preparing his speech, Berle had been tempted to mention the play in which he was appearing, but the thought struck him that although Mount Zion was a Reform temple, the reforms hadn't gone far enough to permit a commercial. (He was wrong. The rabbi, evidently at Berle's mother's suggestion, told the congregation about Milton's theatrical appearance.)

George Burns lived in a kosher home, but became disenchanted with religion at an early age. When his grandfather died, only seven men could be rounded up for the minimal prayer quorum, called a minyan, which required ten men. It became necessary to pay three men fifty cents each to take part. It was the necessity of paying that so bothered the young Burns.

Another crucial common element for many Jewish comedians was having a weak father who was fundamentally a failure in the New World and a strong, intelligent, ambitious mother. Sam Marx was a failed tailor, known in the neighborhood as "Misfit Sam" because he disdained the use of a tape measure, believing, with spectacular inaccuracy, that his tailor's eye was sufficient. There were very few repeat customers. Luckily, Sam was a good cook.

George Burns's father wanted to sing for a living in synagogues, not as a cantor but as a *ba'al tefillah,* a leader of the prayers. However, his voice was not very good, and he rarely had sufficient money for the family. As Burns joked in an unpublished interview he later gave the American Jewish Committee: "After he sang in one little synagogue, the following synagogue, instead of hiring him, they kept it closed during Rosh Hashanah and Yom Kippur." Louis Birnbaum, a failed helper for a kosher butcher and a failure in assisting the cantors in local synagogues, died when the future George Burns was just seven.

Milton Berle's father was such a failure that Berle compared him to Willy Loman from *Death of a Salesman.*

By contrast, Eddie Cantor's grandmother ran an employment agency for servant girls, was a matchmaker, and was arrested for rolling cigars because she didn't have a license. Bert Lahr's mother once saved a child's life by sending money across an alley over a clothesline to a neighbor who couldn't afford to pay the doctor. Minnie Marx and Sadie Berle were the exemplars of ambition for their beloved sons.

In his study of Jewish comedians, psychologist Samuel Janus noted that an astonishing 92 percent "came from families in the lowest socio-economic class." This class factor, seen also in the emergence of Irish and, later, African American comics, is significant. Those in the lower class with quick minds struggled to overcome their fathers' failures and prove the worth of the family to America. Their poverty, their lower-class status, and their failure in school (which would continue to be a tradition among Jewish comedians) added to their desperation, their sense of having to prove their worth to the world, to their mothers, and, not least, to themselves. Janus noted that it takes some level of masochism to "survive the climb to stardom in comedy," and this masochism emerged from these family structures.

The restraining power of a patriarch was missing because these future comedians had weak, absent, or dead fathers. This situation gave the young children what amounted to permission to escape school and take other risks that sons with strong fathers were simply unable to take. It also made them more assertive. The boys especially could assume a sort of familial "leadership" role, filling the emotional space their fathers had vacated.

These children weren't social insiders. They were poor and powerless. That made them skeptical about what others in the society took for granted. But they weren't truly outsiders either, and that fact gave them a belief that they could enter society, though they would have to work extra hard to please an audience, to find the right material, and, most of all, to take what life had to offer, absorb it, and continue working to succeed.

The simultaneity of their condition—being, at the same time, both an American and not quite an American—made for a strong sense of doubt and uncertainty. If one's own identity wasn't clear, after all, it followed that all else was in question, all the supposed truths were, perhaps, simply conventional lies. This in-between status was difficult, unstable, and closer to a tightrope than a bridge. The simultaneity promoted a sense of disillusionment with the society because it wouldn't fully provide admission. These feelings enabled Jewish comics to be part of American life but to look at it with an outsider's eye, with enough emotional distance to see truths that others missed, to laugh at the foibles that others considered simple normalcy, and, in some cases, to confront the culture when others were willing to abide by its rules.

These were invaluable assets as the young comedians made their way onto the vaudeville stage.

2

CURTAIN UP
AND CURTAIN DOWN

THE AGE OF VAUDEVILLE

I t was in 1901, at age five, that young Nathan Birnbaum first felt the stirring passion, the love, that an audience's applause could give him. The youngster, who would shortly become George Burns, had listened with others in the crowd on Mangin Street while an organ-grinder filled the street with music. Nathan, who a year later would enter the first grade at P.S. 22, instinctively started a Spanish dance to the music. The crowd clapped, and young Nathan felt a deep need for approval being partially met. It turned out that his need was such that a lifetime of success and applause could not diminish or fully satisfy it.

This drive to succeed, this fire in every vein, has driven generations of comedians. In Burns's case, this drive needed a channel—

amply provided by vaudeville—and a good deal of help. The first help came from the neighborhood mail carrier who heard Burns and two friends harmonizing to pass the time as they mixed and poured syrup in a candy store basement. Lewis Farley, the mail carrier, suggested a fourth boy for a quartet, and managed them as an act. The Peewee Quartet played on amateur nights at the Cannon Street Theatre, a movie house. The boys also sang on the corner of Columbia and Houston Streets while the crowd gave them money. In fact, they sang almost anywhere: in backyards, in saloons, and on the Staten Island Ferry—where they serenaded young couples and, Burns later remarked, were actually paid to go away and leave the lovers alone.

Nathan left the quartet at age ten and started a dance act with Abie Kaplan, who taught him the rudiments of tap dancing. The two, seeking a stage name, settled on the Burns Brothers. "George" was taken from Nathan's brother Izzy, who had Americanized his own name to George.

In 1905, the Burns Brothers began their career by appearing in Seidman's Theatre, a "presentation house" where live acts were presented between showings of silent films. This first experience was useful to George Burns in more ways than one. There was a Yiddish play also on the bill, in which one of the characters is asked to become Christian. The character replies, "No! A Jew I was born and a Jew I shall die!" Burns used this line whenever he was asked if he had changed his name legally.

Burns would continue to struggle, to change partners, to try any act. As Burns would have been the first to admit, he had more nerve than talent as he made his way into vaudeville. He frequently simply determined what kind of act was needed and presented himself as specializing in that particular talent.

Such a claim was not always accepted. One day at the Farley Theater, the manager heard Burns rehearsing and canceled him before the first show. Burns, characteristically, took this experience and transformed it in his mind. When he retold it, he added to it a "vaudeville shine," a comic exaggeration of reality. Years later, this is how he described what had happened: "I was in the middle of my act . . . and just before my yodeling finish the manager walked out and canceled me. . . . To make matters worse, the audience applauded him. And as he dragged me off the stage, the musicians gave him a standing ovation."

Burns would not succeed until he was in his mid-twenties, when he made his first appearance with Gracie Allen. Throughout the years before that, however, his career was generally considered a failure to everyone but himself. He did tricks on roller skates. He was a dance teacher, and much else. Despite the failures, Burns had great perseverance; his good spirits, his confidence, and his willingness to surrender his ego by giving the best material to a partner would eventually make him one of the most successful Jewish comedians of the century.

According to one story, Burns and Allen were introduced in 1922 in Union City, New Jersey, by Mary Kelley, Gracie's roommate and Jack Benny's girlfriend. Gracie had recently been fired by Larry Reilly, her partner in vaudeville, and she needed a new partner. Mary told Jack Benny, and he told Gracie about his friend George Burns. Gracie approached Burns backstage about starting an act. Burns later recalled listening to her voice and assuming she was a dancer. Another story had them introduced by Renee Arnold, another of Gracie's roommates who was on the same bill as Burns.

However they met, Burns and Allen began by singing and dancing. Burns wrote a routine in which, in baggy pants, he was the comic and Gracie fed him the straight lines. Burns, however, was very sensitive to audience reaction. He immediately saw that audiences laughed when Gracie spoke, even when the lines were not humorous—and they didn't laugh at his jokes. Recognizing the love the audience had for Gracie, Burns immediately rewrote the act, giving Gracie the funny lines and the daffy persona she became famous for displaying.

Burns had built the character on what were then known as Dumb Dora acts, but with a twist. Vaudeville comedians often made demeaning remarks about women, and the typical Dumb Dora act made the "dumb" woman the butt of the joke. Burns changed that. Gracie was not the object of the laughter; her comments and the subjects she talked about formed the source of humor.

This change is revealing. It is an example of how Jewish comedians of the era fitted seamlessly into current show business and did not attempt to subvert it in an obvious way, but transformed it tellingly. Burns kept the form of the Dumb Dora act, but—drawing on the idealization of the *Yiddische* mama—he dignified the woman by making her the center of the act. If the straight man didn't understand this new Dumb Dora, he never got angry. In addition, Burns took the social observations that had been important in Yiddish life, and filtered them not through a shrewd con artist but through a seemingly naive partner.

This smuggling of Yiddish humor into an accepted vaudeville format is emblematic of what the most successful Jewish comedians did. They developed a code, a way to make their Jewish humor seem fully American yet include profoundly Jewish influences.

The Burns and Allen personae were carefully and thoughtfully constructed by the two performers, and writing for them was harder than it looked. In 1934, F. Scott Fitzgerald met Burns and Allen on tour and asked to write for the couple. He prepared an eight thousand–word film treatment for them, titled "Gracie at Sea," but it could not be used because even the great Fitzgerald couldn't capture the Allen character.

Gracie's character saw the world through the lens of what Burns called "illogical logic." She thought she was smart and did not understand why others made obvious mistakes in language and thinking. She would explain the world as she understood it. Burns—and the audience—accepted the logic and never challenged her intelligence or insights. His salty voice and her high-pitched, funny voice were perfect for delivering the lines Burns wrote.

The partnership worked from the start. Their first successful routine began with the two walking onstage holding hands. Gracie would look over toward the wing and wave. She then would let go of George's hand and go over to the wing, still waving her hand. She would signal to the person to whom she was waving to come over. A man would then come out onstage and kiss Gracie, who would kiss him back. They would wave at each other, and he would walk off. Gracie would then come back to George, and the dialogue would begin:

GRACIE: Who was that?
GEORGE: You don't know?
GRACIE: No, my mother told me never to talk to strangers.
GEORGE: That makes sense.
GRACIE: This always happens to me. On my way in, a man stopped me at the stage door and said, "Hiya cutie, how about a bite tonight after the show?"
GEORGE: And you said?
GRACIE: I said, "I'll be busy after the show, but I'm not doing anything now," so I bit him.
GEORGE: Gracie, let me ask you something. Did the nurse ever happen to drop you on your head when you were a baby?
GRACIE: Oh, no, we couldn't afford a nurse; my mother had to do it.

GEORGE: You had a smart mother.

GRACIE: Smartness runs in my family. When I went to school I was so smart my teacher was in my class for five years.

GEORGE: Gracie, what school did you go to?

GRACIE: I'm not allowed to tell.

GEORGE: Why not?

GRACIE: The school pays me twenty-five dollars a month not to tell.

Much of Burns and Allen's material has to do with family, especially the supposedly crazy members of Gracie's family. Her nephew Willy was a favorite.

GRACIE: When Willy was a little baby my father took him riding in his carriage, and two hours later my father came back with a different baby and a different carriage.

GEORGE: Well, what did your mother say?

GRACIE: My mother didn't say anything because it was a better carriage.

GEORGE: A better carriage?

GRACIE: Yeah . . . And the little baby my father brought home was a little French baby so my mother took up French.

GEORGE: Why?

GRACIE: So she would be able to understand the baby . . .

GEORGE: When the baby started to talk?

GRACIE: Yeah.

GEORGE: Gracie, this family of yours, do you all live together?

GRACIE: Oh, sure. My father, my brother, my uncle, my cousin, and my nephew all sleep in one bed and . . .

GEORGE: In one bed? I'm surprised your grandfather doesn't sleep with them.

GRACIE: Oh, he did, but he died, so they made him get up.

In laughing at Gracie, audience members could relieve the stresses of their family life, stresses that were especially acute in immigrant life.

But there was another unspoken family issue that came up whenever Burns and Allen performed. For Jewish audiences sensitive to issues of assimilation, the marriage of the Jewish George to the Irish Catholic Gracie was clearly a conflict. Jewish audience members loved Gracie, but that love was tempered by a recognition that she was a Gentile married to a Jew. Intermarriage presented to American Jews the first clear signs that America's loving arms had unforeseen consequences for their survival as a people. The pain was acute precisely because the embrace was so different from the centuries of hatred Jews had encountered and because Gentiles like Gracie Allen were so attractive.

In a sense, the Burns-Allen partnership mirrored the developing relationship between Jewish comedians and the established American comedic forms. It was a mixing of DNA, and, like many evolutionary factors, just how far-reaching the resulting change was could not possibly be glimpsed at the moment. Also, like most things evolutionary, much of the change was subtle and seemingly minor.

The vaudeville world in which Burns and Allen found such success started as an alternative to the men-only nature of American entertainment. In 1865, an immigrant and former circus clown named Tony Pastor decided that the minstrel shows, then hugely popular, were inappropriate for large numbers of potential audience members. Pastor wanted to provide a place where the entire family could go, so he opened a variety theater and began the tradition of door prizes—usually giving away silk dresses or sacks of potatoes. Pastor allowed only family entertainment. Eventually, he took his show on tour and was quite successful.

Building on Pastor's insights and certain variety-show aspects of minstrel shows, vaudeville emerged in the mid-1880s. B. F. Keith and Edward Franklin Albee staged a variety show in Boston in 1885, made sure all acts were completely suitable for the family, and eventually began expanding, calling their variety shows "vaudeville." This would not be the Albee family's only great contribution to the American theater. Edward Albee's son Reed was the father of an adopted son, the playwright Edward Albee.

The word *vaudeville* evidently came from the Vau de Vive, a valley of the Vive River in Normandy. The valley inspired French drinking songs, and the word itself was transformed to *voix de ville,* meaning street voices.

Keith and Albee developed a circuit, a group of theaters in the East where performers worked. There were also minor circuits with a central booking office and a few locally operated theaters.

The most famous vaudeville house, the Palace, opened in New York on March 24, 1913. It quickly established itself as the venue every vaudevillian aspired to play. There was even a spot on Forty-seventh Street in front of the theater where vaudevillians would congregate, waiting for their next booking, trading gossip, exchanging and stealing jokes, wishing and vowing to play the Palace themselves one day.

There were eventually hundreds of vaudeville houses throughout the country, some of which still survive as theaters for plays or films. It was often a major cultural event for audiences to attend a vaudeville theater. For example, the Paramount Theatre in Seattle opened in 1928 and was among the most ornate. For the fifty-cent admission price, audience members were led by uniformed ushers past figurative adornments and iron handrails, past the floral gold patterns on the walls and the chandeliers with 3 million glass beads to one of the three thousand seats. Performers, however, had far less plush surroundings. The backstage was cramped and little money was spent on the performances apart from some props, musical accompaniment, and some simple and easily assembled materials for shows. There was a single entrance door leading from backstage to the main stage.

The Paramount, like many other theaters, has often been called the secular counterpart to a house of worship in appearance and function. In a secular age, the need for pageant required a majestic setting, a ritualized order of performance, performers to lead the communal "service," and a sense of drawing emotion from the performance—in a theater's case pleasure rather than spiritual solace. Experiences were sought that provided such pleasure.

For the secularized Jewish community, the comedians were especially important as secular rabbis, providing both meaning and a way into American society. This importance would be even more pronounced as the Jewish community itself became more assimilated, but even in the era of vaudeville, some Jewish audiences saw the Jewish comedians as role models for achieving success and providing an identity apart from religion.

The world of vaudeville included people with a variety of different jobs. An agent represented the actors and made arrangements with bookers who signed the actors for performances. Managers ran the actual vaudeville houses and were principally concerned with the box office receipts rather than the quality (or ethnic background) of the actors.

The typical vaudeville show varied, with a brief show consisting of five acts, and a longer one, lasting two hours, made up of eight or nine acts. The opening act in vaudeville, called a "dumb act," didn't include speaking. It might be a trick dog, cyclists, or acrobats, for example. This act was a minor one used to allow latecomers to get to their seats. It was also important for those in the audience who couldn't speak English. No language skills were required to laugh at amazing animals or jumping humans. The aim of vaudeville, after all, was to provide enjoyment for everyone who could pay the twenty-five-cent admission price In fact, successful opening acts did comparatively well economically. Many of the acrobats were paid $150–200 a week.

The second act might be a dancing number or a comedy act, usually performed in front of the curtain. This allowed the scenery to be set up behind on the main stage. A musical or comedy production number followed. The next to last act of the first half was a major star, and the final act of the first half was the headliner, a popular and successful entertainer. After intermission, another number went on to settle the audience. This was followed by another production number, quite often an actor or actress performing a dramatic reading or scene from a play. No matter how many acts there were, the next-to-last spot in the second half was the crucial spot. Because vaudeville audiences loved comedians, a comic often occupied that spot. The show ended with some action, a showy bit that was loud so the audience wouldn't be disturbed by other members of the audience who were leaving.

Each performer, depending on status, went on for about seventeen to twenty minutes. Shows went from early morning until late at night. Performers had the same act, which they simply kept repeating in each city. Because they were on a circuit, it was often the case that they didn't return to a city for a year. Performers thus led nomadic lives, always traveling, performing, preparing to perform, or trying to get bookings. Their private lives therefore inevitably intermingled with their occupation. Marriages were difficult; quick affairs or single encounters with professionals were common and accepted. Economically, the stars of vaudeville did very well, with the very top stars earning as much as $1,500 a week.

By the turn of the century, vaudeville had firmly replaced the minstrel show as the chief form of American entertainment in part because it provided the emotional response to a crisis in American culture, a massive demographic and economic dislocation. The growth of industry had brought to the cities more and more Americans whose principal concern was how to adjust to urban life. Many people were bored by their jobs and worn out at home. They wanted an escape, in a crucial sense from the arc of their own lives.

The very nature of vaudeville, with its quick succession of images and sounds, mimicked urban life and therefore gave audiences an increasing sense of laughing at themselves, their new urban culture, and the emerging revolutionary technologies. The lonely city became considerably less lonely when audience members could be entertained along with others. The sense of rootedness and control that emerged from such laughter provided much-needed emotional security. In mimicking urban life, though, vaudeville also contributed to the subverting of traditional rural values. The focus, by definition, was on immediate sensual pleasure as opposed to delayed gratification. In many ways, then, vaudeville helped usher in modern American life.

The Jews played a prominent role in vaudeville, which made it easier for Jewish comedians to be accepted. There were many Jewish booking agents, stage managers, and theater owners in the new vaudeville industry, and most booking offices were in New York where, of course, a lot of Jewish performers lived. William Hammerstein (father of the lyricist Oscar Hammerstein II), for example, managed the most successful vaudeville house in the country, the Victoria Theater in New York. William Morris (who would later create the hugely powerful talent agency that today still bears his name) was a major booker of talent. Additionally, the entire vaudeville ethos was one of judging talent rather than background. Finally, Jews particularly went into comedy because humor was one of the few acceptable roles available for them. Audiences were used to laughing at ethnic stereotypes, including Jewish stereotypes. The door may have been open for the wrong reasons, but many Jews recognized that at least the door was open, and they walked right in.

The stereotypes, though, were hurtful, focusing on alleged dubious Jewish business practices, a lack of hygiene, and sexual desire. A standard joke about Jews might be one partner saying to the other, "Goldberg, I heard you had a fire last night." The partner then says, "Ssh. It's tomorrow." "Hebrew" masks were sold so people could mimic the dialect-laden ethnic humor at home.

But in time, the complaints against ethnic humor added up. Fanny Brice refused to sing songs she considered as reinforcing anti-Semitic stereotypes. Milton Berle and others of his generation refused to make jokes that mocked Jews. Their decision was important because Jewish comedians were the ones with the license to tell these jokes, and when popular Jewish comedians didn't tell them, the jokes themselves were vastly reduced in number. Also, Albee and Keith had realized that the accumulated complaints (made also by Irish groups) could hurt business. Voluntary restraint began and, over time, offensive humor began to disappear. Clearly, the reduction of such jokes immensely aided Jewish acceptance in the broader culture.

Most important to the Jewish success was the subtle understanding by audiences—Jewish and non-Jewish—that the Jewish experience could provide insights into their own predicament. The journey from farm to city for an enormous number of Americans was traumatic and required a massive effort to adapt. The Jews were rightly seen as the masters of adapting to traumatic change, the veterans of and experts at being uprooted. Jewish comics were accepted because they had gone through a similar experience, and urban audiences knew that the guidance they provided would be invaluable.

A model was thus established for Jewish comedians. When Americans felt uprooted—which they did often in the century—

they found in Jewish comedians people who could simultaneously help them laugh at and therefore control that feeling but also, based on their history, be emotional pioneers, guides to the new frontiers of American life. A new humor was needed, and new people who had actually undergone comparable experiences were needed to perform that humor. The Jews were among those who could fill that need. They weren't the only ones, of course. Will Rogers was so enormously popular because he tied the older western humor to the new experience, an effort that continues to this day through such performers as Garrison Keillor. But after Rogers, this older school of American comedy rarely achieved wide success and even more rarely was able to provide comic solutions to America's very uncomic problems.

George Burns may have been the most successful Jewish entertainer in vaudeville, but he was not the first. There were, for example, earlier comedians who specialized in Jewish dialect comedy. One prominent Jewish dialectician was Joe Welch, whose opening line was, "Mebbe you tink I am a heppy man." His distraught face, long beard, and derby hat made it obvious that he was not a happy man at all. Many audiences liked caricatures not only of Jews but of all immigrant groups. Stereotypes were the heart of much of the comedy, and Welch was important because he would do whole scenes in dialect as opposed to the single jokes others did.

Joe Sultzer and Charlie Marks became famous as the inspiration for Neil Simon's play and the movie *The Sunshine Boys*. Sultzer and Marks met when they got into a bicycle accident and began arguing. Someone told them they sounded like the hugely popular vaudeville team of Joseph Weber and Lew Fields and that they should go into show business. They began singing in saloons. Sultzer and Marks took the name Smith and Dale because Sultzer's brother found a printer with extra calling cards for an act named Smith and Dale whose partners had changed their names.

Using Jewish accents, they created a variety of well-received skits, the most famous of which involved Dr. Kronkhite (*kronkeit* is a Yiddish word meaning "illness") "Dr. Kronkhite and His Only Living Patient" included very corny exchanges such as:

DALE (AS THE DOCTOR): You owe me ten dollars.

SMITH: For what?

DALE: For my advice.

SMITH: Well, doctor, here's two dollars. Take it. That's my advice!

DALE: You cheapskate! You come in here—you cockamamie—

SMITH: One more word and you only get a dollar.

DALE: Why—

SMITH: That's a word. Here's the dollar.

In fact, Smith and Dale differed somewhat from Weber and Fields, who were essentially physical comedians. Among their innovations was the poke in the eye, used so widely later by such teams as Laurel and Hardy and the Three Stooges. But they also further developed the use of twisted language and satiric malapropisms. (Probably their most famous routine included the single vaudeville exchange many people still know: "Who was that lady I saw you with last night?" "She ain't no lady; she's my wife.")

Weber and Fields's physical comedy was certainly influential. The success of knockabout, or slapstick, comedy presaged the American audiences' desire for "action," an entertainment euphemism for violence in sports, in dramatic movies and TV shows, and even in some forms of comedy.

Comedic violence, whether linguistic as in insult humor or physical as in slapstick, is valued by some audience members as an expression of their own emotions. It is misleading, though, to suggest that linguistic violence is completely distinct from physical violence. The Three Stooges (all of whom were Jewish), for example, made clever use of language in addition to purely physical humor. There is a small strain of such physical comedians among Jews, a strain that includes, for example, Soupy Sales, but this physical approach, even when combined with language, never achieved widespread use among Jewish comedians. People of the book, and therefore the word, Jews seemed uncomfortable with the simply physical—which is one reason they were so absent from the silent movies that had begun to compete seriously with vaudeville.

Thus, the Jewish entertainers whose fame outlived vaudeville's were much more focused on language, character, and situation than ethnicity. Many of them, like George Burns, started when they were young.

At age eight, Phil Silvers sang at a stag party for a local hoodlum. Silvers was in the middle of his song when one of the gangsters was shot dead. The man fell at Silvers's feet. At twelve, Silvers sang in Gus Edwards's troupe of young performers—until his voice changed and he was forced to enter comedy.

One of George Jessel's grandfathers was a tailor who would bring out his young grandson to sing while his customers waited to have their pants pressed. From there, Jessel went to his grandfather's lodge meetings, where, again, the child was warmly received. Jessel's mother was a cashier at the Imperial Theatre. At her son's insistence, she talked the owner into hiring Jessel at age nine, after his father had died. Jessel sang with the Imperial Trio at the Imperial Theatre and at a local nickelodeon. Walter Winchell was another member of the trio. Jessel was also a batboy for the New York Giants. If the Giants won, he would sing in the clubhouse. If they lost, Jessel recalled, the Giants' manager, John McGraw, would say, "Get out of here, you little Jew." Jessel (and Winchell) also joined Gus Edwards's company, the most famous vaudeville children's troupe and, teamed with Eddie Cantor, stayed until his voice changed when he was sixteen.

One afternoon, sitting with friends and anguished at his continuing inability to identify some act he could do, Jessel called his mother and told her stories about the day in a comically exaggerated way. His friends immediately encouraged him to use talking on the telephone to his mama as the center of a new act. The humor seems more strained now, but the sentiment comes through.

Hello, Mama. Georgie. Georgie. Your son, from the money every week. How are you feeling? You still see spots before your eyes? Have you got your glasses on? They're on your forehead? Well, how long does it take to get them down? You got them down . . . You see the spots better now.

Say, Mom. How did you like that bird I sent home for the parlor? You cooked it! That's a fine thing to do. That was a South American bird . . . He spoke four languages. He should've said something?

Jessel's "mama" routine, unsurprisingly taken from his real life, reflected the special relationship in Jewish life between mother and son, revealed the strategies Jewish sons used in reviewing their lives for their mothers, gently mocked the mothers in a loving way, and reflected the audience's yearning for such a relationship themselves. In vaudeville, the Jewish mother was the very soul of warmth, kindness, and love. She came to symbolize the love that was missing in so many lives of those in the audience.

Jessel had a more serious side, too. He starred in *The Jazz Singer* on Broadway and never forgave Al Jolson for, as he saw it, stealing the part in what would be a historic film. Jessel gave a powerful performance. George Burns recalled crying when he saw it.

Many comedians and other performers could easily identify with its story of a voyage away from Judaism to show business.

Jessel also was among the first of his generation of Jewish comedians to be attracted to film, appearing in 1911 in one of Thomas Edison's experimental short films. Off camera, he would later become famous as "Toastmaster General" of the United States, never missing a chance to speak, with funerals his specialty. In the 1950s and '60s, he also raised a large amount of money for Israel. In one story, Jessel was supposed to have combined these passions by speaking at a funeral for the actor James Mason's departed cat. After the speech, Jack Benny joked that he hadn't known that Mason's cat had been so generous to Israel.

Ed Wynn knew at age nine that he wanted to be a comedian. He was first onstage at the age of twelve when he went up to assist a magician and announced that he could do the trick; he couldn't, but he acquired a taste of how it felt to get an audience's approval. He ran away from home when he was fifteen, joining a repertory company as a utility boy. Once in a while he did small bits onstage. Eventually, the company failed, and Wynn returned home to Philadelphia to sell hats.

Wynn ran away again, this time to New York where, after success at a benefit, he teamed up with Jack Lewis to enter vaudeville. By nineteen, he was headlining. In 1914, at age twenty-eight, he joined Ziegfeld's Follies. Ultimately becoming known for corny inventions (such as an 11' 4 ½" pole for those audience members who wouldn't touch something with a 10' pole) and silly puns, Wynn had a clear affection for his work and his audience. His infectious giggle, his glasses on an expressive baby face, totally clean material free of suggestiveness and ethnic or racial stereotyping, and use of costumes vastly amused audiences.

Wynn, called "the Perfect Fool" from his role in a play of that name, drew his silly stage character from Yiddish culture. His most important contribution was that he presented his character as fully American, refusing to use dialect. But he was consciously introducing a Jewish character type (with an American accent) to the audience.

The most famous characters of Yiddish folklore are the fools of the town of Chelm. Chelm, a real town, became mythologized as the home of stupid but innocent and self-delusional people. It is crucial to note that the Chelm characters, like Wynn's fool, were seen as foolish but were liked for it. The audience is led to understand that but for the gift of common sense, they, too, might be fools. The compassion for all people, even the simple, even as they are laughed at for their silliness, explains the way vaudeville and later audiences reacted to Wynn.

Yet, Wynn was serious underneath. He was one of the leaders of an Actors' Equity strike in 1919. It was his suggestion that the actors join the American Federation of Labor, and Wynn was the one selected to approach labor leader Samuel Gompers to achieve that goal. Wynn was blacklisted for his union activities, but that did not prevent his continuing success. He was too funny and too popular to keep off the stage.

Eddie Cantor practiced his mimicry at Surprise Lake Camp (his grandmother had had to petition the Welfare Board to send him there) and in the streets. He made his first dramatic appearance at Miner's Bowery Theatre, a place well known to be quick and harsh in its judgment of talent. Buoyed by his success there, Cantor became a singing waiter and, while guests threw bottles at one another, he was paid three dollars for each performance. (Jimmy Durante was the pianist, and the two performers formed a close friendship.)

Cantor's first stage job was in burlesque, a minstrel show offshoot that had evolved into a combination of comedy and women in various stages of undress. Cantor became famous for an act that used a variety of ethnic accents. Florenz Ziegfeld saw him perform in 1917 and offered a tryout, leading to great success in the Follies for the next several years. Cantor's standard opening was to come onstage holding a deck of cards. He'd then request volunteers. Four or five people would be chosen. Cantor would give them each some cards. He'd then tell them to stand up at their seats and hold the cards over their heads with the warning not to let him see any of the cards. Once they had done this, Cantor would then ignore them and continue with his act, especially singing a strange song. Eventually, the audience realized there was to be no card trick, and, as this reality dawned on them, they began to laugh.

Cantor used the stereotypes popular in American entertainment but built on them. Like many other performers of the time, he appeared in blackface, though, with verbal wit, he gave his characters an intelligence missing from the minstrel show.

The blackface tradition had endured for a long while in American culture. Indeed, minstrel shows were the first entertainment form widely seen and admired by Americans. Popular from the 1820s, the minstrel show consisted of white men blacking their faces with burnt cork and speaking in dialect. They portrayed African Americans as happy, carefree, and anxious to entertain white audiences. The shows were psychologically valuable for whites in justifying the continued mistreatment of slaves and, after the Civil War, in justifying continued racial segregation. Minstrel shows typically consisted of three parts. The first part had all the performers in the show onstage in a semicircle. The group would sing, tell riddles, and generally joke around. The second part, called olio, was a variety show, with a great many different acts. The third part was a skit, often a parody of popular plays or music.

The attractions of blackface for immigrant white audiences were different from the attractions for the earlier white generations. The author Michael Rogin has interpreted the blackface, and more tellingly its removal, as a step these performers took as they went from being immigrants to being fully American.

White immigrants (and rural Americans who had moved to cities) were anxious about their status as "real" Americans. This was particularly true of Jews. As James Baldwin once acutely noted, "Jews came here from countries where they were not white, and they came here in part *because* they were not white." Although relatively few of those performers who put on blackface were Jewish, Jews became well known for doing so. Al Jolson was the most famous of those who used blackface. Besides Cantor, Fanny Brice, Sophie Tucker, George Burns, and George Jessel also less famously blackened their faces. Jews and other immigrants had to acquire "whiteness" as part of their new American identity. The fear of being discovered as not white, as foreign, gave blackface comedy a psychological dimension. The blackface comedian or performer appeared to be black but was really white. This was exactly the message immigrants wished to convey to white Americans. Laughing at a blackface comedian allowed immigrant white audiences simultaneously to convey that message and to laugh at their own fears and anxieties. Surely, however, African American audiences (and some performers) must have been far more troubled by such blackface antics.

Besides his blackface act, Cantor also portrayed Jewish characters that were, through a contemporary lens, unflattering. One character, for instance, was a Jewish aviator. This aviator, trying to emulate Charles Lindbergh, named his plane the *Mosquito–Spirit of New Jersey*. He admitted that he couldn't copy Lindbergh, because he couldn't eat a ham sandwich en route as Lindbergh had done.

Cantor had a particularly close relationship with his audience, which was the real secret of his success. Cantor's unending pep was a variation of the nervous energy of Eastern European Jewish life as transplanted to the Lower East Side. His obvious will to please, his nonstop action, and his sense of proximity to the real feelings of those who watched made him popular. Audiences enjoyed his numerous and funny ad-libs and his visible enjoyment of his job. He also took advantage of new technology, in his case the record player. Many of the songs he sang in his career became wildly popular, such as "If You Knew Susie," "My Baby Just Cares for Me," and "Making Whoopee."

The Three Stooges, who would become much more popular in short comedy films, also started their slapstick work in vaudeville. Moe Howard (born Moses Horwitz) was a childhood friend of Ted Healy, a comedian and singer who asked Moe to work with him in 1922. Three years later, Moe's brother Shemp (Samuel Horwitz) joined the team. Later that year, the three were in a theater in Chicago when they saw the wild-haired Larry Fine (Louis Feinberg). The act was set; Healy had what he called his "stooges." Moe had started in films made at the Vitagraph Studio in Brooklyn, playing tough guys and, in so doing, creating his on-screen character. When yet another brother, Jerome Horwitz, better known as Curly, joined the act, it was Healy who insisted he shave his head. The Stooge act in vaudeville depended on a physical violence, marked by eye pokes, double face slaps, kicks, and various objects used as improvised weapons.

At age fifteen, Bert Lahr was in a child act named the Seven Frolics. He soon became successful and developed a variety of interesting routines, some risqué. His most famous bit was as a drunken policeman waiting to arrest an attractive dancer (played by Mercedes Delpino, Lahr's wife at the time). The officer began talking to the young lady, who would then say, "Are you speaking to me?" Lahr would then look at her ample body and say, "Yeah, to you." Then, he'd shift his glance and add, "To you too." In another sketch he tried to lure a young woman out of a tent at the beach when she had no clothes on. Despite these bawdy examples, much of Lahr's unique gift came from wringing pain from his lines. Lahr's sad face was among the most expressive in the business, and his playful work with the sounds of words as he twisted them added a remarkable melancholy to his humor. He also was crucial in extending bits so that they weren't simple jokes, but fitted together in a coherent story line.

The Marx Brothers entered vaudeville in large part because of the drive and vision of their mother, Minnie. In 1905, Minnie saw an ad for a singer in a touring vaudeville act. She convinced the fifteen-year-old Groucho to try out for the job. (The Marx Brothers did not yet have their nicknames, which are used here.) The job called for someone who could also dance, but Groucho couldn't dance at all. Minnie ignored that minor deficiency and told Groucho that he could, indeed, dance. He got the job. On his first trip, he was abandoned in Denver, where his landlady gave him two dollars and got him a job driving a grocery wagon, which he did for two months until he had saved enough money to get back to New York. As soon as he got back, Minnie saw a job for an actor, explaining to Groucho that anyone can act.

Eventually, starting in 1907, Minnie decided the brothers needed their own act. Groucho and Gummo joined with Mabel O'Donnell (or, by other accounts, a woman named Jenny) to create the Three Nightingales. Mabel was a singer who had a glass eye (or, by different stories, a wandering eye or just a bad squint). To hide this, Minnie had Mabel wear a wig with hair long enough to cover the eye. When that didn't work out, Minnie hired another singer named Lou Levy.

At thirteen, Harpo had been a bellhop at the Hotel Seville on East Twenty-eighth Street, but Minnie didn't think that was an appropriate occupation for him. At age fourteen, he was playing piano at silent movies. His repertoire was limited to just a few songs, but Harpo played them with gusto to reflect the action on the screen. With Harpo's addition, Minnie changed the group's name accordingly to the Four Nightingales. The group encountered one failure after another, but Minnie refused to quit. Once, a fire broke out on the stage, and Harpo, unsure what to do, began to recite his bar mitzvah speech in a high voice. They knew they needed an act.

With help from Minnie's brother, the vaudeville comic Al Shean, the brothers in 1910 developed a skit modeled after the sort of juvenile revue pioneered by Gus Edwards. The skit was called "Fun in Hi Skule." Groucho played the teacher. Harpo played a role modeled on Patsy Bolisar, a theatrical country bumpkin popularized especially in shows on riverboats. Harpo practiced a moronic stare and began to, as they put it, "throw" his "Gookie." He puffed out his cheeks and crossed his eyes. There are various stories about the origin of the face. One of the stories is that, as a child, Harpo had seen such a face made by a cigar roller as he worked in the window of a cigar store on Lexington Avenue. The cigar roller's name was Mr. Gehrke, which Harpo transformed into "Gookie." Harpo also slowly developed his character. A reviewer for a Champaign-Urbana, Illinois, paper wrote: "He takes off on an Irish immigrant most amusingly in pantomime. Unfortunately, the effect is spoiled when he speaks." From that review on, Harpo remained silent onstage and -screen. When Groucho had been a delivery boy for a wig company, he had brought home a box of wigs and the boys had tried them on. Harpo tried one for the act. Gummo was pleased with the result, so their aunt Hannah made a wig. Harpo also played the harp, an idea developed by Minnie.

The lines in the "Fun in Hi Skule" skit were invariably corny. For example, at one point in the skit Groucho says to student Gummo, "What are the principal parts of a cat?"

Gummo answers, "Eyes, ears, neck, tail, feet, et cetera, et cetera."

"You've forgotten the most important," Groucho would say. "What does a cat have that you don't?" Groucho would then hint at the answer expected by moving his fingers along his lips, indicating that whiskers was the right answer.

Gummo, though, simply said, "Kittens."

It was in Galesburg, Illinois, possibly on May 15, 1914, during a poker game, that the Marx Brothers acquired their nicknames. By then Chico had joined the act, and they had broadened their repertoire. Art Fisher, a headlining monologist (a performer who today would be called a stand-up comedian), saw their act there. He loved their loud, confident manner; Fisher, who followed their act, immediately knew that in the future he should precede them. Fisher had developed a habit of nicknaming people in the style of a popular comic strip called "Sherlocko the Monk." Harpo's nickname came, of course, from his playing the harp. Groucho was named because of his quarrelsome personality (though Al Shean and Harpo, at least in his autobiography, maintained that Groucho's name came from the "grouch" bag vaudevillians hung around their neck to protect money or other valuable items). Gummo's name came from the gumshoes (the name then for the rubber coverings for shoes when it rained) he always wore. Another story is that he wandered around backstage sneaking up on people like a "gumshoe," a detective. Chico was named because of his penchant for chasing chickens, as young women were then called. Therefore, the correct pronunciation of his name is Chick-o, not Cheek-o, though such a pronunciation became common after a typesetter made a mistake and printed cards with "Chico" rather than "Chicko" on them and even more so when Chico created his Italian character—with an accent taken from a barber he knew. (In private, the brothers continued to pronounce the name as Chicko.) Zeppo was named later, perhaps from the zeppelin or perhaps, as

Harpo suggests, after Zeppo, the trained chimpanzee, since Zeppo did acrobatics and looked simian in his efforts.

After Gummo was drafted into the army, Zeppo replaced him. The four other brothers reportedly appeared at a recruiting station in Chicago but were all rejected. But their career in vaudeville, meteoric as it was, didn't last. They had quit the Albee circuit to sign up with the Shuberts, but soon the Shuberts decided to abandon vaudeville and Albee would not take them back. Luckily, Chico ran into someone in Philadelphia who needed an act, and soon an agreement was reached. After a year in Philadelphia, the show *I'll Say She Is!* came to Broadway in 1924. The play came from a failing show called *Love for Sale* written by Will B. Johnstone and his brother Tim. An extremely positive review by Alexander Woollcott, part of the famous Algonquin Club Roundtable, guaranteed the brothers' success. During the run of *I'll Say She Is!* Woollcott asked the brothers why they still used their real names instead of the much funnier nicknames. They expressed concern about retaining their dignity. Woollcott was astounded at the reaction. "Dignified? You?" he responded. They changed the billing.

Even as early as this show, Groucho's character was set. In one scene, Groucho played Napoleon and Lotta Miles played Josephine. The interplay between them is vintage Marx Brothers.

NAPOLEON: Forgive me, my queen. I don't doubt your love. When I look into your big blue eyes, I know that you are true to the army. I only hope it remains a standing army . . .

JOSEPHINE: Napoleon, when you go, all France is with you.

NAPOLEON: Yes, and the last time I came home all France was with you, and a slice of Italy, too.

The wild romps of the Marx Brothers had a particular Jewish

flavor. Like the Keystone Kops and similar American antic comedians, the brothers were wild, but the Kops were—at least presumably—on the side of the law. They may have been comically
inadequate, but they were not subversive. The Marx Brothers,
though, were directly challenging the forces of social order. They
deliberately wished to subvert power and the controlling forces of
society; they acted out against authority in a way their Eastern
European Jewish ancestors daydreamed of doing but were unable
to do in reality.

Jack Benny began his relationship with music when he got his
first half-size violin on his sixth birthday, a gift from his parents,
who dreamed of a career in classical music for their son. He hated
to practice, but he did like to perform. At age fifteen, he began to
play the violin at the Barrison Theatre in Waukegan, skipping
school on matinee days. In 1911, the Marx Brothers played the theater, and Minnie Marx (then known professionally as Minnie
Palmer) was impressed enough by young Benny to offer him a job
as a violinist in the pit for their act, but Benny's father refused to
let him travel.

When Benny was seventeen, the theater closed, and Cora Salisbury, the Barrison's pianist, decided to go back to vaudeville. She
invited the young Benny to form an act with her. This time, he did
leave home—after Cora Salisbury promised that young Benny
would keep kosher. He eventually got a new partner and then
joined the navy, applying to enter the theatrical company.

Up until then, Benny's act was entirely musical. He didn't think
of himself as or try to be a comedian. In the navy, though, he
began to tell jokes when David Wolff, another sailor, urged him
to save a failing violin performance. (One writer suggests that the
actor Pat O'Brien, rather than Wolff, was the one who did the urg-
ing.) The sailors had booed, and Wolff went out onstage in the
middle of the performance and told Benny to talk to the audience.

Benny reacted by telling a few jokes. Warming up, he continued, "I heard that you sailors complain about the food. Well, I want to tell you that the enlisted men get the same food as Captain Moffett gets . . . only his is cooked." The audience loved it, and Benny, surprised by their warm laughter, suddenly found himself with a new career.

He left the navy and began reading humor magazines for jokes, gradually using his violin less and his jokes more. He was using the name Ben K. Benny, but someone with a similar name complained. Sailors had a habit of calling each other Jack, so Benny adopted it as his own first name.

Benny became famous for his opening. He'd walk out onstage, go up to the musical conductor, and ask, "How's the show so far?" The conductor would say the show was fine. "Well," Benny would respond, "I'll fix that." This self-deprecating trait, later displayed on his radio and television shows by allowing himself to be the butt of jokes and by giving the other actors wonderful lines, may have emerged from Jewish humor. As noted earlier, Benny later became famous for his persona as a cheapskate, a popular anti-Jewish prejudice. In fact, Benny's cheap character didn't come from Jewish life. The cheapskate was a stock vaudeville persona, and, like Burns, Benny was simply modifying the template with a small dollop of Jewish sensibility, or *Yiddishkeit.*

Fanny Brice, at age thirteen, was used to singing for customers in her parents' saloon and with local newsboys in poolrooms. The newsies convinced her to enter an amateur contest at Keeney's Theatre, a famous vaudeville house in Brooklyn. Fanny won the ten-dollar first prize. (The audience liked her so much, they threw money onstage, and she collected an additional three dollars this way.) Fanny began to enter other amateur shows and always did well. She got a job as a chorus girl but was fired by George M. Cohan after he saw her dance. At nineteen, Fanny was given a song called "Sadie Salome" by Irving Berlin. Berlin suggested she sing it with a Yiddish accent, and it was a great success. In 1910, she appeared in the Ziegfeld Follies and spent more than a decade in each of the annual Follies, which she supplemented with vaudeville and other work. Hers was a face that could traverse the range of emotions that vaudeville audiences found so enticing. Brice never thought of herself as pretty, but her drive to perform, her effervescent enthusiasm, and her sheer charm always radiated through during her performances. She was a first-rate satirist with a great gift for caricature, and until her later radio career, Brice was clearly immigrant and Jewish, her humor often revolving around her inability to grasp English correctly.

Fanny Brice was one of several prominent women performers in vaudeville. Sophie Tucker, like Brice a singing comedian, grew up washing dishes in her family's restaurant. She met actors traveling in the area who came into the restaurant for a meal, and she saw show business as an escape from what looked like a suffocating life. She had liked singing and been successful at amateur concerts. Her excessive weight seemed to add rather than detract from her performance. Eventually, Tucker left her marriage, gave her son to her mother, and fully entered the vaudeville world. Though constantly unhappy about it, she was forced to wear blackface for a long while. Tucker sang songs that were frank about sex and often humorous. She gained the most fame for her song "My Yiddische Mama."

There were other singers with a comedic touch as well as Yiddish actresses who sometimes did comic roles, such as, most famously, Molly Picon. But the social roles assigned to women precluded large numbers of talented women from entering show business.

Milton Berle's fame as a television performer was built on his radio career, and that, in turn, was built on his vaudeville career. As a boy he had been a model in Buster Brown shoe advertisements and worked in silent films at the Biograph Studios in Fort Lee, New Jersey. He was invariably accompanied by his mother, not just at these early efforts but for every one of his performances until Sadie Berle's death in 1954. Berle worked in "kid shows" modeled after Gus Edwards's efforts. He became increasingly popular during the 1920s for a variety of acts that were not great models of comic sophistication. His most famous bit involved meeting a young woman on the stage that was set up with water and a phony dock. The young woman then told Milton that she was planning to kill herself. Milton made an earnest effort to relieve her of such urges. She would begin to flirt with him, eventually coaxing him to give her all of his money. Then a second woman would appear, and she, too, would tell of her plans to commit suicide. Berle would then push her into the water.

Far from being embarrassed about his background, Berle was proud to be a Jew. Once in 1925, a popular comedian named Frank Fay and Berle were on the same bill. Fay was annoyed that Berle was standing in the stage entrance and told the stage manager to "get the little kike out of the entrance." Berle's mother, a strong woman and brilliant at defusing problems with improvisation, told an angry Milton that "maybe he said 'tyke.' Why don't you go back there tonight and listen again." Berle did just that and heard Fay say to the manager, "I told you to keep that little Jew bastard out of the wings." A furious Berle physically attacked Fay, sending him to the hospital.

Berle's encounter with Frank Fay, though, illustrates the situation that American Jews found themselves in during the 1920s. It was an era of increased anti-Semitism reflected in job discrimination and in many other ways. For example, Harvard University's president, A. Lawrence Lowell, limited Jewish enrollment to 10 percent, in order, he claimed, to prevent anti-Semitism. *Variety* included an ad for ushers that required applicants to have blond hair and "straight noses." The Ku Klux Klan, revived in Dallas by a dentist in 1922, had grown in 1924 to a group with a membership of more than 4 million people in forty-three states. The anti-Semitic forgery *Protocols of the Elders of Zion* was serialized in Henry Ford's *Dearborn Independent*, which by 1925 had a circulation of seven hundred thousand. Ford made his dealers distribute a monthly quota of his paper. The anti-Semitic campaign lasted for ninety-one issues, eventually charging that Benedict Arnold had been "a Jewish front." Anti-immigration laws were enacted that would have a profound and horrible effect in the 1930s when Hitler came to power.

Anti-Jewish sentiment was ironically increasing as the secularization of American Jews dramatically continued. From 1914 to 1924, for example, consumption of kosher meat fell by 30 percent. The generation that came of age in the 1920s was a transitional one that felt neither fully Jewish nor fully American. Immigration had itself weakened families because of separations, desertions, and the inevitable temptations the New World offered. Contrary to popular mythology, prior to World War I, the Jews had the highest divorce rate in New York City because of the tensions of immigrant life and the long separations. Jews felt a sense of their own Jewishness, but they weren't quite sure how to define the content of that identity. Increasingly, popular culture became the most crucial bond uniting the varying segments of the Jewish community. In particular, it was the comedians who helped Jews deal with the world.

Perhaps not surprisingly, the Jewish comedians who thrived in vaudeville and survived to be remembered were specifically the ones who did not do "Jewish" bits. Joe Welch, Smith and Dale, Weber and Fields, and other Jewish dialect comedians such as Benny Rubin are not as widely recalled and did not define American culture nearly as much as George Burns, Jack Benny, Milton Berle, and the Marx Brothers. These successful comedians provided an assimilationist model based on a subtle contract offered by the culture: Jewish comedians, more specifically male comedians, were fully accepted so long as their humor was, or seemed to be, universally applicable. This message, combined with the anti-Semitism of the era, made the Jews of that generation uncertain of their own identity.

They wanted American approval, but they deliberately chose not to discard their Jewishness. They hid it, but did not surrender it. These immigrant Jewish comedians developed a "double consciousness," a sense of being Jewish but having to hide it to win approval and a sense of being American, but not fully so. Such a "double consciousness" in many ways defined American Jewish life and the Jewish comedians who found success in America.

World War I and its aftermath added to everyone's uncertainty. The effect of the war, coupled with the dislocations of urbanization and the adjustment to new technology, was devastating. Suddenly, the future didn't seem so clearly headed toward progress. Putting off pleasure was chancy and immediate satisfaction much more attractive. The Roaring Twenties unleashed a pent-up sexual energy held down by Victorian morality and a belief in progress. Women, who had finally been given the vote in 1920, were joined by men in seeing evolving sexual attitudes as a new freedom in America.

By the time the 1920s ended with the stock market crash, the whole of American life was about to change. The economic collapse, the technology that led to radio and sound films, the emergence of a new generation, and the rising horror in Europe all combined to make the 1930s and 1940s an entirely new world. By the 1930s, vaudeville would be dead, fatally wounded by the skyrocketing popularity of radio and sound motion pictures. Jewish comedians did not play a major role in silent films or in radio much before 1930. And as the 1930s dragged on, the smiles on Jewish faces would emigrate when faced with the reality of the Nazi menace. When those smiles returned, they would be newly haunted not just by the centuries of hatred of the Jews but also by the unspeakable memories summoned by a single word: "Holocaust."

II

THE YEARS

OF FEAR

1930–1950

3

THEATER
OF THE MIND

RADIO'S FINEST HOUR

E arly in 1932, Jack Benny decided to take some time off from his vaudeville act to learn about radio, the new guest being invited into the homes of an increasing number of Americans. "I'm going to study this thing backward and forward," he said. "The big future in our business is the radio."

By March 29, Benny was ready for his first appearance, as a guest on Ed Sullivan's show. His initial words were: "Hello, folks. This is Jack Benny. There will now be a slight pause for everyone to say, 'Who cares?'" The self-effacing jokester actually was not the Jack Benny who emerged later in radio. That character would take time, even after Benny began his own program on May 2.

As he developed his character and shaped his program, Benny

55

and his writers transformed American entertainment. Typical radio performers, unsurprisingly, drew on their vaudeville experiences and made radio a vaudeville extension sent into living rooms rather than being performed in theaters. The gags, puns, and quick patter of repartee and the reliance on a "stooge" (often an announcer) to feed the comedian straight lines worked well enough, but Benny saw—in a way others didn't—that the new medium had its own environment, one that made change necessary.

All the performers were shocked at radio's requirements. In vaudeville, a comedian could survive on a single twenty-minute skit. The comedian would go from theater to theater around the country repeating the same routine. By the time a comedian returned to a city, the audience had long forgotten the skit or remembered it with enough fondness to want it repeated, and so the whole process could begin again. Radio was completely different. A skit done once could not be repeated the following week; new material was needed all the time.

Struggling to deal with such a reality, the comedians found several potential solutions. Some added variety to their comedy shows, effectively copying a vaudeville program by having a singer perform during the comedy show. Some tried to keep repeating material and failed. Almost all quickly realized they would need writers to create the jokes. Experts at quick gags found themselves in high demand. A generation of writers who had planned to be the next Hemingways decided that their creative urges could be much more lucratively satisfied by turning to radio.

Many of these humor writers were Jewish as well. The widespread perception that Jews were the masters of comedy writing is illustrated by a perhaps apocryphal but nonetheless telling story as told by George Burns. An advertising agency supposedly sent a memo to a producer of a show: "We suggest you hire several young writers to work on the show." The producer fired back his own memo: "I'll be glad to hire as many young writers as you like, but if you want the scripts done on time, I also need two old Jews and a typewriter."

Part of Jack Benny's special genius is that whereas many comedians famously maltreated the writers who labored long and hard to create jokes for them, Benny just as famously had a special relationship with his writers. When Groucho Marx once refused to follow the script the writers had prepared, Benny declared that Groucho simply would not be a guest on the show. Benny's support produced not just loyalty but also an atmosphere in which inspired work could be produced. Benny served as a comedy editor, going painstakingly through each show with a perfect ear. He knew, as the writer George Belzer once put it, that "every line has a rhythm." Benny's musical training was invaluable, as was his comic sense. He trusted his own sense of humor, once expressing gratitude that he hadn't gone to college because doing so would have robbed him of the same sensibility as the common listener. Benny timed jokes, silences (which he called "waits"), and laughs, and lines were written based on the voice rhythms of the actor. Over many years, Benny made character comedy central and put his character in a variety of situations. A continuing cast, with each actor having identifiable characteristics, was assembled. A conversational style that increasingly de-emphasized jokes was developed.

Stinginess was the most famous part of the Benny persona, one that he often claimed had been invented accidentally because audiences had laughed at some "cheap" jokes, and so they were added. But, as noted, the stinginess was not based on a Jewish stereotype. (It's unnerving to watch Benny out of his character in the early movie short *A Broadway Romeo* [1931] pursuing a young woman and mocking a Scotsman who is reluctant to buy a magazine at a stand Benny is caring for.) The most famous of Benny's cheap jokes involved a robbery. The Benny character was walking home at night. There was a sound effect of footsteps behind him. A man's voice asks for a match, and Benny says he has one. Then the man's voice gets harsher.

"Don't make a move. This is a stickup."

"What?"

"You heard me."

"Mister, mister, put down that gun."

"Shut up. Now come on. Your money or your life."

Benny paused, and the thief said, "Look, bud, I said your money or your life."

"I'm thinking it over!" Benny replied in what might be the most famous comedy line in radio history.

Many people mistakenly believe that this joke got the longest laugh in all of radio, or at least the longest laugh Jack Benny ever got. Benny himself recalled the laugh going on in waves. But listening to the March 28, 1948, show is illuminating. The laughter is loud but lasts for just seven seconds, a good laugh but hardly historic. Evidently, the legend began because John Crosby, a well-known radio columnist, was a guest on that show, liked the joke, and wrote about it several times, giving publicity to an individual joke that eventually took on mythic proportions.

Jack Benny is justly famous for his timing. He very frequently asked writers to insert unfunny words into the dialogue, words that could easily be removed. Benny used these weak lines to measure laughter or applause (he called the time for such laughter and applause the "spread"). If the laughter was weak, Benny could say the next line quickly to get on to the next gag line. If the laugh was strong, Benny would say the line more slowly, giving the audience a second's pause so he wouldn't trample on the laughter for the next line.

Listeners loved the Benny character. Once at a nightclub (variously reported as Earl Carroll's or the Moulin Rouge), Benny gave a large tip to the hatcheck girl. She returned it and said, "Please, Mr. Benny, leave me with some illusions."

In developing the cheap character, Benny showed his genius by making himself the scapegoat. In this way, Benny could not be accused of ascribing cheapness to an ethnic group or to another person. More important, by making himself the object of derision, he created a character who could be put in a variety of situations, with a distinct personality that could carry over from situation to situation and thus from show to show. Had the butt of jokes remained a stooge, such a character would be used sparingly and could not, in any case, carry the entire program.

The attraction of such a character during the depression is obvious. Economic necessity made many radio listeners cheap themselves. They had to be very careful about how they spent their money. Such cheapness, though, brought with it guilt, emotional depression, and anger. Parents believed they were unable to provide for their families. Those out of work worried about whether they'd ever get a job again. Even those who survived comfortably were worried about how widespread the depression would become and how long it would last, concerned that their own comfort might evaporate. The Benny character helped audience members laugh at that frightening part of themselves. Additionally, because of his exaggerated stinginess, Benny made "normal" cheapness much more sensible. He was giving his listeners emotional permission not to feel bad about watching their money. As Benny himself put it, "My character sustained . . . because I played a character who had all the faults and frailties of mankind. . . . Every family has that kind of a person."

The cultural historian Susan J. Douglas makes an astute observation that the Benny character had what at the time were considered feminine traits—vanity about age and appearance, regular giggling, and a lack of sexual assertiveness. Douglas reads the character as an attack on both masculinity and upper-class pretensions. Upper-class males, the rulers of America, had failed their country by leading it into the depression. The anger that audiences felt toward such a group was palpable. That audience was made up of unemployed men who blamed either themselves or the government for their predicaments, and their families who simultaneously wanted to blame the male head of the household but did not do so in order to keep the family together. The Benny character subtly attacked the leaders without ever being political. Audiences may not have realized the emotional effects the character was having, but they recognized that they felt better after the program.

Of course, Benny himself was Jewish, and cheapness was a characteristic that anti-Semites ascribed to Jews. Worse still, anti-Semitism was growing in America and dramatically so in Europe. Benny also mocked his own prowess with a violin, a musical instrument widely identified with Jews, and the Benny program produced two Jewish ethnic stereotypes as characters, Mr. Kitzel and Schlepperman.

But the Benny character did not encourage anti-Semitism. People liked Benny as a performer and found his character weaknesses endearing and personal rather than venomous and applicable to an entire group. The audience response was more empathetic than antipathetic, and empathetic laughter doesn't go well with prejudice.

Audiences found Benny's incompetent violin playing to be funny and not self-hating. (He was so well known for his lack of ability that he once approached the White House gate with his violin in a case. As he approached, a marine guard stopped and asked him what was in the case. Benny responded that it was a machine gun. The marine smiled and said, "You can pass, then. For a minute I thought it was your violin.")

Also, it is unclear how many Gentile listeners even knew Jack Benny was Jewish. Indeed, a young Tommy Smothers was among those listening to Benny and learning the lessons of comic timing without ever realizing that the hilarious Benny was Jewish. Those who did know could find comfort in Benny, whereas others might also find it comforting that so many people did not seem to care or know what Benny believed in.

In addition, in limited number and in small doses, audiences enjoyed the clearly Jewish characters on the shows. Mr. Kitzel was illustrative of this point. His cry of "mit a pickle in the middle" became a national catchphrase. On one program Benny encountered Kitzel rooting at a baseball game.

"I didn't know you liked baseball so much, Mr. Kitzel," Benny said.

"Like baseball, Meestah Benneh? I'm crazy about this national pastime, what you call. In fact, I'm telling you something, Meestah Benneh, in my youngeh days, I was a professional player. I used to pitch baseball."

"I didn't know that, Mr. Kitzel."

"Once I even had a no-heet game."

"What was the score?"

"Twenty-six to zero. We lost."

"How could you? I thought you pitched a no-hitter."

"I did—but hoo hoo HOO—deed I walk them!"

On another occasion, Benny encountered Mr. Kitzel at Union Station in Los Angeles and asked him where he was going.

"Gung? Who's gung? I'm vaiting. A train I'm meeting, Meestah Benneh. I'm vaiting for mine son to come home from college."

"And what college does he attend?"

"Southern Methodist, Meestah Benneh." (To Benny's surprise,

he got letters from Jewish students who actually attended Southern Methodist University. Several hundred Jewish students were enrolled there, and there were two Jewish fraternities; one of the fraternities invited Mr. Kitzel's son to pledge.) Kitzel's habit of ascribing Jewish names to people (Nat King Cohen, for example) was another source of great humor for audiences.

It wasn't just with regard to Jews that Benny realized playing to humorous stereotypes opened the door for more progressive reconsiderations. The use of white actors for African Americans, most famously in the *Amos and Andy Show*, was radio's substitute for blackface. Nevertheless, radio was a rehearsal for desegregation. Benny hired Eddie Anderson, an African American actor, to play his servant Rochester. Anderson had permanent laryngitis as a result of yelling as a youngster selling newspapers to support his family, and his distinctive voice was what attracted Benny. Until 1943, the Rochester character was filled with stereotypes. He gambled, he drank gin, and he went after women. However, even then, Rochester was an equal in mocking the Benny character. This was crucial because a servant—a black servant—was given lines putting down his white boss with the same verve and skill as others in the cast. Benny once said, "I never felt and I do not feel today that Rochester and Mr. Kitzel were socially harmful. You don't hate a race when you're laughing with it." Indeed, Benny seemed to resent the charge: "Everybody loved ethnic humor during vaudeville and often the people who were being ridiculed most enjoyed the kind of ethnic humor aimed at their own group. During World War II, attitudes changed. Hitler's ideology of Aryan supremacy put all ethnic humor in a bad light. It became bad taste to have Jewish jokes." Benny even saw a socially redeeming purpose in ethnic humor: "I think it was a way that America heated up the national groups and the ethnic groups in a melting pot and made one people of us—or tried to do so."

Benny countered any anti-Jewish elements in his character by being quietly but unmistakably Jewish in his personal life. He married a Jewish woman in an Orthodox ceremony. When he and his wife wanted to adopt a baby, they went to a Jewish agency. One Sunday afternoon, Benny was preparing for his show that would be finished by four o'clock in Los Angeles, before sunset and the beginning of Yom Kippur. Benny was concerned by the fact that on the East Coast the program wouldn't air until after sundown and listeners might believe it was a live show. He told an assistant that he didn't "want people to think I'm desecrating this holiday by working on it." The assistant joked that all the Jews on the East Coast would be in synagogue. Benny shook his head and said, "I wasn't thinking of the Jews. I wouldn't like the Gentiles to think I didn't respect my religion."

Benny also used his influence to confront anti-Semitism. In 1939, at the New York World's Fair, Eddie Cantor gave a speech while holding a photograph of a check given by the German American Bund to an American who, according to Cantor, was "playing footsie with the Nazis." The courageous Cantor specifically named Father Coughlin as the recipient. Headlines that evening read "Comedian Blasts Priest," and Cantor's radio program was canceled the next day. Cantor was out of work for a year until Jack Benny personally intervened. Benny called up the advertising agency Young and Rubicam. "If radio's going to go on, Eddie Cantor must be part of it. . . . Why should he be punished just for having more guts than the rest of us?" Shortly thereafter, Cantor was back on the air.

In 1948, Cantor would again call on Benny, this time to give to the State of Israel, then fighting its War of Independence. Golda Meyerson (later Meir) met with a group of people at Cantor's house, seeking the desperately needed funds. Benny sent over a signed check with the note: "Eddie, fill in this check for whatever you need." Cantor filled the check in for twenty-five thousand dollars, which he knew was the minimum Benny would have given.

But most of these Jewish commitments were made as private figures, not public celebrities. If later Jewish comedians would be Jewish and demand that audiences accept that identity, radio Jews were trying to forestall criticism by accepting the stereotypes themselves.

This East European–like passivity in the face of authority was a clear indication of how uncertain American Jews felt in their new land. Their sensibilities could be unleashed only subtly, as Benny did. They could use language as a weapon, but only within carefully restricted American subject matter. The structures of Jewish comedy could be seen in Benny's parodies of movies or Cantor's quick patter. But the full gift of Jewish comedy could not be used on radio.

There had been specifically Jewish characters on radio. One famous one was Mrs. Nussbaum (played by Minerva Pious on Fred Allen's show) who also did dialect and gave Jewish names to clearly non-Jewish people, even enemies (such as Emperor Shapiro-hito). But whereas a small number of clearly Jewish types were encouraged, they were—except for Gertrude Berg playing Molly Goldberg—not accepted as leading actors. The Jewish character actors had foreign accents and engaged in silly behavior. They were harmless and peripheral. Smart and skilled Jewish characters, fully integrated into the spotlight of American society, would have been far less tolerated. Such a reception gave Jewish entertainers such as Benny a cruel choice: consciously suppress their Jewishness and Jewish involvements or lose an audience. The comedians mostly conformed to audience desires. A lot of the Jewish comedians changed their names; presented themselves as non-Jewish (as mentioned earlier, many people thought George Burns was Irish; Groucho Marx believed audiences thought the Marx Brothers were Italian); were careful to avoid overtly Jewish content, which, however, did sometimes appear in many subtle ways; married Gentile women or, more commonly, several serially; and in other ways tried to purchase some insurance against failure by assimilating into the society and being recognized only as an American by their audiences.

Still, even if their gifts were restrained, Jews made enormous contributions to radio. Here, after all, was a medium entirely built on sound and voice, and talent in radio comedy was based on verbal wit. Jews, more than any other ethnic group, had relied on language as the basis for their religion, as a source of the humor that sustained them, and as a weapon. Radio seemed built for Jewish comedians. It is unsurprising that they succeeded both as writers and as performers.

Much has been made of radio as a "theater of the mind," with audience members as coproducers of the show, supplying the images that went along with the voices and sound effects that constituted radio reality. Television, on the other hand, required a minimum nod to reality, if only because the images had to be actually seen by the audience, and therefore sets had to be built. Partially for this reason, almost every radio comedian who made a successful jump to television, including both George Burns and Jack Benny, found radio better despite the fact that they couldn't use facial gestures or props or funny costumes developed in vaudeville.

The humor of radio, as in vaudeville, frequently focused on puns. Ed Wynn was the master. His show, on at 9:30 P.M. on Tuesdays, at one point drew 74 percent of those listening to their radios. "I was just carrying a jar of jelly wrapped in newspaper when it fell on the floor and broke. You should see the jam Dick Tracy is in today" was a typical Wynn routine. Eddie Cantor, another punster, talking about bullfighting with the Mad Russian, a character on his show:

"So what happened?" Cantor asked.

"The bull ran towards me."

"He lunged?"

"Lunged? He looked like he didn't even have breakfast."

Though silly, puns are also subversive. They undermine the authority of language by ignoring certain rules as well as emphasizing the way language can be twisted to impart surprise. In addition, they illustrated the postimmigrant generation's inability to speak English correctly (a clear symbol of their continuing outsider status), and served as a way station to later generations that handled English well. One additional important reason that puns were so prevalent is that radio comedians were severely restricted in the material they could use. Sponsors had ruled out controversy and ethnic jokes. Censorship rules eliminated obscenity or overtly sexual material. Given the particular audience and these many restrictions, puns were the safest, surest way to construct jokes. However, to many contemporary ears, a series of weak, obvious puns seems inferior comedy.

With its mass audiences, radio homogenized taste. Listeners in Dubuque and Brooklyn alike laughed at Jack Benny. And the pervasiveness of radio—by the mid-1930s, three out of four homes had at least one—its relatively cheap cost, and the comic qualities of its programs eventually doomed vaudeville. The three hundred vaudevillians who quit the circuit in 1929 knew that radio was the future and vaudeville the past. Their departure signaled the end of vaudeville's power but simultaneously fed a lot of talent into radio.

The radio audiences may have been large, but methods to ask them about their tastes were rudimentary and relied on memory rather than tracking during the actual listening to the program. Not knowing how mass audiences would react, advertisers were understandably cautious. Sponsors insisted on clean, inoffensive material. Perhaps the depression and the eventual world war also made audiences themselves seek the safe comfort of familiar material rather than wanting to explore the new. Additionally, the experiences of motion picture scandals (from Fatty Arbuckle being accused of mutilating an actress to a deaf audience lip-reading actors in a silent film and uncovering a common practice—the actors passed the time not speaking the dialogue but swearing at each other) and the emergence of the Hays Office provided a sobering lesson to radio producers.

There were, of course, numerous prominent Gentile radio comedians, such as Fred Allen, Edgar Bergen, Bob Hope, Jimmy Durante, Bob and Ray, Abbott and Costello, Fibber McGee and Molly, Freeman F. Gosden and Charles J. Correll (who played Amos and Andy), and many others. Some of these comedians relied on standard American humor, especially tall tales and folksy, warm sentiment. But the prominence of Jewish comedians served to expose large numbers of Americans to Jewish sensibilities, and by and large they found those sensibilities congenial indeed.

Not every Jewish vaudeville star made a seamless transition to radio. Ed Wynn, for example, suffered from "mike fright." When he spoke on the radio, his voice sounded more like a shriek. His nervousness made him perform in costume in front of radio audiences and in makeup; he was the first performer to do so. His mimicry of the vaudeville performance, of course, was sad, and he once admitted, "I simply cannot work unless there is a theater atmosphere."

George Jessel was also lost in the new medium. He loved to ad-lib, and vaudeville audiences were used to his doing so. Like Groucho Marx, he resented the time limitations imposed by radio, limitations that made it necessary to stick to a carefully crafted script, which had been tested against the clock. In addition, too many ad-libs interrupted the tenuous reality that scripts established. Jessel would wander away from the microphone and ignore the strict time constraints. Jessel's overt Jewishness, illustrated by his New York–centric humor, was also unappealing to audiences outside New York. The mass audience demanded that performers lose their specificity and find subjects and personae that could be understood, appreciated, and, most important, laughed at by enough Americans to attract advertisers. Jessel's career withered.

Milton Berle frequently ad-libbed in such a way as to break the rhythm of the script, which contributed to his failure to master radio even though he was so gifted a comedian. Eddie Cantor was an ad-libber who succeeded on radio because he was able to keep the lines both brief and relatively few in number, and he intuitively or consciously knew not to interrupt the script at the wrong time. But much of Cantor's appeal, so obvious to vaudeville audiences, rested in his skipping and hand clapping as he sang. All this energy and charm was lost on the radio. His voice was thin and high, neither strong nor distinctive, especially in comparison with the more recognizable voices radio produced. The comedy was there, but even that was merely good, not original.

Even the Marx Brothers were unsuccessful on radio. Their first show was titled *Flywheel, Shyster, and Flywheel*; it lasted for only one season, 1932–1933. Though unpopular, the radio show nonetheless proved fruitful; fifteen routines from the series later wound up, in one form or another, in their film *Duck Soup*. (The Flywheel name also was later used in *The Big Store*.) The humor was classic Marx Brothers—without, given radio's limitations, a place for Harpo.

GROUCHO: This is an outrage, Ravelli—locking us out of our own office on Christmas Day. . . . A fine Christmas this is. When I woke up this morning I looked in my stocking and what do I find? *Your foot.*

CHICO: Ah, what'sa matter? You *gave* me that stocking.

68

GROUCHO: *I* gave you that stocking?

CHICO: Sure, lasta night. I ask you what you give me for Christmas, and you say you give me a sock.

GROUCHO: Just for that, Ravelli, you get no present from me.

CHICO: You got a present for me, boss? At'sa fine. What is it?

GROUCHO: I can't tell you, Ravelli. It's a secret.

CHICO: Ah, I no smoka segrets. I smoka cigars.

GROUCHO: One more crack like that and you'll get cigars. Scars all over your body.

The better-known comedians succeeded in radio by learning to adapt. No one did this as well as George Burns. At one point, Burns noted that his ratings were slowly falling. He knew that a large ratings drop in a single week was less troublesome because it indicated another event was taking place. Incremental, small drops were more dangerous. Concerned, Burns turned to friends such as Jack Benny and Eddie Cantor for advice, but no suggestions seemed to help. Then, one night, unable to sleep, he found the problem. He and Gracie were married and older, and their humor was that of a young, unmarried couple. He simply went on the air and told the audience that from then on the characters would be a married couple. The ratings rose, and Burns and Allen never looked back.

Growing as characters over their radio careers, Burns and Allen learned from Jack Benny that gags had given way to character and what would later be known as "situation comedy." Those who couldn't grasp this, or couldn't develop a likable character to put in a variety of situations, eventually lost their audiences.

Milton Berle had an energetic but too eager-to-please radio voice. Berle, unlike Benny and Burns, did not do character comedy but relied on an endless supply of one-liners. If an audience didn't like a particular gag, another one was right behind it:

69

For some reason I can't forget my school days. What memories. I can still remember that little black schoolhouse. It was in Pittsburgh. I may not have been the smartest boy in the class, but I wasn't far away from the smartest—about three seats away. How we kept the teacher on her toes. We put tacks on her chair. Mathematics was a pipe for me. One and one is two, and two and two is four, four and four is eight, eight and eight is sixteen, sixteen and sixteen—and then there's geography.

The Jewish women comics of the era were generally less successful, less accepted by audiences. The most important exceptions were Fanny Brice and Gertrude Berg.

Fanny Brice's most successful character was Baby Snooks, a four-and-a-half-year-old child she played with a cute, easily recognizable voice. The character was based on a bit of improvisation done by Brice at a party in 1921 and had been used in sketches on Broadway. The choice to speak through the voice of a little girl was especially clever, for such a character could deflect the troubles audiences had in accepting Jewish women as comics, and, like the puppet Charlie McCarthy, a child had permission to make comments that would be offensive or cruel if said by an adult. There is the natural human tendency to see in childhood a lost freedom from responsibility, even from reason, that is not acceptable in adults.

For Jews, though, there were special anxieties about growing up in a world long hostile to Jewish interests. The ability to utter truths without serious repercussions—a luxury available to child characters such as Baby Snooks—had often been denied to Jews through much of their history. The literal safety afforded by childhood, coupled with a release from economic hardships and dealing with anti-Semites, made feeling like a child emotionally attractive. Moreover, Jews sometimes had to withhold their real intelligence and feelings to survive; they had to pretend that they had a stunted intellectual and emotional growth. In this sense, Jewish performers pretending to be children metaphorically represented their ancestors' very real acting in everyday life.

It was against such a background that Fanny Brice succeeded in creating her Baby Snooks. A typical show had the child annoying her father by getting into trouble and then getting out of it. The plots were thin and the jokes were relatively weak:

(A phone rings)
SNOOKS: Hello.
MAN: Hello, I want to talk to Mr. Higgins.
SNOOKS: He ain't here. Who's calling, please?
MAN: This is Mr. Mudge from across the street. Who is this?
SNOOKS: This is Hortense, the maid.
MAN: Well, listen, Hortense. You tell Higgins to call me as
    soon as he gets in, see? It's about that brat kid of his.

But the humor did not come from the cleverness of the writing; rather, it rested almost entirely on the comic inflections and sound of Brice's voice.

If Brice's gift was a child's voice, Gertrude Berg's gift was a warm, motherly voice. Berg's creation, *The Goldbergs,* stood out in being a clearly ethnic comedy, with a woman as the moral head of a household and a Jewish woman as writer, director, and producer of the show. Indeed, the early shows (when the program was named *The Rise of the Goldbergs*) focused on humor that emerged from the Yiddish-induced mangling of English. The sentiment was as thick as the accent.

Originally, *The Goldbergs* didn't have a sponsor; the network broadcast it whenever space in the schedule needed to be filled. Yet, *The Goldbergs* survived. In part this was a tribute to Berg's great energy, drive, and genius.

Berg's rise to radio began at Fleischmann's, a resort hotel in the Catskills that was run by her father, Jacob. After writing skits there, she wrote a five hundred–word script, filled with dialect, but didn't know what to do with it. She called all her friends, but no one had a connection to someone in radio. Berg's husband, Lew, knew Herman Bernie, the brother of the comedian Ben Bernie. Berg finally got up the nerve to call him, and he agreed to read the script. Herman Bernie called a Mr. Schwartz, who was then in charge of programming at WMCA. Schwartz got Berg a job doing a commercial for a Christmas cookie. The commercial was supposed to be read in Yiddish, but Berg couldn't read the language so she memorized the commercial, establishing the voice that would work so well for her.

Berg went to CBS Radio in 1929 with a new script. Her show got on—and was immediately canceled after the first broadcast. Someone at CBS didn't like it.

Soon after the stock market crashed, NBC asked for a copy of a new script Berg had written called *The Rise of the Goldbergs*. Bill Rainey, the program director, asked Berg to read the script for him. He then gave Berg a four-week contract. A week later the show was on the air.

Berg developed an interesting mix, creating a show that was a cross between a situation comedy and a soap opera. Each show skillfully wove together laughter, some sadness, and a moral lesson. A principal strategy was to have strife between the immigrant generation played by Berg and the new, more fully American generation. There was a perceptible difference over the years, with Molly Goldberg and her husband, Jake, subtly losing some of their thick Yiddish accents. Finally, the show changed its setting, having the Goldbergs move out of New York.

The secret of Berg's appeal was rooted in the warmth she projected. She was the mother audience members had or wished they had. It was an era in which Jewish mothers were the models of perfect mothers, sacrificing all for their children's happiness. The warmth of Yiddish, as constructed by Berg, was infectious.

MOLLY: Reading the paper, David?

DAVID: What else?

MOLLY: So read me.

DAVID: Listen. A gangster shot a man in the telephone booth and left him standing.

MOLLY: Yeah? What'll we have for supper, David?

DAVID: Whatever.

MOLLY: I thought maybe noodles—soft—it shouldn't be too hard for your new teeth . . .

DAVID: For me you don't have to bother.

MOLLY: For who else would I not bother?

Many of Berg's common phrases were copied nationally, such as "So who's to know?" or her opening call to a neighbor, "Yoo-hoo, Mrs. Bloom." Berg also used Yiddish intonations with English words, an especially clever strategy because it Americanized the language just enough while keeping the humorous charm of the original:

MOLLY: Jake, it's Shabbes. You must go to voik also today?

JAKE: Molly, how many times must I tell you. I go to beezness, not to voik.

MOLLY: But Jake, don't you alvays tell me you're voiking hard?

JAKE: Yes, Molly, bot vhen it's for yourself, it's beezness.

Berg clearly and unabashedly presented the Jewish struggle to succeed, and she had the charm and skills to make audiences see that a story about Jewish immigrants in New York trying to adapt was a perfect symbol of the American people struggling to survive in the depression. Berg's nonthreatening warmth and clear lack of any assertiveness made her acceptable to American audiences.

Radio comedians were not only valuable to the country in dealing with the depression, but also vital as America entered World War II. By the early 1940s, about 90 percent of American families had at least one radio in the home and listened to the radio for, on average, between three and four hours a day. The popular shows had 30 million listeners. (There were then about 130 million Americans.)

Working with the War Advertising Council, a strategy known as the Network Allocation Plan was developed. Sponsors and advertisers were to have a message about the war on every fourth show. Daily shows had a message biweekly.

One example of the coordination between the government and radio comedy had to do with wartime gasoline rationing, which was introduced because there was a shortage of rubber. Reduced driving, it was believed, would reduce the need for tires. Whereas in the past there might have been a strictly comical sketch about the hardships, audiences now heard the following exchange among Eddie Cantor, Jack Benny, and Gracie Allen:

CANTOR: Gracie, haven't you heard that gasoline is being rationed?

GRACIE: Well, of course I know gasoline is being rationed. My goodness, what do you take me for, a dunce? I've read all about it. You're only allowed one cup a day.

CANTOR: Gracie, that's coffee.

GRACIE: Eddie, don't be silly. A car won't run on coffee . . .

BENNY: Gracie, look. What they're really rationing is mileage. The less we drive our cars the more rubber we save. And the rubber we save is vital to essential industries and to the army.

GRACIE: The army? Uses rubber?

BENNY: Sure.

GRACIE: Gee, wouldn't you think with all the modern weapons
that soldiers wouldn't have to sling shots?

Jack Benny was, of course, a natural to do material on rationing.

DON WILSON (BENNY'S ANNOUNCER): Well, Jack, gas isn't the
only thing being rationed nowadays.

BENNY: No, there are a lot of things, Don. A half pound of
sugar a week, no whipped cream, one cup of coffee a day,
a meatless Tuesday . . . But we'll have to get used to it.

MARY LIVINGSTONE (BENNY'S REAL-LIFE WIFE): Get used to
it . . . You've been rehearsing for this all your life.

Radio comedians traveled to various military bases and broadcast from them. They went on tours to entertain troops in Europe
and the South Pacific, putting on live shows. They actively promoted the sales of war bonds and appeared at events to raise funds
for the United Service Organizations (USO) and Red Cross. The
comedians were even called upon to deliver messages prepared by
the Office of War Information telling Americans about the war
effort.

And they were eager to help. Jack Benny donated a violin that
was auctioned for funds and at the end of his show reminded audience members to buy war bonds and delivered messages from the
Office of War Information. He began camp shows in 1942, traveling Mondays through Thursdays and flying back to Hollywood
for rehearsal and to broadcast his show. Benny's own experience
in the navy gave him key insights. "I knew that the basis of all military humor is griping—about the food, K.P. duty, weekend passes
and the brass," he said. Benny also walked through hospital wards,

telling jokes, just talking, and playing his violin, especially his theme song, "Love in Bloom." In 1943, Benny made his first USO tour overseas. In Benghazi, in North Africa, a B-17 crew painted some words on a bomb: To ADOLF HITLER—WITH LOVE IN BOOM. In Ismailia, Egypt, Benny searched out a kosher restaurant. He also traveled to Tel Aviv and Jerusalem, then under British control. The next summer he went to the South Pacific, and after the war, in 1946, Benny met with General Eisenhower in Berlin.

Even more than Benny, Eddie Cantor was explicit in attacking the Axis powers. Indeed, *Variety* published a letter from him on January 14, 1942, saying that after Pearl Harbor, all humor was political. "High spirits," he wrote, "are one of this country's first priorities." On one show, in a German accent, he said there was "no food shortage in Germany. Last night we had a big wienie roast. The Allied planes came over and cooked Frankfurt." On another show he announced confidently, "They'll never bomb this studio. [There is a sound of bombs.] Why can't I keep my big mouth shut?" On January 29, 1944, Cantor broadcast for twenty-four straight hours over KPO in San Francisco in order to sell war bonds. He sold $37.6 million worth.

George Burns recalled in a later interview with the American Jewish Committee the effect that Hitler's coming to power had on him: "I found myself getting very Jewish when that happened. I imagine that affected everybody the same way." He and Gracie had traveled to Poland before the war, where they saw many Jews in their beards and hats. This made him comment later that when Hitler started the war, "It was so easy to find them [the Jews], it was so easy to locate them. Half of them would have been saved had they taken off their hats. But they died with their hats on." Burns admired the Jews' stubborn pride and fierce loyalty. Though he couldn't understand religion and had never tried to raise his children as Jews, he nonetheless retained a clear sense of Jewish identity: "I've always felt Jewish ever since I can remember, and I'll always feel the same way. I've never tried to be anything else."

Milton Berle claimed to have flattened a Nazi sympathizer in Chicago and said in a 1977 unpublished interview, "I'm a proud Jew. I'm glad that I'm a Jew. . . . I feel more Jewish today than I ever felt."

The Nazi regime and its treatment of the Jews provided a unique situation and obligation for Jewish comedians. Although the Holocaust's scope and its unbearably horrific details were not fully known to the general public until after the war, the Nazi mistreatment of Jews and others was obvious from the moment of Hitler's emergence as chancellor in 1933. If the Jewish comedians had trouble conceiving of genocide as a real possibility, the more conventional elements of anti-Semitism were all too familiar.

The sad fact is that the comedians were limited by their lack of political knowledge; their reliance on hostile, indifferent, or silent American officials to provide that knowledge; and their concern to stay popular and not be too obviously Jewish, especially before the war when isolationism was popular and American Jews were frequently accused of fanning a war fever. Humor was their most potent weapon. Mel Blanc played Hitler on a Jack Benny program as a crazed maniac chewing a rug. But that was about as far as any of the Jewish—or, for that matter, non-Jewish—radio comedians went.

The support for the war effort was certainly crucial. Yet, there was no concerted effort by comedians on radio to alert the country to the full nature of the Nazi menace. The comedians' desire to be accepted by audiences restrained them from confronting European anti-Semitism. The comedians were a symbol for all American Jews, unbearably worried about Nazism, trapped in a society that didn't fully trust Jews and was reluctant to go to war. The comedians wanted continued success and American Jews wanted social acceptance, and that meant staying quiet. In 1936, even Eddie Cantor, who would later do so much for the war effort, sang an isolationist song called "If They Feel Like a War, Let Them Keep It Over There" on the *Rudy Vallee Show*. One of the lines he sang was: "Our job is to protect our loved ones over here." The war changed Cantor as it did others, but the focus was on Americans alone and did not include reference to the Jewish victims in Europe. The jokes during the war changed comedy and led to the acceptance of topical humor after the war, but for the victims and survivors of the Nazis the sounds of American laughter were hollow indeed.

And whatever Jewish comedians joked about after the war, their own smiles, whether consciously or not, would be haunted by the comedic failure to confront the anti-Semitism of American society and the genocidal plans of a madman.

4

LAUGHING
IN THE DARK

FILMS

The oldest comedic gag on film, in a French short film, was one in which a child steps on a garden hose. The water stops running and so the man holding the hose looks into the nozzle. The youngster then lifts his foot and water squirts out. The aggressive nature of film comedy and its ability to release tensions were immediately made evident. It is also telling, of course, that the humor was physical and at least marginally cruel.

Jewish characters were present in motion pictures virtually from the invention of the art form. Early one-reelers about Jews focused on Jewish stereotypes. Jewish characters were identified by their long beards and heavy mustaches. They were pawnbrokers, tailors, con artists, and cowards.

The film critic Leonard Maltin has suggested that because pantomime and visual comedy were not their strengths, Jewish comedians did not go into silent films. But there were still some Jews who made it onto the silent screen. The Jewish vaudeville team of Weber and Fields was in various films. Max Davidson played Izzy Davidson, a lazy and clearly Jewish character in a series of films for Hal Roach Studios. Sammy Cohen, a comic actor with a very large nose, had a perfect appearance for the exaggerated Jewish characters he played.

George Sidney, born Sammy Greenfield, was the most important Jewish comedian in the silent era. He began his screen career in 1915 after a time in vaudeville, where he became famous for the character of Busy Izzy. The character lent his name to the title of Sidney's first film. He then made *In Hollywood with Potash and Perlmutter* and *Partners Again, with Potash and Perlmutter* for Samuel Goldwyn and appeared most famously in *The Cohens and the Kellys* (1926) and its six sequels. Once again, the characters Sidney played were stereotypical. The Sidney character, Jacob Cohen, was overweight, wore an ill-fitting suit, had constantly moving hands and a large nose, and was unshaven. He was socially inept. He cheated at business.

Silent film obviously emphasized physical appearance and physical movement. By definition, it could not include verbal humor, the Jewish comedians' strength. Given the demands of the medium, the Jewish comedians of the silent era simply did not have the talent of those comedians whose fame has survived. Silent film comedy's greatest stars were all Gentiles and include, most prominently, Charlie Chaplin and Buster Keaton. A few commentators claimed that Chaplin was himself Jewish. Clearly, his tramp character could be seen as Jewish, though Chaplin was generic enough in appearance so that the tramp could be from any ethnic group. Still, the gossip about his being Jewish and his clearly sympathetic portrait of put-upon immigrants contributed to a sense of accepting Jews and other immigrants as comic figures not through stereotypes but through sheer talent. Both Keaton and Chaplin, though, were essentially physical comedians. Chaplin's economic movements, his uncanny use of props, and his brilliant ability to top one sight gag with another all stemmed from a physical not a verbal wit.

There were more prominent Jewish comedians in the early era of talking pictures. In *It Might Be Worse* (1930), George Jessel wants to kill himself and is even called a schlemiel. Smith and Dale made a series of films including *What Price Pants?* (1931), about a boss who is tricked into giving his worker a piece of the business when the worker tricks him into believing the worker has gotten a huge inheritance. Jack Benny, Milton Berle, George Burns, Fanny Brice, Bert Lahr, and Ed Wynn all appeared in film comedies, but none that were memorable.

And then there were the Marx Brothers.

It may well be the case that no group of movie comedians was more difficult to work with than the Marx Brothers. Chico frequently couldn't be found for a scene. While frantic searches were being undertaken for Chico, Groucho and Harpo would wander off. Zeppo was perpetually late. Harpo enjoyed setting up elaborate practical jokes much more than rehearsing scenes or even showing up on the set.

This free-spiritedness, though, belied a tremendous work ethic. The brothers had spent years traveling around the country with their mother from city to city, perfecting their act. Groucho, in particular, was endlessly exploring alternative lines, sometimes settling on the first one but only after convincing himself that the other options were less funny. He was terrifically demanding, mostly of himself. When he saw a Sunday matinee of *The Cocoanuts*, the Marx Brothers' first feature film, he was so dismayed he left, planning to buy back the film. Groucho approached Walter Wanger, who represented Paramount in New York, but it was too late. By then the reviews were in, and the movie was on its way to success. (Movie exhibitors, who had originally complained that audiences wouldn't understand the film because Groucho talked too fast, smiled as audiences returned again and again simply to make sure they got all of Groucho's witticisms.)

The Cocoanuts, made in 1929, was based on the huge stage hit of the same name, and was filmed while *Animal Crackers*, the Marx Brothers' newest Broadway show, was still running. Because the Marx Brothers were so familiar with the material, filming began with no rehearsals. That soon had to be changed; the crew laughed too hard hearing the lines and watching the antics for the first time. The film was a potpourri of pretty women in bathing suits, musical numbers, Marx madness, and a flimsy plot. There were also Yiddish words and slang, much more than in any other Marx Brothers movie. Some of these terms were so deeply hidden they almost constituted a secret language available only to Jewish audiences. The most subtle occurs when Chico and Harpo are planning to sign into the hotel. Groucho shows them the register and says: "Now step this way, boys, and just put your moniker on there and everything will be A.K." Instead of saying "O.K.," Groucho says "A.K.," an abbreviation for the Yiddish phrase *"alter kocker,"* which is usually used to describe an old, crotchety man. Its literal meaning is more vulgar. *Alter* means "old" and *kocker* means "human waste."

In another scene, Groucho says: "All along the river, those are all levees." Chico says, "That's the Jewish neighborhood," and Groucho responds, "Well, we'll pass over that." Such an interplay was at least more obvious to urban audiences who had met Jews named Levy and understood that Passover was a Jewish holiday. Rural audiences, though, were probably much more confused by the talk.

Chico is involved in other Jewish references. When leaving a detective, Chico mutters, "Ah, shalom." Chico is introduced as "Señor Pastrami" as he prepares to play the piano. Chico says to another character, "Bravo, Galitzianer." A Galitzianer is a Jew from Galicia, a province in Poland (later Austria) as opposed to a Litvak, or Lithuanian Jew. The two were often at odds.

These minor linguistic additions were prizes offered to Jewish audiences as well as a small number of outsiders. The outsiders in society were able to put one over on society by communicating without the "other" understanding.

The Marx Brothers were never religiously Jewish. Their Jewish identity was familial, ethnic, urban, and linguistic. They took being Jewish for granted but were quiet about it. In an effort to blend into American life, they had traditional Christmas trees in their homes to celebrate what they considered an American not a religious holiday. Groucho's character was not even originally Jewish. Only when the Germans sunk the *Lusitania* in 1915 did Groucho, then in vaudeville, change his character from a German to a Jewish one. Groucho was as cynical about religion as he was about all else. When his son Arthur was married in a Jewish ceremony, Groucho went up to the man performing the marriage and said, "Is it true you fellows breed like rabbis?" Indeed, nothing of a spiritual nature appealed to him. One of Groucho's wives took him to a psychic. Groucho was told she could answer any question. He turned to her and said, "What's the capital of North Dakota?" He was asked to leave.

But whether religious or not, the brothers could not avoid all anti-Jewish sentiment. There was a famous Groucho story about his son (or, in other versions, one of his daughters) at a "restricted" club, being told that he could not use the swimming pool. Groucho's reply was that since the child was only half-Jewish, could he walk in up to his knees?

The other brothers had comparable experiences. Chico and his family were once refused a room at a hotel near Lake George in upstate New York. On another occasion, Harpo arranged to stay at a hotel in Montauk, on Long Island. The hotel wired him back saying, "RESERVATIONS CONFIRMED. TRUST YOU ARE GENTILE." Harpo was furious, but he didn't want to upset the two men who were traveling with him, so he didn't send a wire back to the hotel. Instead, he went to the hotel, his pants rolled above his knees, a tam-o'-shanter on his head, holding a crooked cane, smoking a pipe, and registered himself as "Harpo MacMarx." Over dinner, he told the others what had happened, and they insisted on leaving. As they were checking out, the manager came over and Harpo said, "Lad, could ye dir-r-rect me to the near-r-rest Jewish temple?" Harpo then threw a Gookie, and they left.

Much of the Marx comic genius—and its religiously subversive nature—can be seen in such anecdotes. The Marx Brothers showed an intense willingness to mock the very society they wished to enter. In doing so, they changed the rules for future Jewish comedians who wished to entertain American audiences.

In contrast to comedians such as George Burns, Jack Benny, and Ed Wynn, who were models of assimilation, the Marx Brothers sought not to change themselves but rather to change the audience so that it could understand secular but distinctly Jewish sensibilities.

The Marx Brothers' revolution was incomplete, and it included retreats. Over time, they reduced the number of Jewish references in their films, but they maintained their commitment to alter the traditional materials at which audiences laughed. They lived their lives and they made their films on their own terms. Society would have to accept them for what they were—poor children of immigrants struggling to understand and adapt to the wider American culture. After the Marx Brothers, Jewish comedians would be freer to be themselves.

The Marx Brothers' revolution began with their characters. Groucho was irreverent, a cynical trickster who shamelessly sought money by seducing wealthy and dignified widows, a con man who ridiculed all he saw. He talked so quickly that his targets were still trying to understand the last insult while Groucho had uttered two more. Groucho inverted the Jack Benny approach of providing appropriate audience pauses. When some in the audience complained that the laughter in the theater prevented them from hearing the next line, Groucho refused to retreat. The fast-talking urban wisecracker became an American comedy type and allowed generations of Jewish comedians through the door.

Groucho's unbridled verbal attacks undertaken at breakneck speed were supplemented by his appearance. Unlike Burns or Benny, Groucho created his character by using exaggerated visual effects. His greasepaint mustache and eyebrows, his cigar, his bent way of walking, and his energetic dances made him funny in appearance and voice.

Groucho's mustache, glasses, and cigar are a sort of mask hiding his real self from outsiders and a sign of insecurity about being found out. As with all the Marx Brothers, Groucho was an outsider, even when his character was president of a country or president of a college. He didn't belong in any social environment. Harpo and Chico also wore disguises. The masks and disguises represented immigrants having to disguise their true identity, sometimes grotesquely, to adapt to life in the Golden Land. Immigrant audiences could find their own emotional identity in the Marx Brothers wearing masks precisely because the immigrants were fearful that their foreign nature might emerge and betray them, unmasking them as foreigners and making them feel like failed Americans. In wearing the masks, the Marx Brothers allowed audiences to laugh at themselves and their most deep-seated anxieties.

Fear of the exposure of the real self was most famously portrayed in the film *Duck Soup*. In a classic scene, Harpo is trying to hide from Groucho. Harpo breaks a mirror and, to continue hiding, pretends he is Groucho's reflection. Only Chico's entrance ruins Harpo's brilliant imitation. The scene made exquisite psychological sense to an immigrant audience. Harpo was trying to hide by imitating someone else, just as many immigrants and their children believed they had to hide their true selves to imitate Americans. Yet, the outsider also could find himself on the inside, as a hotel manager or doctor, for example. The two brothers, that is, portrayed the anguish of assimilation; the self that felt outside society and the self that felt inside society faced each other with the insider attempting to outwit the outsider, but with the outsider, for a time, keeping up. The pain of having both sides, with the outside self trying desperately to mimic the inside self, was thus made palpable.

Many of the Marx Brothers' routines were about those on the outside trying to get inside by seeking the key. Consider, for example, "The Password" routine from *Horse Feathers*.

CHICO: Who are you?
GROUCHO: I'm fine, thanks, who are you?
CHICO: I'm fine, too, but you can't come in unless you give the password.
GROUCHO: Well, what is the password?
CHICO: Aw, no! You gotta tell *me*. Hey, I tell what I do. I give you three guesses . . . It's the name of a fish.
GROUCHO: Is it Mary?
CHICO: Ha! Ha! Attsa no fish.
GROUCHO: She isn't. Well, she drinks like one . . .
CHICO: Now I give you one more chance.
GROUCHO: I got it. Haddock.

CHICO: Attsa funny. I gotta haddock too . . . You can't come in here unless you say "swordfish." Now I give you one more guess.

GROUCHO: Swordfish . . . I think I got it. Is it swordfish?

Again and again, questions of welcome and entry come up in the Marx Brothers' movies. In *Monkey Business*, the brothers are stowaways struggling to get into the country. In one scene, Harpo and Chico can't get in a door to a party. Harpo and Chico are also stowaways in *A Night at the Opera*.

And their plight wasn't just about Jewish immigrants. Chico's character was an Italian immigrant who held a variety of jobs, mostly of an extremely modest nature. He sold fish or peanuts. He tried to peddle toosy-frootsy ice cream or dirty postcards. He struggled, that is, for a living even as he schemed to improve his life. He also always defended the innocent Harpo, perhaps the most extreme symbol of the immigrant who cannot speak the language. Chico was the interpreter of Harpo for the world. Chico sometimes pretended to be stupid, a strategy that often worked because people confused his appearance, accent, and seeming ignorance with a lack of cunning and intelligence, both of which Chico had in ample supply. Chico's assimilationist strategy was similar to Groucho's in the acquisition of a disguise but the opposite in how he handled language. Groucho became a master of English, whereas Chico pretended he couldn't use it well.

Chico was often crucial, though by no means alone, in emphasizing a common emotion of immigrant life: the desire for food. His first question in *Animal Crackers* concerns finding the dining room. In *Monkey Business*, he, along with Groucho, steals the captain's lunch. In *A Night at the Opera*, Groucho orders a meal that Chico also eats. A central part of *Room Service* involves the struggling acting troupe's attempts to get food. Harpo is also frequently portrayed as hungry. In *A Night in Casablanca* he tries to bite Chico's thumb. This constant theme of needing food reflected not only the Marx Brothers' real early life, but the underlying anxiety of the immigrants who still felt uncertain that their next meal would be forthcoming.

Harpo embodied a third linguistic strategy: silence. Harpo's silence in the face of humiliation and hunger and his innocence in a corrupt world made him embody the pure goodness of those who don't fit into society. He gave hope and dignity to those who continued to feel like outsiders. His seeming innocence was balanced by his physical chasing of women. Here the childlike Harpo shows grown-up desires, though ones not typically satisfied. In chasing the women, Harpo complicates the tradition of Jewish comedians playing characters who are children or childlike such as Fanny Brice playing Baby Snooks. Harpo played a childlike character, but he let his mask down and revealed himself to have very adult desires. In partially revealing his adulthood, Harpo was a perfect representation of America's Jews, who were just beginning to feel comfortable in revealing their true selves to Americans. Of course, the Marx Brothers' playful, anarchic childishness also served as an outlet for the simple human desire to be freed from social inhibitions.

On the economic ladder, Harpo was even below Chico. Harpo was a bum. With Groucho as a con man or fraud, Chico as a vendor, and Harpo as a tramp, the Marx Brothers stood outside normal commercial life. In their portrayal of economic outsiders, they reflected the common feelings, especially of immigrant Jews but also of all immigrants, that they were not being allowed into the wider society.

Many Americans in the 1930s felt locked out not just from economic life but also from social life. The depression had made them lose confidence in the institutions that made up society. The Marx

Brothers mercilessly lampooned those institutions that had so deeply disappointed Americans, thus allowing audiences to vent their anger on the institutions that had failed them (the government) or that ignored or condescended to them (the wealthy and powerful). This attack, though, was skillfully controlled, the anger rationed out as carefully as gasoline or coffee would later be during the war. Groucho spoke on behalf of the audience. Harpo suffered on behalf of the audience. Chico struggled on behalf of the audience. If audiences were hungry, so would the Marx Brothers be hungry. If audiences believed they were without power, so, too, would the Marx Brothers have that belief. The brothers' funny costumes and props were exaggerated examples of their being outsiders. Like Jack Benny, who was so cheap that no audience member who had to save money could be as cheap, the Marx Brothers were so outside society by their looks and behavior that no audience members could feel more outside. By serving as comic exaggerations, the brothers made audience members feel more like insiders. This can be seen, for example, in the various ways the brothers help troubled romantic partners find true love, whereas they generally, but not always, are deprived of such love. Harpo must always chase the blondes. Groucho must always woo not because he truly loves the woman in question but because of her wealth and status. Both of these pursuits, in turn, reflect aspects of Jewish assimilation: pursuit of the non-Jewish mate (the blonde) and the non-Jewish social class. It should also be noted that Zeppo, who wore no mask or disguise, often found love in the films.

The Marx Brothers, in this respect, mirrored Jewish life. They were outsiders who didn't feel comfortable or fit into the wider society or, more commonly in Jewish history, weren't let into the society. Their assault on the kinds of political and social institutions that had been historically hostile to Jews was so fervent because the desire to attack them had been repressed for so long.

Jewish audiences, then, could emotionally identify profoundly with the various assaults of the Marx Brothers. In ways they perhaps didn't understand, mass film audiences were beginning to absorb and appreciate a Jewish sensibility and see that its concerns were their own. The emotions unleashed by Jewish comedians strangely met the needs of American audiences. Those American depression audiences could suddenly understand the Jewish experience with poverty and feelings of powerlessness.

By their third film, *Monkey Business*, there was the first clear indication of a decline of overtly Jewish elements. The brothers do hide in barrels of kippered herrings, but Yiddishisms are gone. Even more critical, at one point Groucho turns to the audience after one of Chico's remarks and says, "There's my argument. Restrict immigration." That's a remarkable line in a film in which restrictions on immigration are being mocked, but it indicates the slow move in the films away from ethnicity and toward straightforward humor.

Horse Feathers, their next feature, with its satire of higher education and college sports, was clearly aimed away from urban audiences and more toward middle Americans who would enjoy mocking college life and watching a bit of funny football. During the filming of the football game, Harpo noticed an adorable little girl, three or four years old, on the sidelines. She was part of the local population used to make up the crowd at the game. Harpo found the girl so cute that he offered her parents fifty thousand dollars if he could adopt her. The parents replied that their daughter could not be bought. Whatever the ethics, Harpo certainly had a good eye: The girl was Shirley Temple.

Duck Soup is often considered one of the best of the Marx Brothers' films. Leo McCarey, the man who had suggested that Stan Laurel and Oliver Hardy form a team, primarily provided the antiwar, antigovernment political sensibility of the film. Groucho thought McCarey was the only great director they ever had. Chico liked him because they could gamble. (Once, Chico brought a bag of walnuts and bet a hundred dollars he could throw a walnut farther than McCarey. The director, not knowing that Chico was a huckster's huckster, agreed, and threw his walnut about a hundred feet. Chico then picked one up and tossed it much farther. The impressed McCarey paid up, not knowing that Chico had filled his walnut with lead.)

The Margaret Dumont characters in the films were the embodiments of the upper crust of American society, struggling to resist the entreaties of those who sought to seduce them. In *Duck Soup*, Groucho continued his assault on Margaret Dumont and what she stood for. "I welcome you with open arms," she says, to which he replies, "Is that so? How long do you stay open?"

Sometimes Groucho's assault lasts longer:

DUMONT: I've sponsored your appointment because I feel you are the most able statesman in all Freedonia.

GROUCHO: Well, that covers a lot of ground. Say, you cover a lot of ground yourself. You'd better beat it. I hear they're going to tear you down and put up an office building where you're standing. You can leave in a taxi. If you can't leave in a taxi you can leave in a huff. If that's too soon, you can leave in a minute and a huff. You know you haven't stopped talking since I came here? You must have been vaccinated with a phonograph needle.

Duck Soup also took on political structures. In one scene the minister of war speaks about "taking up the tax."

GROUCHO: How about taking up the carpet?

MINISTER: I still insist we must take up the tax.

GROUCHO: He's right. You've got to take up the tacks before
you take up the carpet.

This mockery of taxes continued with Chico and the Minister
of Finance:

MINISTER: War would mean a prohibitive increase in our taxes.
CHICO: Hey, I got an uncle lives in Taxes.
MINISTER: No, I'm talking about taxes, money, dollars.
CHICO: Dollas! Thatsa where my uncle lives. Dollas, Taxes.

After *Duck Soup*, the Marx Brothers left Paramount for MGM,
and more particularly for the producer Irving Thalberg, the man
F. Scott Fitzgerald had nicknamed the Boy Wonder. Thalberg
developed a clear plan for the Marx Brothers: more of a story line
and fewer gags. The result was what may be their best film, *A
Night at the Opera*. In this film, Groucho could mock high art
("On account of you I nearly heard the opera"), lawyers, and
spoiled celebrities. Here was subject matter that average American audiences could enjoy.

The sparkling dialogue is illustrative of the enormous contributions made by the brilliant writers who tried to work with the
Marx Brothers—"tried" because the Marx Brothers frequently
changed the dialogue. But George S. Kaufman (who found Margaret Dumont for them), S. J. Perelman, and others made vital
contributions.

One scene in *A Night at the Opera* involves a contract Groucho
wants Chico to sign. This is a frontal assault on lawyers:

GROUCHO: Now, pay particular attention to this first clause
because it's most important. Says the, uh, the party of
the first part shall be known in this contract as the party

of the first part. How do you like that? That's pretty neat, eh?

CHICO: No, that's no good.

GROUCHO: What's the matter with it?

CHICO: I don't know. Let's hear it again.

GROUCHO: Says the, uh, the party of the first part should be known in this contract as the party of the first part.

CHICO: That sounds a little better this time.

GROUCHO: Well, it grows on you. Would you like to hear it once more?

CHICO: Uh, just the first part.

GROUCHO: What do you mean? The—the party of the first part?

CHICO: No, the first part of the party of the first part.

GROUCHO: All right. It says, the, uh, the first part of the party of the first part should be known in this contract as the first part of the party of the first part should be known in this contract . . . Look. Why should we quarrel about a thing like this? We'll take it right out, eh?

The scene continues, with Chico being opposed to the sanity clause because he knows "Sanity Claus" doesn't exist.

There were also more explicit emotional elements in *A Night at the Opera* than in earlier films. For the first time, Harpo was hit in a film. The childlike innocent evoked instant sympathy and made identification of a villain easy. There was even indirect reference to urban life, with its crowds, cramped conditions, and hunger in the famed stateroom scene when Groucho and three stowaways are joined by the engineer, the manicurist, the engineer's assistant, a woman looking for her aunt Minnie, a woman who wants to mop the floor, the steward and his assistants, and Margaret Dumont who opens the door, causing all inside to fall out.

Thalberg allowed the brothers to try out comic bits in front of live audiences, vastly improving some of the scenes. The stowaway scene developed its crucial elements before live audiences prior to filming. Although this cost a lot of money, Thalberg correctly surmised the film would be field-tested in a unique way.

A Night at the Opera was the peak for the Marx Brothers. Never again were they as vital in their films, though they were often extremely funny.

The Marx Brothers were not the only Jews to succeed once the movies had sound. Eddie Cantor made some one-reelers, such as *Getting a Ticket* (1929), which is essentially an excuse to film a vaudeville skit about a police officer who wants to give Cantor a ticket unless Cantor can prove he is really Eddie Cantor by singing a song. In *Whoopee!* (1930), the first of six films he made for Samuel Goldwyn, Cantor sang songs and appeared in blackface. He wore a disguise as a Native American, one who spoke in a Yiddish accent and identified himself by saying "Me Big Chief Izzy Horowitz" in a distinctly Jewish chant. *Whoopee!* was quite successful in New York, but less so in such places as Chicago, Louisville, and Seattle; Cantor's reliance on his clearly Jewish character was inhibiting his wider approval. So, like the Marx Brothers, over time Cantor steadily de-emphasized the Jewish aspects of his film personality, a process the social critic Irving Howe called "de-Semitization." This attempt at assimilation, which producers forced to try to sell pictures to wider audiences, became more and more pronounced.

Whoopee! dealt with intermarriage. The Jewish Cantor character, Henry Williams, is in love with his Gentile nurse, whereas the other white female is in love with Wanensis (whom she believes to be a Native American). The Jewish-Gentile relationship was in fact common in popular entertainment and reflected a widespread belief that in the melting pot that was America, love was more important than ancient religious traditions.

Jewish audiences found this premise troubling. In the 1930s and
'40s, very few American Jews intermarried. Jewish comedians, on
the other hand, frequently married Gentile women (for example,
George Burns, George Jessel, Phil Silvers, all the Marx Brothers,
and Bert Lahr). Had the American Jewish community known that
Jewish comedians were prophetic in their romantic attachment to
Gentiles, perhaps the concerns would have been greater, but interfaith marriages did not rise precipitously until the beginning of the
1960s; by 1990, more than half of Jews who were getting married
chose a Gentile partner. The comedians did not see themselves as
romantic Jewish forerunners. They saw themselves as Americans
and did not want to endanger their assimilationist success by
reverting to a traditional pattern of Jewish life. Not always handsome, Jewish male comedians found themselves able to date and
wed beautiful Gentile women. The lures of Gentile America were
powerful indeed.

At the end of *Whoopee!* the white–Native American romance is
able to proceed only when Wanensis's Native American parents
reveal that their son is actually white, that he was left as a baby and
raised in the tribe. This retreat from confronting a difficult issue
takes away from the power of the film, but clearly raises the question of what exactly the melting pot is willing to melt. *Whoopee!*
also contains a scene that, in retrospect, is quite disturbing. At one
point Cantor crawls into an oven and comes out in blackface,
enabling him to sing. The blackface remains offensive, but the
scene of a Jew in an oven is horrifying after the Holocaust. Amazingly, a similar scene is in the later Cantor film *Kid Millions* (1934).
The first time Cantor appears he is hiding in an oven—and he has
a brother in the film named Adolf. Cantor also appears in blackface in this film during "Minstrel Night." The plot, about Eddie's
character inheriting $77 million, is weak. Eddie plays a reluctant
groom ("A wedding is a funeral where you smell your own flow-

ers"). At one point, he does say to an Arab sheik, "Let my people go," but that is about the only Jewish reference.

Like the Marx Brothers, the Three Stooges also reflected immigrant life. But whereas the Marxes tended to band together to fight the outside world, the Stooges turned inward. They used their physical antics, the face slaps, nose punches, and hair pullings, on each other. That is, theirs was a sadder comedy because they showed that the much touted closeness of family life brought tremendous internal strife. Audiences uncomfortable with their spouses, their siblings, their parents, or their children could find a family replicated in Moe the parent and Larry and Curly (and later Shemp and others) the children. The themes of close family, confusion about a place in society, and feeling like a victim were tangibly Jewish in origin. And the American laughs at the Three Stooges are releases from family tensions, aggression sublimated to humor, anger let out in art so that it is not let out in life.

The Stooges exaggerated the attacks with clever sound effects. When a character sat on a flame, the sound used was butter that was being fried in a pan. The plucking of ukulele strings aurally enhanced an eye being poked. A whip was cracked to add an effect to a slapped face. A cloth was ripped to accompany a shock of hair being pulled. When someone was knocked out, there was often the sound of a bird chirping.

Sizzling butter and cracking whips weren't the only Stooge sounds; there were also a few Yiddishisms. In *Hokus Pokus* (1949), they generously applied a talcum powder named Schlemiel Number Eight. In *Malice in the Palace* (1940), they struggled against the emir of Shmow, a term that later applied to a train car in *Cuckoo on the Choo Choo* (1952). (*Schmo* is not actually a Yiddish word, but a combination of Yiddish and English. It is a more polite substitute for the obscene Yiddish word *schmuck,* which can refer to a schlemiel, the way *schmo* does, but more literally refers to the male organ.)

Danny Kaye made several movie shorts during 1937 and 1938, but his major movie career developed in the mid-1940s by making a series of films for Samuel Goldwyn. Kaye had, like so many comics, left school, and, after working in the Catskills, he gained fame on Broadway in *Straw Hat Revue*. He then starred, also on Broadway, in *Lady in the Dark*. Goldwyn enjoyed the show and wanted to sign Kaye but didn't like the young man's looks. His large nose, Goldwyn thought, made him look too Jewish. Goldwyn settled for just having Kaye dye his red hair blond.

Kaye was a great mimic and master of language. Expert at "scat" songs, which sounded like jazz music but contained syllables that made no sense, he was also impressive in singing complex, funny lyrics often written by his wife, Sylvia Fine. Kaye's intelligence was always evident as was his charm and emotional vulnerability, all of which made audiences feel close to him. Kaye represented not the literal outsider, as did the Marx Brothers, but the confused insider. In this, Kaye was a transition figure for Jewish comedians. He felt much more fully American than the Marx Brothers, but his role was not yet clear.

One aspect that some critics have noted is the sexual nature of some of his unmasculine characters, which enabled Kaye to present an alternative mask to the one the Marx Brothers wore. The Jew could enter the society but not fully as a man. The American identity, that is, is not yet fully formed even in Kaye's movies.

Kaye's films, beginning with *Up in Arms* (1944), were generally unremarkable except for Kaye's vocal manipulations. That movie—a remake of *Whoopee!*—is a love story set during World War II, but on the Japanese front. The movie, that is, avoided directly dealing with the sort of Jewish issues that the original version tackled. In that, *Up in Arms* was like much of the rest of Hollywood. Ironically, just as the Jews of Europe were disappearing from the Earth, the Jews of Hollywood—as characters, if not performers—were vanishing.

Despite the popularity of the Marx Brothers, Cantor, and others, the number of Jewish subjects in Hollywood films dropped dramatically in the 1930s. In the 1920s, there had been numerous Jewish-related films, including some about Jewish treatment under the czars. As the film historian Patricia Brett Erens notes: "Beginning in the thirties, Jews were pushed off center . . . although they remain as identifiable minor characters in many films up through 1933. From 1933 to the end of the decade even these types disappear. Thus from 1933 to 1940 few stories about Jews and Jewish life are filmed." Erens does not believe that any studio had a policy effecting this diminution.

Leonard Maltin is not so sure. He recalls speaking with the comedian Benny Rubin, who claimed that he was blackballed. According to Rubin, a meeting of the movie moguls (most if not all of whom were Jewish) took place in the late 1930s after the anti-Semitism in Germany grew worse. The moguls, Rubin believed, decided they would no longer put Jewish characters on screen. Maltin doesn't know if such a meeting did actually take place, but he says there is supporting evidence in the fact that, as Erens suggests, the characters simply disappeared. Maltin notes other ethnic stereotypes—the Irish cops and the Italian organ-grinders, for example—were still present in consistent numbers, whereas the Jewish characters disappeared. Tom Tugend also reports hearing about the meeting in which the moguls purportedly agreed to "one, keep Jewish names off the screen; two, all Jewish executives to sell their Cadillacs and Rolls Royces; and three get rid of their *shiksa* [Gentile] mistresses." The most charitable reading of any such effort is that these policies were meant to avoid providing ammunition to the anti-Semites who complained about Jewish influences in Hollywood.

There are other possible explanations for the disappearance. Corporations had gained control over the film studios that had been privately owned. The corporations, aiming for a national audience, downplayed Jewish elements. This move fit seamlessly into efforts to remove Jewish stereotypes. The Hays Code, beginning in 1934, added to the blandness and the desire to avoid offense.

There are, though, more troubling possible motives. By the mid-1930s, the major studios in Hollywood received 30–40 percent of their gross revenues from distributing films overseas. In 1939, about 150 million Europeans went to see an American-made film every week. The studios were concerned that by angering the Nazis they would lose this business. Louis B. Mayer of MGM went so far as to ask William Randolph Hearst to speak with Hitler to protect the studio's German film interests. Hearst did so.

The Nazis placed restrictions on the content of the films they imported, and most studios seemed to comply, although by 1940 only three studios (MGM, Twentieth-Century Fox, and Paramount) were allowed to export their films to Germany, and this permission ended in September of that year.

The Hays Office, concerned about the economic consequences of angering the Nazis, and deeply influenced by the isolationism at home, pressured filmmakers to resist making any "propaganda" films. Indeed, from September 15, 1939, until January 1940, the Hays Office explicitly banned the production of anti-Nazi films. The State Department, which favored neutrality, supported the idea that studios should not make films that would anger any other country.

Whatever the real causes for the decline in Jewish characters, Hollywood reacted to the emerging anti-Semitism with silence. Michael Birdwell, in his book *Celluloid Soldiers: The Warner Bros. Campaign against Nazism*, argues that Harry Warner created anti-

Nazi films, though disguised as allegory. Birdwell sees, for instance, Warner pictures that focused on organized crime actually as attacks on fascism and suggests that Errol Flynn as Robin Hood was metaphorically fighting against the Nazis. Birdwell notes the general silence of the other major studios, seeing Warner as a brave and lonely figure.

There were, in fact, some real and rare exceptions, films that did not hide behind metaphor. Charlie Chaplin's *Great Dictator* (1940) was the first film made in Hollywood to attack Nazi anti-Semitism. Despite the comedic elements, the film remains a powerful indictment of Hitler. Chaplin received a large number of threatening letters during the film's production.

It is a startling fact that Moe Howard of the Three Stooges was the first American actor to portray Adolf Hitler. The Stooges made three anti-Nazi films. In *You Nazty Spy* (1940), cabinet members in the Kingdom of Moronica want power but need someone "stupid enough to do what we tell him." They settle on Moe Hailstone, a paperhanger. As the cabinet members try to convince Moe, a black feather appears and lands on his upper lip, making him a Hitler look-alike. With Curly functioning as Field Marshal Herring and Larry as the minister of propaganda, Moe functions as a ruthless dictator. At the end of the film, all the Stooges end up thrown into a lion's cage. The film was probably prompted by the Warner Brothers film *Confessions of a Nazi Spy*, released in 1939, which, in keeping with the mood of the industry, opened with a disclaimer: "Any resemblance between the characters in this picture and any persons living or dead is a miracle."

I'll Never Heil Again (1941) was a sequel to *You Nazty Spy*. Once again, Nazi cruelty is ruthlessly portrayed. For instance, Curly as field marshal reports to Moe as dictator: "We bombed fifty-six hospitals, eighty-five schools, forty-two kindergartens, four cemeteries, and other vital military objects." The dictator Moe and his supporters become trophies for the true ruler of Moronica at the end of the film.

Back from the Front (1943) has the Stooges in the merchant marine. Their boat explodes and the three end up on a Nazi warship, the SS *Shickelgruber* (Hitler's real family name). Moe disguises himself as Hitler and then orders the ship's officers to shoot themselves. Moe then sneezes, dislodging his fake mustache. In the resulting panic, the Stooges knock out all the members of the ship's crew. Their anti-Nazi attack is direct. When they salute German officers they say, "Hang Hitler!"

Unfortunately, the Three Stooges' audiences were not in politically, socially, or economically important positions, and a reputation for what some critics considered sadistic physical comedy prevented the Stooges' message from being heard. On the other hand, perhaps because critics or influential audiences did not take them seriously, they were free to do what other stars were not.

The only important Hollywood comedy about the Nazis was *To Be or Not to Be*, which was made in 1941 and released the next year. That is, planning and production took place before the United States entered the war, making director Ernst Lubitsch more daring than if he was simply supporting an ongoing American war effort. Jack Benny, in what he called "the best picture I ever made," starred as Joseph Tura, a Polish actor whose Warsaw troupe plans to put on an anti-Nazi play titled *Gestapo* just as the Nazis are entering Poland. This fact is unclear at the beginning of the film when we see the troupe rehearsing. For moviegoers, it first appears as though Benny is portraying a Nazi. He wears a Nazi uniform and says "Heil Hitler" fully six times. Indeed, when Jack Benny's father saw the film for the first time, he walked out after one minute, as soon as he saw his son give a Nazi salute and say "Heil Hitler." Benny wrote to his father about the incident, but Meyer

Kubelsky didn't answer. The comedian called, but his father never would come to the phone. Then one night he answered the phone himself.

"Hello, Dad," Benny said to him. His father didn't answer. Benny went on. "This is Jack—your son."

His father exploded. "You're no son of mine! I got nothing to discuss with you."

Confused, Benny asked what he had done.

"You gave the salute to Hitler is what you did."

Benny then asked him, "Did you stay for the whole picture?"

"I should stay for such a picture? I was never so ashamed in my life. I don't tell people anymore I'm the father of Jack Benny."

Understanding the problem, Benny said, "But that was only the beginning of the picture. If you had waited you would see that I'm *against* the Nazis. I'm fighting them. Please go back and see it all the way through."

Jack Benny's father went on to see the film forty-six times.

Meyer Kubelsky was not the only critic of *To Be or Not to Be*. Many people saw the film as being in bad taste in trying to extract humor out of horror. Using farce to depict dangerous killers was to deflate what was really serious. There are some lines that are comic but chilling in retrospect. For example, in one scene Benny is pretending to be the Gestapo leader "Concentration Camp" Ehrhardt and says, "We do the concentrating, and the Poles do the camping." At one point Carole Lombard, who plays Benny's wife, notes the fancy dress she will wear "in the concentration camp scenes."

Besides *To Be or Not to Be* and the Three Stooges, there was little in the way of Holocaust-related films from Jewish comedians. The Marx Brothers did make *A Night in Casablanca*, which was distinctly anti-Nazi. A Nazi who utters openly sadistic statements such as "It would soothe me to see someone in pain" strikes Harpo. At the end of the film Groucho mocks "the Master Race." This might have been a daring film had it not been made in 1946 after the war's end.

Me and the Colonel was another postwar anti-Nazi comedy. Danny Kaye stars as a kind Jewish refugee who is seeking to escape the Nazis as they head toward Paris. He is aided in his escape by a most unlikely ally, a Polish colonel who is an anti-Semite. Kaye's character is cheerful and helps the colonel, who begins to alter his feelings toward Jews. Kaye's bright optimism—especially in confronting the Nazis—seemed light-years from the sensibilities of the era. The willingness of Kaye to play the part, though, is significant since he was playing a Jew and since films about Nazis were not very popular with audiences even in the late 1950s.

These postwar films only underscore the silence in the face of Nazi anti-Semitism, a silence that remains a stain on Hollywood's name.

There were general efforts to fight the war. The Bureau of Motion Pictures, a division of the Office of War Information, was established to review screenplays, provide technical support to films, and even suggest appropriate film subjects that might aid the war effort. None of this, though, was aimed directly at the Nazi slaughter of the Jews.

American audiences laughed during the darkness of the era through comedies about a lot of subjects, but humor, or even serious drama, was never effectively harnessed to confront the Nazi Holocaust. The shame of this reaction would not be completely felt until years after the full extent of the Nazi horrors was discovered.

5

THE

JEWISH ALPS

THE RISE OF THE BORSCHT BELT

As radio changed American entertainment and as the Great Depression and World War I forever reshaped the culture, the Jews had continued their own twin struggles at home. They faced external threats from an intense increase in anti-Semitism and an internal challenge from assimilation.

The children of the immigrants, American Jews who came of age in the thirties, found themselves wrestling more than their parents did to define the nature of their Jewish identity. Some wished to retain a strong sense of their Jewish identity while reaching out to embrace compatible parts of American culture to create a new self: the American Jew. Others were more enamored of the wider American culture without reference to their Jewish heritage. Most, though, wandered between these poles, caught in a crucial struggle for self-definition.

The Jews were never large in numbers; in 1937 they reached their high point as a percentage of the American people: 3.7. (By the end of the twentieth century Jews were only 2.2 percent of the American population.)

More than three-quarters of Jewish parents did not give their children a religious education. Surveys during the 1930s showed a larger decline in religious belief among Jews than among other groups. A 1935 survey showed that three-fourths of young Jews had not been to a religious service during the past year. American Jews were giving up their immigrant past as well. In the 1930 census, only one in four Jews declared Yiddish as their mother tongue. Jews also began a dispersion to the South and West.

The voluntary absorption of American values by the children of immigrant Jews is usually called assimilation. A more technically correct word for the process, though, is *acculturation*. Acculturation is a process by which two cultures borrow from each other so that what emerges is a new or blended culture. That is what happened to Jewish culture and American culture. By the 1920s, '30s, and '40s, many Jews actively sought to assimilate American values into their identities.

At the same time, slowly, but especially after World War II, American culture would begin to absorb aspects of the Jewish culture. The acculturation, exemplified by Jewish comedians, would be virtually complete by the end of the century.

In the 1930s, though, Jewish efforts to absorb American culture were retarded by the refusal of some Americans to let them into the culture. Father Charles L. Coughlin, the Detroit priest Eddie Cantor had attacked, exemplified this refusal by broadcasting his racist and anti-Semitic sermons over the radio in the late 1920s. In October 1930, Coughlin began a weekly CBS show, eventually reaching 10 million listeners. The timing was not accidental; the depression, beginning after the stock market crash in 1929, had led to both an economic crisis and a resurgence in anti-Jewish sentiment.

Still, widespread anti-Semitic feelings did not grow dramatically until Hitler's rise to power and Franklin Roosevelt's inauguration of the New Deal program. Hitler and American pro-Nazi attacks on Jewish financiers were an attractive explanation to some displaced farmers and poverty-stricken Americans. In 1933, William Dudley Pelley founded the Silver Legion, better known as the Silver Shirts, one of the hundred or so anti-Semitic groups founded between 1933 and 1941. The depression's effects were compounded by a Christian fundamentalism that sometimes saw Jews as the descendants of those guilty of deicide, hardly to be absorbed in a God-loving American culture, and whose European brethren could be, and were, seen as being divinely punished for their continuing heresy.

The feelings against Roosevelt, who was sometimes accused of having Jewish ancestry, were profound. In October 1934, Roosevelt received a letter from a woman in New York. Her sentiments reflected the attitude of a growing number of disaffected Americans: "On all sides is heard the cry that you have sold out the country to the Jews, and that the Jews are responsible for the continued depression, as they are determined to starve the Christians into submission and slavery. You have over two hundred Jews, they say, in executive offices in Washington, and Jew bankers run the government."

American religious media and leaders contributed to the growing anti-Semitism. In 1937, Edward Cardinal Mooney, who had recently been appointed in Detroit, tried to stop Father Coughlin from continuing his public broadcasts. After a lapse of three months, Father Coughlin returned on an expanded radio network, advocating the end of political parties "because most politicians are

Communists." He warned in December 1937 about "world Jewish domination."

Fundamentalist Protestant leaders, and some of their supporters in Congress, joined in the attacks.

All these factors had an effect on ordinary Americans. In a 1938 public opinion poll, 45 percent of Americans believed Jews were less honest than Gentiles in business dealings, and 35 percent believed that the Jews of Europe were mostly responsible for the oppression they faced. In response to one crucial question asked in the poll—"Should we allow a larger number of Jewish exiles from Germany to come to the United States to live?"—77 percent of those responding said no.

The America First Committee was formed in July 1940. Although its actual membership was probably about 850,000 (including Henry Ford and Father Coughlin), its influence was large and profound.

Charles Lindbergh spoke before them in September 1941 and blamed the Jews for fomenting war with Germany. Lindbergh said about the Jews: "Their greatest danger to this country lies in their large ownership and influence in our motion pictures, our press, our radio and our Government."

Anti-Semitic sentiments were widely heard even by those who were not themselves anti-Semitic. In 1940, 46 percent of respondents replied affirmatively to the question: "Have you heard any criticism or talk against the Jews in the last six months?" In 1942, 52 percent of those surveyed responded that they had heard such views. In 1944, the number was 60 percent, and in 1946, the year after the war ended, fully 64 percent said they had heard criticism of Jews.

When the war began, Jews were frequently accused of avoiding military service, whereas Christian soldiers were fighting to save the Jews of Europe. (Actually, although Jews made up only 3.33

percent of the population, 4.23 percent of the armed forces were Jewish. Jews didn't just enlist in disproportionately high numbers. Approximately eleven thousand American Jews were killed in the war, and another forty-two thousand were wounded. Fifty-two thousand received some decoration, citation, or award.)

Anti-Semitic feelings sometimes even resulted in physical attacks on individual Jews. In June 1939, a person selling Father Coughlin's publication stabbed a New York City Jewish high school teacher. In December 1939, Father Coughlin's followers picketed WMCA in New York because it refused to run his broadcasts. The picketers attacked and beat passersby they believed were Jewish.

In Boston, gangs so frequently threatened and attacked young Jews that the governor of Massachusetts ordered an investigation be undertaken. Eventually, Boston's police chief was prevented from being reappointed because the police had stood by while Jews were attacked.

All this anti-Semitism made Jews reluctant to be seen as promoting the war. Although Jews found a political home after 1928 generally in liberalism and specifically in Franklin Roosevelt's Democratic Party, and efforts were made to confront Nazism, they were limited in their ability to influence middle America or, for that matter, Roosevelt himself.

This limitation, combined with a timidity grounded in fear and an as yet not fully shaped American identity, prevented organized Jews from getting popular Jewish entertainers, not to mention American society, to take up the fate of Europe's Jews. American Jews did not wish to appear to be asking for special treatment and were worried about the fight against Nazism being a "Jewish war." American Jews, like American Jewish comedians, accepted the Roosevelt assertion that focusing on winning the war was the best way to save the Jews.

Jews had some advantages in facing hostility. They never faced legal segregation as African Americans did. Jews were not rounded up as were Japanese Americans on the West Coast. In addition, Jews had great internal resources. They were a diverse and energetic community. And though anti-Semitism delayed a fuller assimilation of America's Jews, while they waited they were able to develop a full range of cultural and communal activities, safe from the psychological demands of Gentile society and the emotional and sometimes physical demands of dealing with anti-Semites.

One principal resource was a ten-by-twenty-five-mile strip of the Catskill region a hundred miles northwest of New York City. The Catskill Mountains, first sighted by Henry Hudson, got their name from two Dutch words: *kat*, a wall of earth, and *kill*, a creek. The Jews had first come there in small numbers. Jewish farmers from the Old World, unhappy with the rigors of urban life, tenement living, and an economically precarious life in the city, made their way to Sullivan and Ulster Counties. There, in a thousand hotels and bungalow colonies, Jews could escape the heat of the city and the tensions of trying to fit into the wider American society.

They could be themselves. They could eat all they wanted, play all day, relax, look for husbands and wives or more transient romantic partners, and, most of all, laugh. The Catskills allowed the Jews to escape.

Unlike the crowded life of New York, the Catskills had fresh air, plenty of room, and were free from the city's unbearable summer heat. Relatives of the Jews who lived in the Catskills began to come up in the summer, and their descriptions of the area made it seem like a Jewish Eden.

These visits combined with unsuccessful farming efforts to result in a crucial new industry. Farmers began to turn their houses into boarding rooms. Especially after World War I, these boardinghouses began to expand. Hotels emerged, as did bungalow colonies, made up of groups of cottages.

The idea of leaving the city for an escape from work, the idea, that is, of a vacation, was foreign to Jews. Their "vacations" were the Sabbath and Jewish holidays. But the notion of getting away from the daily requirements of work was attractive, and the idea of vacating their urban dwellings was extraordinarily alluring. Still, however attractive the very American idea of vacations was, Jews were not welcomed in places where other Americans could easily go.

Jews also had to undergo a more subtle psychological transformation to appreciate the Catskills. A vacation was meant exclusively for pleasure. This idea of pleasure for its own sake was foreign to the East European Jewish mind. Many Jews felt guilty about enjoying themselves when no moral lesson was taught, no religious lesson learned, no social good accomplished. The hedonism inherent in such an idea of pure pleasure, though embedded in the 1920s American culture exemplified by Prohibition and Jazz Age excesses, had to be learned by the Jews. But many were eager pupils.

Beyond accepting pleasure as an allowable, legitimate feeling, American Jews after World War I began to make a sufficient income to afford such a vacation. Most often a family would stay for a week or two with the husband staying in the city for the workweek and coming up for the weekend. Some wealthier vacationers could stay for a month or even for the whole summer season.

The new resorts of the Catskills tried at first to mimic Old World pleasures or to provide simple rustic experiences. Vacationers picked berries, listened to klezmer music, played games, and went swimming. Entrepreneurial owners offered entertainment, provided by singers and others.

The increasing sense of wanting to be more American combined with frustration at being unable to enter American life fully. The Catskills responded by making the resorts much bigger and providing American, not East European, attractions. Golf courses, tennis courts, and huge swimming pools rendered picking berries obsolete.

But however American these resorts became, they were unquestionably Jewish in various ways. Of course, most of their clientele were Jewish. Catskill hotels were modeled not on the emotionally indifferent resorts of America, but on the warmth of a Jewish home. As Joey Bishop noted: "It looked like a home. When you walked in, there was bread on the table, pickles on the table. . . . You could ask for more food." The abundance of food was a deliberate statement by the resorts; here, Jews would not have to worry about their next meal. This feeling freed immigrant Jews emotionally in ways that nonimmigrant Gentile Americans could not understand.

Borscht, a beet soup that was served either hot or cold, frequently topped with sour cream and sometimes with small potatoes or cucumber slices, was commonly served at the resorts. Because of its popularity, the resorts that dotted the area became affectionately known as "the Borscht Belt." (The area was also called by other names, such as the Sour Cream Sierras, the Jewish Alps, or the Derma Road.)

The familiar food, the presence of families and other Jews, and the warm environment combined to provide a deep sense of security. The Borscht Belt was almost a substitute for a shtetl, a village or small town in which Jews lived in Eastern Europe. In the Catskill resorts, Jews were the majority, and there was no external pressure to conform to American values. They had a homeland in America for a week.

This security allowed Jews the freedom to explore American

culture, to rehearse a wider assimilation in their everyday lives. The resorts recognized this need and sometimes took names with a distinctly American or Gentile flavor, especially with intimations of peace: the Avon Lodge, the Concord, Harmony, Ideal House, the Raleigh, Tamarack Lodge, and others. Not only did the guests play American games, but they also tried out American dating customs and other aspects of American culture. The resorts were the Jewish way station between immigrant life and comfortable assimilation.

Milton Berle, Fanny Brice, Mel Brooks, Lenny Bruce, George Burns, Myron Cohen, Jack Gilford, Moss Hart, Willie Howard, George Jessel, Jack E. Leonard, Sam Levenson, Carl Reiner, Neil Simon, and his brother Danny Simon were just some of the Jewish comedians and comedy writers who worked in the mountains.

Many Jewish comedians began their careers in Catskill resorts as "tummlers," or social directors and entertainers. The word *tummler* (pronounced "toomler") comes from the German *tummel*, or *tumult*, and means someone who makes a lot of noise, someone who is always trying to have fun. The tummler's job was to provide virtually constant entertainment for a resort's guests. They were social directors—a job that required them to be, among other roles, comics, singers, masters of ceremonies, producers and directors of shows, and leaders of games.

The poor tummler was often called upon to report some outrageous exaggerations of the truth in order to promote romances. He might, for instance, be told by a young man not to mention that the young man had just inherited a fortune. According to the accepted rules, this meant the tummler was supposed to tell every attractive young woman of the man's supposed financial condition.

On Sunday nights, the traditional arrival time for guests, the tummlers introduced the new arrivals to each other, frequently having to draft male resort workers to even out the sexes. A typical week might include Campfire Night on Monday, Costume or

Dress-Up Night on Tuesday, Amateur Night on Wednesday, Nightclub Night on Thursday, Basketball Night on Friday, and a big variety show on Saturday night, leading to a checkout on Sunday afternoon.

Tummlers loved Thursday nights when they could perform. The audiences also loved the performances, but for a different reason: Heckling the tummlers was a time-honored tradition. The young tummlers had to develop a series of responses to hecklers: "You want to match wits? Sorry, I never attack an unarmed man." "The floor is yours. Wash it." "You've got great lines, but they're all on your face."

The tummlers were in constant search of new material. That search often meant borrowing material from the more famous comics. As Sid Caesar recalled years later:

My first job in show business was . . . at a place called the Biltmore Hotel . . . I was the social director and master of ceremonies. I was twenty years old. I got thirty-five dollars a week. But my deal was that Saturday nights I could go out and do an act at other hotels, which was a terrific deal except that I didn't really have an act at the time. I stole four minutes from Larry Best, four minutes from Larry Alpert, six minutes from Myron Cohen, and that was my act.

There were actual places in Manhattan where jokes and gags could be bought and sold. The most famous of these "supermarkets" were Kellogg's Cafeteria on West Forty-ninth Street and the Palace Cafeteria and the Theatrical Drugstore, both on West Forty-sixth Street. Joey Adams would copy down George Jessel's routines and then auction them off and also perform them himself. One of Jessel's "Mama on the Telephone" routines could get Adams twenty dialect jokes and a used monologue.

The comedians would also stop at the Red Apple Rest, a roadside restaurant exactly halfway between the mountains and the city. There, late in the night, they would go over the acts, describe the audience, and gather gossip about the other comedians and about routines ripe for buying or "borrowing."

Comedians, of course, found that training as a tummler was incredibly valuable. They could face the toughest of audiences. They had to perform live—constantly. They had to learn how to get new material, whether or not the material was original. It is no wonder that so many comedians who succeeded, especially in live television or in nightclubs, got their training when they were young in the Catskills.

Red Buttons (born Aaron Chwatt) used to sing on street corners. His red hair and the forty-eight buttons he wore on his uniform at Ryan's, a tavern, resulted in his nickname. But he really began his career at Beerkill Lodge in the Catskills where he was a bellboy, waiter, prop boy, and entertainer. At the Beerkill Lodge, he earned a dollar and a half a week, though Buttons earned a bit more by getting a fountain pen, filling it up with sweet cream, and bringing it to paying guests at dinner and charging a quarter a squirt to put the cream in coffee, cream being strictly forbidden to be served with meat at the kosher hotel.

Danny Kaye began his career at White Roe Lake in 1933. He was twenty years old at the time and put on a play each week while also appearing in a new variety show each night. Because he also had to entertain for each meal, he could rehearse only late in the night. Kaye spent five seasons there, before going to Camp Tamiment where he was the chief emcee. Kaye learned how to amuse every guest. If he had to, he was not above "accidentally" falling into the swimming pool while wearing all his clothes. He and another worker would regularly chase each other wielding meat cleavers and then jump into the fishpond. Kaye became well known for performing at night on a porch as audiences watched, their cars parked in a semicircle around the porch with their headlights on because the hotel had no outdoor lighting. Regulars who knew him cheered his later success in films.

Judy Holliday (who translated her birth name, Tuvim, which means "holiday" in Hebrew, adding an extra *l* for distinction) was another Catskill graduate. Holliday had been a switchboard operator for Orson Welles's Mercury Theater, but the job did not lead to any acting opportunities. After six months she left for the Borscht Belt, where she worked at several hotels.

Her career, though, really took off when she returned to New York in the fall of 1938. She was sitting with Adolph Green in the Village Vanguard, a tiny café in Greenwich Village. The two offered to put on a free performance once a week if the manager would provide them with rehearsal space. The deal was made and the two, along with Betty Comden, Alvin Hammer, and John Frank, began to perform as a group (called the Revuers), eventually attracting a wide audience. Holliday's distinctive, funny voice and her brilliant comic timing were widely noted. She received offers to be in the movie *Greenwich Village*, but she refused to sign until similar offers were made to the other Revuers.

She appeared on Broadway in *Kiss Them for Me*, but it wasn't until her Broadway appearance in *Born Yesterday* that she attracted wide attention. (She won the part when another actress left the show in Philadelphia. Holliday had three days to learn her lines.) She eventually starred in the 1950 motion picture based on the play, for which she won an Academy Award, beating out Gloria Swanson in *Sunset Boulevard* and Bette Davis in *All about Eve*. Holliday portrayed a dumb blonde, a former chorus girl hooked up with a crooked junk dealer who has come to Washington to buy off members of Congress and make even more money.

But Holliday was not a blonde, and she was certainly not dumb.

When she was ten, her IQ was measured at 172. She was forced to hide behind the dumb blonde image to achieve success, just as she constantly had to fight a problem with weight so that she wouldn't look too heavy for her roles. She could never be her real self. Her career, then, was also a good metaphor for American Jewish life. Acceptance was possible—at the price of an altered self.

Caught at a time of transition, having starred in few films, none of which was distinctive without her, Judy Holliday's name has faded, but she was an important representative of how women had to struggle to be accepted. She died young—at age forty-three in 1965—right on the cusp of a cultural revolution that would change not only Jewish lives and women's lives but also the lives of all Americans.

Jackie Mason, then Jacob Maza, was at Sunrise Manor. He walked out onstage and uttered his first words, "This place stinks." However accurate the observation might have been, the enraged owner didn't give Mason a chance to continue. He was thrown out of the hotel. Mason became the master of ceremonies at the Pioneer Hotel, and, as most comics did, he used borrowed lines as he introduced comics with bigger names. Once Phil Foster was appearing and Mason used much of Foster's own material in the introduction. Foster walked out and said, "How do you do, ladies and gentlemen? You just heard my act, so good night." Foster walked out of the hotel.

Alan King also had some clever remarks to make about a hotel. He was fifteen and was told at the Hotel Gradus that if he did well he could stay for the summer. King walked to the stage and opened with: "When you work for Gradus, you work for gratis!" He was fired the next day.

Buddy Hackett (born Leonard Hacker) had begun his entertainment career in a striptease act at Coney Island. Hackett and his father both worked the Catskills. Hackett worked as a waiter—

a bad waiter, he admits. One day a comic scheduled to appear didn't show up, so young Hackett had his chance. "I was sixteen and the five dollars looked good. . . . It was a disaster. They not only didn't laugh, but also looked as though they were comin' up onstage to kill me. I finished out the season in another hotel—but as a waiter!" Later, Hackett succeeded as a comic at the Concord. One of his most famous routines there, later used on a record, was Hackett's act as a Chinese waiter. Despite the ethnic stereotype, which in itself came straight from burlesque and vaudeville, Hackett's waiter was proud and refused to be beneath the customers he served.

Henny Youngman played the violin at Swan Lake Inn, but when, in 1932, the social director didn't show up, Youngman began his professional life as a comic. He particularly liked to make fun of his boss with a line he would later adapt and ride to fame:

> Now take my boss—please. He's got borscht instead of blood in his veins. He's the biggest man in "Who Owes Who." If he can't take it with him, he'll send his creditors. . . . You wanna drive your wife crazy? When you get into bed tonight, don't talk in your sleep—just grin. You wanna drive a friend nuts? Send him a telegram saying "Ignore the first wire." . . . I went out with a girl last night. She wasn't a Lana Turner. She was more of a stomach turner.

Joan Rivers got booked because she owned a car. Her old Buick was crucial, for she could bring other acts with her. At one hotel, no guests spoke English, so an interpreter translated her lines into Yiddish. "Every line bombed twice," she recalled. Rivers finally decided on a strategy. She'd go on and say she wasn't doing a comedy act but a lecture. There were no expectations for laughter from a lecture, and so any she got would be perceived by audience members as an extra benefit. Rivers would "lecture" about being single: "I have very high standards. If he doesn't have a pulse, forget it."

Jerry Lewis (born Joseph Levitch) had seen his father, Danny, working as a comedian at Brown's Hotel. Young Jerry started by mocking the movements of those he saw around him. His first gag was on a Sabbath evening. The rabbi was delivering a blessing when Lewis went through the kitchen door, bumped into a waiter, and dropped the tray filled with dishes. Even the rabbi laughed.

Lewis learned quickly that his clowning during meals could bring laughs. Working as a busboy he pulled all kinds of stunts just to get a smile. At night, he went from hotel to hotel performing. He quickly learned that it was difficult to get noticed in the Catskills, and so he eventually decided to take his training and go elsewhere, but that training remained invaluable and shaped Lewis's later comic ventures.

The turning point in Lewis's post-Catskill career came in July 1946, while he was working at the 500 Club in Atlantic City. The head of the mob in Camden owned the club, though a man named Skinny D'Amato ran it. D'Amato liked Lewis, who did a pantomime act mugging along to songs, but didn't like a singer playing in the club. Apparently there was just no chemistry between the comic and the singer, and D'Amato was thinking about firing them both. Lewis suggested that D'Amato keep him but hire a young Italian singer he had worked with at the Glass Hat in New York. The singer—Dean Martin—was eventually hired with the promise that he and Lewis would do some funny bits together.

Martin arrived and started at the club on July 25. Martin sang and Lewis did his pantomime act, but D'Amato was furious. The promised humor between Martin and Lewis was nowhere to be found. The comedian was threatened with being fired if there wasn't humor in the second show.

It was ten o'clock. The next show was at half past twelve. Jerry Lewis desperately needed the $150 a week he was being paid. He and Martin went into the dressing room with one simple goal: they had, immediately, to come up with an act that they would perform in two and a half hours.

Working on the greasy brown paper from the pastrami sandwiches they had ordered, Lewis came up with an idea he dubbed "The Playboy and the Putz." Martin would start off being himself, the suave singer. Lewis would dress in a busboy's outfit, and, he told Martin in an alleyway that led to the stage, "Then we'll grab some things out of the kitchen and make a lot of noise." Jerry Lewis was emotionally back in the Catskills.

The show started. Martin began and then Lewis came out. From there, he followed the best Borscht Belt tradition. There was no action he would not do if it might get a laugh. He juggled dishes and then dropped them. He walked over to the band and tried to conduct it with one of his shoes. Then he burned the music. He ran wild in the crowd (so small, Lewis remembered it as "literally four"), sitting with them, spilling wherever he sat.

Eight minutes had gone by. Martin was still singing. Lewis kept interrupting. They went after each other. They threw celery, tripped waiters, and turned off the lights.

The hysterical crowd was witnessing entertainment history. For the next ten years, Martin and Lewis were the most successful comedians in America. Their first film, *My Friend Irma*, appeared in 1949. Over the next seven years they made fifteen additional films, widely admired especially by young viewers. The pair split up in 1956, and Lewis went on to write, produce, and direct other films, most notably *The Nutty Professor* (1963), though others were also successful. Indeed, Charlie Chaplin requested a print of *The Bellboy* (1960), claiming it was Lewis's best film, though he probably liked it because it was a throwback to silent comedy since the title character was unable to talk. This was also the first film for which Lewis received writing credit.

Jerry Lewis did not fare well among many intellectuals, who found his infantile, manic, uncontrolled comedy silly and embarrassing. His writing and directing fascinated some critics; he was then the only comedian to have started in sound films that not only starred in a comedy but also directed it. Most, however, saw an annoying child in an adult's body.

Instead of fighting this image, Lewis nurtured it. In one of the last Martin and Lewis films, *You're Never Too Young* (1955), Lewis actually pretends to be an eleven-year-old child in order to hide out from a gangster. This connection Lewis had to children is crucial. To Lewis, being a child meant being innocent and free. The requirements imposed on a person by adulthood (sexual maturity, order, responsibility, even rationality) restrained that innocence or freedom. Lewis wanted to let the freedom loose, and even in his adult body, he looked for the nine-year-old inside himself. That Jerry Lewis lacked control. Inhibitions were foreign to him. He had chaotic energy. He enjoyed making mischief. His emotions burst out in all directions.

For many years, Lewis raised vast sums of money as he hosted a telethon to help those, especially children, with muscular dystrophy. It is understandable that he would be emotionally attached to such children. The children who had such a disease were widely neglected by society until Lewis came along. Such children lack motor coordination, they face ridicule and ignorance, and they require extraordinary strength and bravery in the face of their plight. Lewis could see in them the tragic underside of all he was trying to say about children comedically. He could see in their struggles a dramatic and more tragic metaphor for his own life.

Lewis's attachment to Jewish sources and his effects on other

Jewish comedians are underappreciated aspects of his comedy. The clearly Jewish influences of the Borscht Belt were supplemented by his own encounters with anti-Semitism. The first prominent one occurred when Lewis was a student at Irvington High School, in New Jersey. A teacher had sent him to the principal, and the principal asked why he behaved as he did. Lewis replied that he didn't know. The principal then said, "Is it that you're just a Jew and don't know any better?" Lewis hit the principal, who fell against the desk and lost two teeth. Young Jerry Lewis was expelled.

Despite his clearly Jewish background, Lewis's characters were not explicitly Jewish, as Woody Allen's and Mel Brooks's would be, but they weren't sanitized, purely American characters either.

The reason that *The Nutty Professor* is so successful as a film is that it mirrors the struggles Lewis was going through. The protagonist, Prof. Julius Kelp, is a shy, weak, accident-prone schlemiel. His white socks, glasses, and prominent buckteeth make him the physical nerd. Early in the film one of his students, a football player, humiliates him by locking him in a cabinet. Only the concern of another student, Stella, moves him. He falls in love with Stella, and, to impress her, he engages in a scientific experiment to transform himself from the nerd Kelp into the smooth Buddy Love. Buddy is a loud, physically bold, attractively cool guy who sings to adoring fans. Stella seems both fascinated and repelled by Buddy's interest in her. She clearly doesn't like his self-assurance, his rudeness, his lack of courtesy, and his aggressiveness. When at the end of the film the Buddy Love persona disappears at a concert and it is revealed that Kelp and Love are the same person, Stella tells him, "I wouldn't ever want to spend the rest of my life with someone like Buddy." They plan to marry.

Kelp, of course, was a stereotypical Jewish male: smart, socially inept, in love with a beautiful, blonde Gentile woman. He tries to change himself to become more American, smoother, more attractive by prevailing social standards, more secure with women, more willing to confront bullies. This mask, though, falls off and reveals the true Jew underneath. Nevertheless, it is the true Jew that wins the (Gentile) heroine. It is the true Jew that is admired. It is Buddy—the ugly, oily American—that is rejected. It is the outsider rejecting the insider's beckoning call.

But, perhaps not surprisingly, Lewis's attempt to come to terms with being Jewish was not entirely successful. Many in the young audience saw in Buddy Love not the repulsive monster Stella did, but a person they'd like to be like if only they could similarly transform themselves.

Some American Jews were indeed closer to Buddy Love than Julius Kelp. They were becoming increasingly comfortable in their Golden Land, their confidence spurred on by several factors. One, of course, was the rapid decline in anti-Semitism in the 1950s and '60s. In addition, the Jews rooted their lives more deeply on American soil. They moved from the cities to the suburbs where they built large and beautiful synagogues. They left behind the communal institutions of immigrant life, the *landsmanshaften*, Yiddish newspapers and books as well as daily use of the language itself, and socialist clubs and organizations. They moved among, went to school with, and increasingly married Gentiles. They, or at least their children, went to college and became professionals. American Jewish confidence was also boosted by the emergence of the State of Israel in 1948. The fighting Israelis transformed the image of the Jew in Gentile eyes, and many American Jews liked the transformation.

Despite these successes, however, there lurked a dormant concern among many American Jews. They instinctively believed that in embracing American values they were losing their Jewish selves. Although some American Jews may have been relieved by the changes, others accepted Jerry Lewis's view: The Jews should be happy with their Jewish identity and not try to assimilate or transform just for acceptance.

American Jews, though, could not in real life find the simple solution that Jerry Lewis put in a film. They continued to struggle. The daughters and sons of those who had moved to the suburbs rebelled against what they saw as a vacuous life. Some turned to the Judaism of their ancestors. Others turned to the political Left. All of them continued to struggle with their secure but still fragile American Jewish identities.

Jerry Lewis made another film about being Jewish, though one that has never been released. It was the 1972 film *The Day the Clown Cried*, in which Lewis played a Jewish circus clown who was forced by the Nazis to lead children to gas chambers. Lewis did enormous research for the project. "I went to Belsen, Dachau, and Auschwitz. I saw the killing camps, the sprinklers which unleashed Zyklon B, and I saw the nail scratchings on the walls." Although reaction among those who saw the rough cut was mixed, Lewis believed it was a masterpiece. Had it been released, it would have certainly affected how critics and the audience saw Lewis, and, for better or worse, would have connected the possibility of pathos and humor with the Holocaust decades before the commercial success of Roberto Benigni's 1998 film *Life Is Beautiful*.

The Jews who went to the Catskills to see the young Jerry Lewis wanted to escape anti-Semitism and the increasingly horrifying news from Germany and later from the war. Joking about such subjects, and even about Nazism, was the standard strategy. George Jessel, for example, resorted to the technique of making fun of himself before others did so. He would tell audiences that his draft board had classified him 12-F. "That means I go when the Japs are in the lobby." A favorite anecdote at the Laurel was about Hitler's visit to a fortune-teller. The tummler would tell the joke about Hitler. "He wants to know on what day he will die. The gypsy says, 'On a Jewish holiday.' Hitler then asks, 'What holiday? Rosh Hashanah, Yom Kippur, Hanukkah?' The gypsy says, 'My leader, any day you die will be a Jewish holiday.'"

Such humor was not always appreciated. It made the Jews defensive, as if they were cowardly to use humor instead of fighting. Realizing this, the resorts posted lists of former guests who had won military honors. GIs who were convalescing were invited to be guests at no charge. Large war-bond rallies were held. Eddie Cantor sold a quarter of a million dollars worth of bonds on one August evening at Grossinger's.

And, however much Jews may have wanted to leave their concerns behind during their vacation in the mountains, those concerns sometimes followed them. Totem Lodge, located twelve miles east of Albany, was subject to anti-Semitism during the war. One Saturday night, a group calling themselves the "Friendly Neighbors" put a burning cross on a rowboat and sent it across the lake to Totem Lodge. After this happened several times, a group of men from the lodge crossed the lake and waited. Several members of the "Friendly Neighbors" ended up in the hospital, and all anti-Semitic activity stopped.

After the war, the Catskill resorts would begin a slow decline, due mostly to a growing acceptance of Jews by the wider society (so that Jews went to the same resorts that other Americans did) and by two inventions: air-conditioning and television. The air conditioners made city life in the summertime much more tolerable at a much cheaper price than a vacation. Televisions, which cost $500 but could be bought with a down payment of only $20, provided for free the very entertainers that guests had formerly paid to see. The strong American economy also added to the decline of the Catskills. With money, the Jewish patrons could fly to Miami or even to Europe.

Still, the mountains continued to be a training ground for some comedians even after the war and for several decades continued to attract Jewish guests and name performers, as did similar hotels in other areas, especially the Poconos in Pennsylvania. Woody Allen spent three summers, starting in 1956, at the Tamiment. He received about $150 a week. For this, Allen had to put on a new show each week. After doing typical television sketches, Allen began to stretch. One Allen routine featured experts in psychological warfare facing each other on the battlefield. They carried no weapons, but would shout at each other: "You're short. You're too short, and you're unloved." After the third summer, Allen decided to move on, fearful of spending his career in the mountains. Like many American Jews, he had decided it was time to take on America at large.

The Jewish comedians' efforts to enter American culture were about to meet with unparalleled success.

THE YEARS
OF ACCEPTANCE

1950–1965

6

THE
MAGIC BOX

THE AMERICAN
TELEVISION REVOLUTION

M ilton Berle returned to New York from California in early
1948 just as Texaco decided that it wanted to enter the
new medium of television. There had not, as yet, been a
major entertainment show, and Berle was approached for some
ideas. He suggested a variety show, modeled on vaudeville, with
himself as host.

Berle's show aired on June 8, 1948, as one of three competitors
for Texaco's sponsorship. He was given a ten thousand–dollar
budget and used it to hire the singer Pearl Bailey, a comedian, and
the ventriloquist Señor Wences—whose real name was Wences-
lao Moreno and whose father was a Sephardic Jew. (It is remark-

able that at a moment when his future in television was on the line, Berle would use a black performer and a foreign-sounding Jew who presented himself as Hispanic.) Berle's first show even had some circus acts. NBC, lacking a television studio, was forced to alter one of its radio studios, creating Studio 6B in the RCA Building in Rockefeller Center.

The show was a success, and, in September, Berle was chosen as the regular host for the Texaco Star Theatre. The show was scheduled for Tuesday nights at 8:00 P.M. and debuted on September 21. Guests included Phil Silvers and Smith and Dale. History was about to be made.

There were no monitors in the studio, so audiences had to look around the raised cameras. This forced Berle to avoid subtle movements and play loudly and broadly, just so the audience could see and hear the act. The studio audience's laughter was, of course, crucial in providing guidance to home audiences, giving them permission and prompts to laugh and creating an electronic community.

Berle had hired the writer Hal Collins to revive old vaudeville, burlesque, and radio routines that Berle had used successfully. It took just those few weeks to use up all the material, forcing Berle to create new routines specifically aimed at television audiences.

The show was an enormous success. In Detroit, water levels dropped in the city's reservoir immediately after the show when the viewers rushed to their bathrooms. Nightclubs changed their closing nights to Tuesdays. A theater manager in Ohio put a poster in his lobby: "Closed Tuesday. I want to see Berle, too." Berle acquired the nickname "Mr. Television" and was widely credited for the rapid increase in sales of television sets. In 1947, there were 136,000 sets. By the end of 1948, just months after Berle's meteoric show, there were 700,000 sets reaching about 4 million people. (Joe E. Lewis commented: "Berle is responsible for more television sets being sold than anyone else. I sold mine, my father sold his.") People would go to a neighbor's house or a tavern or stand in front of an appliance store window showing the program, watch the grainy and snowy black-and-white show, and the next day rush out to buy their own television set. By October, Berle's show recorded the highest ratings ever received by a regular radio or television program. As columnist Jack Gould shrewdly observed, "Berle's rapid gags, broad clowning, versatility, and hard work added up to video's first smash hit."

The shows were clearly vaudeville brought into the home. Berle used a curtain to open and close an act. Camera work was unexceptional; the director saw the show for what it was: a representation of a standard vaudeville program. The audience didn't expect the camera to move.

Berle was the ringmaster, the master of ceremonies who did his opening monologue and introduced each new act. Keeping to his own vaudeville tradition of entering into the acts of other performers, Berle often interrupted or joined in the act. When "Buffalo Bob" Smith came on, Berle appeared dressed as Howdy Doody. He sang with Elvis Presley. Other guests included Sid Caesar, Dean Martin and Jerry Lewis, and Frank Sinatra.

Vaudeville and Borscht Belt traditions required Berle to do anything for a laugh. Whenever the word *makeup* was spoken, someone would charge onstage from the wings and smack Berle with a giant powder puff. He was hit with cream pies. Actors squirted seltzer at him. He mugged for the camera while people pulled at his hair.

He also liked to tease audience members: "Don't laugh, lady. . . . Look at the old bird you came in with. And you're no chicken yourself. Boy, what an audience tonight . . . That cute blonde over there. You look like Judy Holliday, and the guy next to you looks like 'Death Takes a Holiday.'" These confrontations could have been offensive, but Berle instinctively knew the limits his audiences allowed.

Part of the fun came from the fact that Berle's show was live. The ad-libs were frequent and effective. Of course, performing live for the nation inevitably led to unexpected events, sometimes funny and frequently incredible. The most famous of the unforeseen incidents during live television involved Red Buttons. The bit was called "Confidential Auto Loan," an act Berle had performed many times. Buttons played a character who wished to borrow five hundred dollars from a finance company. A crucial part of the sketch involved Buttons taking off his clothes for a physical examination. Berle's sister Roz had made a breakaway suit for Buttons. They used it several times during rehearsal and all went well. Berle would pull the suit off, and Buttons would stand there in funny drawers. During the show, Berle pulled at the suit, but it didn't break off properly. Needing to have the clothes come off for the gag, Berle pulled harder. Berle, however, pulled too hard. All of Red Buttons's clothes—including the funny underwear—came off. He stood there naked for a second until the camera could turn its attention elsewhere.

Berle was comfortable with Yiddish and sometimes used it on the air. In one show, Berle wore a sailor suit and screamed, "I'm *schvitzing* in here." The audience laughed, understanding the Yiddish word for "sweating." During the same program, Berle dressed as a contessa, and while fixing his hair said, "My *sheytal* is falling," using the Jewish word for the wig that Orthodox women wear.

Berle was perhaps most famous for his costumes. He might be dressed as George Washington standing in a bathtub instead of a boat in the Delaware River. He'd be dressed as a caveman wielding a club and a dummy that he'd hit and toss into the audience. He'd then run into the audience and return with a mink coat. He was

Superman, Sherlock Holmes, Charlie Chaplin, and many other famous characters.

Then there were the performances in drag. Berle had done this in vaudeville with great success, and his cherubic face made his appearances as women all the more plausible. The costumes were meant to be outrageous. He was Cleopatra. He danced the can-can in costume. Because a picture of him dressed as Carmen Miranda, a then famous Brazilian singer, appeared on the cover of *Newsweek*, this impersonation was perhaps Berle's most famous. Audiences roared as Berle appeared with a pile of artificial fruit atop his hat and huge earrings. Miranda herself was a frequent guest on the show. Once, however, during a quick change between numbers, she had forgotten to put on the needed undergarments. As Cesar Romero twirled her, her skirt was raised, and, like Red Buttons, Miranda was exposed to the American public.

Berle's blatantly Jewish use of language, his fusion of slapstick onto such Jewish humor, and his wild energy and desire to explore any method for provoking laughter were all signs of an urban, American Jewish sensibility. That sensibility extended to Berle's sense of his audience as a family and his responsibility to children who stayed up late to watch his show. At one point he ended his program like this: "I want to say something to any of you kiddies who should be in bed getting a good night's rest before school tomorrow. Listen to your uncle Miltie and kiss Mommy and Daddy good night and go straight upstairs like good little boys and girls." Berle's self-assignation as a family member was crucial to his popularity. He was the crazy uncle, the one who made everyone laugh at family get-togethers and also the uncle who had, beneath the laughter, deep emotional ties to everyone in the family. The nickname "Uncle Miltie" stuck.

Berle's Jewish sensibility was an urban one, but he was careful to avoid the stereotyping that had marked vaudeville. He noted in an unpublished interview that "I never, never used ethnic material. . . . Very vicious, very anti-Semitic."

Berle was crucial in meeting an audience's postwar need for linguistic liberation. Berle's wildness in style, language, and behavior was just what his audience wanted. They needed to feel a release after the tensions of a life marked by depression and war. They wanted to let go. It would take a decade for the full fury of liberation to be let loose into the culture, but midcentury audiences began their efforts by finding people who could locate their emotions and express them, people who could give them models for liberated behavior without endangering their sense of self or morality. They wanted a comedian to do this, and, with his Jewish comedic roots, Berle became that comedian. In this sense, Berle was a forerunner of Lenny Bruce and later comedians who would more radically free Americans from the public linguistic restraints under which they had lived.

But, in the end, Berle proved too Jewish for America. This might seem like an odd observation given Berle's tremendous success. But Berle's popularity is deceptive. Television audiences in those early days were actually urban. Wealthier urban areas were the first places where televisions were bought, and it was Berle's success there that prompted more rural populations to purchase televisions. When they did, however, they did not find Berle particularly appealing. He was too exotic in an age of conformity, too slick, too urban, too Jewish. From 1949 to 1952, when Berle was achieving his greatest success, about 5 million people a week watched his show. The radio historian Arthur Wertheim believes that fully 35 percent of that audience lived in New York City, a city with a large Jewish population. As television expanded westward, Berle's popularity declined. Berle's show, now sponsored by Buick, fell to the sixth-highest-rated show in 1953–1954 and number thirteen the following year. By 1955, Phil Silvers as Sergeant Bilko was able to beat Berle in the ratings so that, effectively, his meteoric and historic television career was over.

In its early years, television promised a considerable amount. Of course, the sheer invention was itself incredible. The technological magic box, after all, produced pictures and sounds of famous stars for free. The marvel of such an invention prompted understandable overstatements about the beneficence of the new medium and misunderstandings about its value. In one New York City junior high school, for instance, teachers demanded a meeting with their principal. At the meeting, the teachers expressed concern for the future of their profession. After all, they asserted, youngsters would now be able to watch television and soon would be as smart as the teachers. The principal tried to calm them down, but he, too, was unsure about the potentially expansive educational contributions of television.

Television seemed to offer an intimate window on reality, providing what seemed to many to be an unmediated view of the world. Television made it possible for large numbers of Americans to watch and be affected by the same programs at the same time. To some extent, this had already happened with radio, but television's illusory intimacy gave audiences an even more profound sense of a shared experience.

These early promises were, of course, mostly unfulfilled. Audiences didn't want to do a lot of thinking. They didn't want their views of the world challenged, but rather confirmed. They didn't want to hear discussions of controversial social issues. Eager not to alienate audience members, television sponsors—like radio sponsors—quickly fell into the established patterns of providing simple fare aimed at entertaining mass audiences while convincing them to purchase the products offered during the program breaks or on commercials embedded as part of the program.

Television, crucially, not only recorded the enormous transformation of American postwar society but also made its own contribution to that transformation. The magnificent American war victory over an enemy that was, by common consent, morally evil had buoyed American spirits. This enthusiasm combined with the robust economy to produce a zest in the culture unmatched since the years just before the 1929 stock market crash. Americans were more confident than they had been in decades, not only in their country but also in themselves and the families they planned to have.

The American emphasis on hard work and family and the rise of suburban living made television a perfect medium for the times. It was in the home, keeping families together. It provided easy, free, family-oriented entertainment, a release from the long workday. It was also emerging as the perfect electronic baby-sitter, freeing busy parents from having to entertain children all the time.

Television altered American lifestyles. Viewers stayed up late and so slept less. People began eating meals on small, portable tables in front of the television set. Television watching reduced time for other activities, such as reading or exercise. By 1951, movie attendance had declined in a large number of cities where television was available.

One of television's more subtle effects was crucial for the rise of Jewish comedians. Television's value as home entertainment made families withdraw somewhat from community activities. They were at home more with each other than they might otherwise have been. In addition, with often just one television set in the home, families had to sit together to watch, and so families became prominent in numerous American comedies (such as *Father Knows Best, Leave It to Beaver*, and *The Adventures of Ozzie and Harriet*). But the strains of increased closeness—and the realization that family life hardly ever matched the idealized versions on those shows—created a need for a humorous escape from family tensions. Jews, however mocked for other reasons, were widely noted to be good at family life. Jews had had the experience of intense family relations across the centuries and specifically in America during the immigrant generation as they crowded together in packed tenements. Jews used humor to help other Americans locate the emotional landscape where families could live in peace.

But even in the 1950s the changing American culture was wonderful for Jewish comedians, if for no other reason than the fact that anti-Semitism had precipitously declined. Whereas in 1946, 64 percent of Americans told pollsters that they had heard criticism or talk against the Jews in the preceding six months, just five years later, in 1951, that number had dropped to 16 percent—and to 11 percent by 1956.

The reasons for this abrupt and welcome change were many. A flourishing economy made Gentile Americans feel an emotional generosity to minorities, at least to white minorities such as the Jews. And the very optimism and success of the postwar years encouraged people to concentrate on their own careers and families rather than nurse grievances against others. Soldiers who had fought against anti-Semitism in Europe were more conscious of it when they came home.

Of crucial importance was a gradual awakening to the extent of the Holocaust. The International Military Tribunal held in Nuremberg in 1945–1946 had put the architects and builders of genocide on trial, and revealed to the world the crucial facts about their unbearably cruel and inhumane activities. *The Diary of Anne Frank* was also widely read in the 1950s, further stirring readers' sympathies toward the Jews. In 1961, Israel put Adolf Eichmann on trial, and televised the proceedings. Americans reacted with horror to the Nazi crimes, helping to create an atmosphere in which public expressions of anti-Semitism became increasingly unacceptable.

The heroic and dramatic birth of Israel in 1948 was also crucial in reducing anti-Semitism in America. Such an utterly improbable rebirth of a Jewish homeland in the ancient land of Israel was itself a dramatic and interesting story. The fact that Jews could fight and win a war against multiple enemy nations not only increased Jewish pride around the world but also transformed the view of Jews in the eyes of some Gentiles; Jews were no longer simply history's chosen victims. And for an increasing number of fundamentalist American Christians, the birth of Israel was a crucial sign of the Second Coming; Jews could not be ridiculed if they now were pivotal in what would be for some fundamentalists the end of the world.

Finally, the decrease in anti-Semitism can be ascribed to the decades-long work of American Jewish entertainers, especially comedians. Without their realizing it, many Americans had, across the decades, been absorbing a Jewish sensibility as they laughed at Jewish comedians.

Sid Caesar was, with Milton Berle, the most important of those comedians. Caesar had studied classical music and had been a professional saxophonist. This background let him clearly see the relationship between sound and silence. He was second only to Jack Benny in the effective use of silence, and second to none in his ability to mimic languages (so much so that as he spoke gibberish he appeared to be speaking in another language). This ability came early. As a youngster Caesar would listen to the customers at his father's delicatessen. They spoke Italian, Russian, and many other languages. Soon Caesar began to copy the distinctive sounds he heard. Eventually feeling himself prepared, he ventured over to a table of Italians. The tiny Caesar began to speak in seeming Italian, though the words, of course, made no sense. Their musical sound and their cadence, however, were perfect. The diners loved the sound, though it took them a minute to realize what the youngster was doing. Then they laughed and brought him over to another table so he could do the same, only this time in Polish.

Even as a youngster, Caesar knew that this method of eliciting humor was better than what he had seen, especially the ethnic stereotyping, the mockery of stooges, and slapstick, such as pie throwing or seltzer squirting. Instead, Caesar found humor in making fun of events in ordinary life.

The musical juxtaposition between silence and noise extended to Caesar's personal life. He was a shy man in many ways, someone who, he admits, hid behind his characters. Yet, he was not above violence. In the marines, while in a hospital, he heard two other marines using abusive anti-Semitic language and calling Jews cowards. One came over to Caesar's hospital bed while Caesar was away to check the chart for his religion. When Caesar returned, the marine said, "I *told* you this one was a yellow Jew." Caesar, deceptively calm, walked over, picked up a glass water pitcher, and smacked it against the bed stand, shattering it. He grabbed one of the marines and held the jagged edge of the glass against the marine's throat, saying, "Now, how yellow are these Jews?" Orderlies rushed to the scene. Caesar later told a psychiatrist that he might not have killed the marine, but "I would have cut him."

During another occasion at the Palmer House in Chicago, Caesar in a rage attacked Mel Brooks, who was then a writer on Caesar's television program, *Your Show of Shows*. Caesar had been drinking. At one point Brooks said, "I don't want to sit around all night looking at you drinking Scotch. Let's go out."

Caesar walked over to the window and looked out to the street eighteen floors down. Then he grabbed Brooks. "You want out?" Caesar asked. "I'll *show* you out." Caesar lifted Brooks off his feet and ran to the window. He dangled the young writer, who was half inside the room and half hanging outside. Caesar's brother Dave, also in the room, grabbed both of them and pulled until they were back in the room and safe.

Caesar also punched out taxi windows, and once, when a horse threw his wife from the saddle, he punched the horse, an event later re-created in Mel Brooks's film *Blazing Saddles*.

Caesar's first television program, *Admiral Broadway Revue*, premiered on January 28, 1949. The show looked like a sophisticated Saturday evening show at a Borscht Belt hotel. This may have been because it was created by Max Liebman, who got his initial training there. (And, of course, Caesar himself was a Borscht Belt veteran.)

Although the show received good reviews (one critic called it "the find of the year"), it was canceled after nineteen weeks.

Its successor, *Your Show of Shows*, debuted on February 24, 1950. *Your Show of Shows* was a perfect stage for Caesar's extraordinary skills. Mixing comedy sketches with popular music, as well as ballet and operatic performances, it offered, as all variety shows did, some act to please everyone.

Caesar, in keeping with his distaste for the gags and wisecracks so popular with other comedians, instead created sketches and focused on characters. "I didn't use one-liners," he recalls, "because for me the fun came through the characters."

As the Professor (best remembered when Carl Reiner was added as the straight man interviewing Caesar), Caesar could be a variety of characters. He was Professor Ludwig von Snowcap, an expert on mountain climbing, or Professor von Sedative, an expert on sleep, or one of many other similar characters. One memorable sketch was based on John Gilbert, the silent-screen star whose high voice rendered him unable to succeed in sound movies. Caesar played Rex Handsome, a vain star with a high-pitched voice. In this version, "Handsome" did finally succeed because his voice lowered when he conveniently caught a cold. In other sketches, Caesar was a Teutonic "general" getting dressed in a precise military manner by his assistant, played by Howie Morris. Both spoke in "German" during the entire sketch. (Morris's abilities in keeping up with Caesar were remarkable.) At the end of the sketch, the "general" turned out to be an apartment doorman. Caesar also liked to do "movies," such as "The Cobbler's Daughter" in which Caesar plays an Italian trying to marry off his daughter. Once he did a takeoff on *The King and I* in which, as the barefoot king, he steps on a cigarette. The show, broadcast on September 15, 1956, was the first performance an eight-year-old named Billy Crystal saw on television that made him laugh.

These characters, along with the husband Caesar played in many sketches, were urban, with a Jewish sensibility, and also particularly rooted in Caesar's own psyche. The characters each had divided selves: Rex Handsome was a good-looking, masculine star with a decidedly unmasculine voice; the Professor was a self-confident, well-educated fool. In this division, they were like Caesar himself: a driven genius who claimed (and still does claim) that comedy can't be learned; a shy man who turned vicious when drinking; a man who thought highly of his writers but frequently belittled them and those around him. He was, in a sense, the most complex of the Jewish comedians of his era.

It is unclear to what extent such a divided self was even grasped by the audience and, if so, to what extent it was the source of interest. Clearly, it was the quality of the entertainment and Caesar's unique ability to mimic that was most attractive. Still, in retrospect, Caesar was a symbol of his time. America was torn between two selves: the America of the depression and the America of postwar prosperity; the America tired of war and the America increasingly concerned with communism; the America of suburban families and the fringes who went on the road to rebel against the culture. Caesar's characters located the dark undersides of the vibrant, new America. Presented through humor, they were acceptable to audiences who were themselves grappling to control those undersides and build a postwar society.

Shows were broadcast live for thirty-nine weeks a season. There were no cue cards and no TelePrompTers. However difficult and brave such an effort was, it carried rewards. Without having to rely on prompts, Caesar could look at the eyes of the other actors and listen to their voices. This kind of contact provided incredible timing and a genuine comedic exchange. To this day, Caesar remains proud of his work without the normal safety nets of television. "There's nobody today who could do a live show. They can't go two minutes without looking at a cue card." When asked how he could do it, he laughs and says, "You drink a lot of water."

Caesar is also proud of his clean material and compares it favorably with current tastes. "Today they depend on *shmutz*. Anybody can get a laugh by dropping their pants. After you drop your pants, now what are you going to do?"

There were a variety of brilliant writers who helped Caesar create his characters. Mel Brooks joined during the fourth show of the *Admiral Broadway Revue*. Brooks had been a neighbor of Don Appel, who had worked with Caesar. Brooks followed Appel around the Borscht Belt and then followed Caesar around nightclubs. Brooks was deeply attracted to Caesar's humor.

According to Caesar, just an hour before the fourth show of the *Revue*, he realized that one of the skits was seriously in need of revision. No one could come up with a solution to the problem, which was how a jungle boy could explain to the Professor how he would order breakfast in the wild. Brooks, hanging around but not on staff, was asked for his idea. Brooks developed a strange sound (a perfect idea that played to Caesar's key strength) called "the Cry of the Crazy Crow." Brooks was then offered a job.

Brooks has a slightly different memory of the event. Brooks says that Caesar invited him to come by a rehearsal for *Your Show of Shows*, which aired the following year. Brooks says Caesar was concerned about a bit in which an airport interviewer talks to people coming off a plane. Brooks says he then came up with the idea of a jungle boy.

The comedian Milt Kamen showed up one day with a young man named Woody Allen, who was promptly hired. Allen and another writer, Neil Simon, were shy; they couldn't present their ideas in the wild and raucous writers' room. Instead, Simon would lean over to Carl Reiner, whisper an idea, and Reiner would present it. Simon's brother Danny was Allen's mentor. Larry Gelbart (who later developed *M*A*S*H*), Joe Stein (who later wrote the book for *Fiddler on the Roof*), Mel Tolkin, Selma Diamond, Aaron Reuben, and Gary Belkin were also there. Reiner would later use this group as the basis for *The Dick Van Dyke Show* with Van Dyke playing the head writer of a comedy show.

Of the writing, Caesar said, "We all wrote together. Nobody was writing by themselves. It has to be in your style, your language. They have to put it in your mouth." Caesar himself was a brilliant editor, instinctively knowing good material and very obviously incredibly capable of getting that material from the writers.

Your Show of Shows was on the air for four years on Saturday nights. *Caesar's Hour* replaced it for an additional three years. (Although many who recall Caesar blend the two shows, there were crucial distinctions, the most important one being the replacement of Imogene Coca by Nanette Fabray. Because Fabray could sing and dance, there were more production numbers in *Caesar's Hour.*)

By the end, Caesar's use of liquor had begun to affect his performance. He would repeat material, making sketches go too long. His delivery, famous for its musical rhythm, was off-key. By 1958, ratings began to fall, and competitors finally forced the show off the air.

Gertrude Berg also found a home in television. Berg wanted to please her audience every bit as much as Berle. But whereas Berle's audience was more secular, Berg wanted to reach a broader Jewish community without losing an American audience. It was a difficult and delicate balancing act, one that was at first successful, but eventually could not be sustained.

Berg decided early on that she wanted to take her successful radio show to television. She approached NBC, but the network executives didn't think television audiences would welcome the show. Berg then went to CBS, where, again, executives didn't think the show would be successful. Berg then arranged a meeting with William Paley, the head of CBS. He arranged an audition that went very well.

The Goldbergs started on January 10, 1949, and ran on CBS until June 1951. It then switched to NBC in 1952 and stayed on until the summer of 1953. In 1954, the show aired locally in New York on the independent station WABD. Although Berg later denied it, the early shows sometimes focused on an explicitly political message. There was, for example, a 1949 episode called "The Rent Strike." In the show, Molly's husband, Jake, is angry at a new rent increase and decides not to pay it. By the end of the show, however, it is not a strike that solves the problem but Molly's cooking. She bakes the landlord a cake for his birthday. As she declares: "A landlord is also a person."

This use of food as a substitute for confrontation and a means to negotiation and eventual accommodation was commonplace on *The Goldbergs*. It was an example of the limits of the series: bring up an important subject, especially to Jews with memories of poverty, and find a way to deflect antagonism by relying on ethnic and folk skills. The approach, that is, was a classic Jewish survival strategy: don't annoy the Gentiles or those in power but find a way to solve the problem. The show was a generation behind real American Jews.

Berg also had shows about Yom Kippur and Passover, but in both cases the episodes were less about the holidays and more about family relationships or attachments to marks of ethnicity, again especially food. As she told Morris Freedman, a writer for *Commentary*, "I don't bring up anything that will bother people. That's very important. Unions, politics, fund-raising, Zionism, socialism, inter-group relations, I don't stress them. . . . The Goldbergs are not defensive about their Jewishness, or especially aware of it."

But Berg's show and observations were not quite consonant with the views of most young parents. The show was increasingly at odds with an emerging materialism, a belief that if children could be given what their parents were deprived of, they would be happy. The well-meaning antimaterialistic messages of the show seemed quaint even if charming.

The show also had practical problems. Philip Loeb, who played Jake, had been listed in *Red Channels*, the anticommunist publication that sought communists and communist sympathizers in the entertainment industry. Although Berg tried to defend him at first, he was forced off the show in 1952 and later committed suicide. And the critics were not always kind. A *Variety* critic didn't like the episode about Passover, which included a seder. A writer for *Television* was upset at a show about anti-Semitism, an episode in which the Goldbergs were visiting Gentile residents of an apartment on Park Avenue. This episode, said the critic, "made for uneasy viewing for the TV audience." Indeed, the critic continued, the Goldberg family should have been "in their own element in the Bronx." The notion of keeping Jews in an ethnic ghetto was a middle ground for American audiences. They could appreciate the warmth of a Jewish family if the family did not directly threaten their own social life. Berg misread this. She moved the family out of the Bronx to a suburban landscape to show the movement of American Jews outward in American life. But it was just such a movement that large audiences were not ready for.

The most important reason for the eventual demise of the show, however, was its overt ethnicity. Understandably, Berg was popular with Jewish audiences. She still lived by the rhythms of immigrant life, and her attempt to bridge two cultures had perfectly matched the efforts by large numbers of American Jews in her generation to navigate the assimilationist waters of American life without drowning.

However, in television the trend was away from ethnicity and toward bland, nondescript situation comedies about middle-class WASP families. Television sponsors sought a larger voice in defining programming. The wild, unpredictable antics and ad-libbing of Berle and Caesar were beyond the sponsors' control, but a sitcom could be filmed and edited to the sponsor's taste. Moreover, there were many fewer television stations than radio stations, which meant that television programs had to have wider appeal. Finally, declining anti-Semitism notwithstanding, the presence of so many Jews in television was clearly a cause for concern among some segments of American society. During the 1950s, for example, some Americans believed Jews were more likely to be sympathetic with communism if not outright communists themselves. There were, for example, a huge number of Jewish performers listed in *Red Channels*. The perception of Jews as potential or actual allies with America's archenemy made many entertainers—and other Jews— more reluctant to identify themselves openly as Jews.

Suddenly, the Jewish comedians began to disappear in a scene eerily reminiscent of the 1930s film industry. Shows that seemed too Jewish were modified. Carl Reiner's attempt to create a show with a clear Jewish sensibility and based on Reiner's experiences as a Jew in the Bronx was completely transformed. Dick Van Dyke replaced Reiner, and the setting was moved to suburban Westchester County.

Still, Jewish sensibilities filtered through. Such a sensibility could be seen in Sergeant Bilko, the character played by Phil Silvers on his show. The series itself started off improbably when Silvers hosted a White House show for President Eisenhower. A CBS vice president in charge of programming was there and called Silvers's agent about developing a program. Silvers was reluctant, until CBS suggested he could work with Nat Hiken, a writer widely recognized for his comic genius. The two developed idea after idea before settling on an army sergeant. Not lost on Silvers was that there was an enormous number of viewers who had been or were going into the army. The potential audience was projected to be 10 million. Silvers could play a bit of a con man, but one protected by the uniform. Being in the army also protected the actor against criticism. He may have been a bit of a fraud, but such a character could be sympathetic if he had a warm heart, war experience, and served the country.

Hiken and Silvers named their character after Steve Bilko, a minor league baseball player who had hit sixty-one home runs and whose name—with its connotations of "bilking" someone—fit the character perfectly. Thus was Sgt. Ernest Bilko born. Other characters were also given names from the world of sports. One was named after an umpire named Paparelli; Corporal Barbello had Rocky Graziano's real name. Harvey Lembeck played Barbello, although Silvers originally wanted Buddy Hackett for the role. Another actor, Maurice Gosfield, looked to Silvers like a Doberman pinscher, and so Pvt. Duane Doberman was created

The show, which debuted on September 20, 1955, and ran for four years, was immensely popular. The president expressed his appreciation for the show, and the army provided a technical adviser.

Silvers believed, and most critics and viewers agree, that the best episode was "The Trial of Harry Speakup." The premise of the show was itself a challenge. The army has decided to speed up induction time. A chimp is smuggled into the barracks with a new recruit, and the chimp is dubbed by accident "Harry Speakup." (An anxious person on the induction line doesn't get a response when he asks the new recruit his name and so, looking down at his papers, says, "Come on, Harry. Speak up." The WAC typing out the names believes that is the new recruit's name.) At the psychological test, the chimp jumps on the desk, and the psychologist, again looking down, notes, "rejected by mother . . . violence under control." Bilko switches names on the intelligence tests, so that Harry places fourth highest. Finally, Harry is sworn into the army. Only then is the discovery made. Somehow, Harry has to be forced out of the army without the public finding out that he is a chimpanzee. Bilko comes up with an idea: Harry had bitten a sergeant and so should be court-martialed. Bilko would serve as the defense attorney. Zippy, the chimp playing Harry, loved telephones, and grabs one at the trial. Silvers, forced to ad-lib, says: "I plead for adjournment. My client is calling for a new attorney."

The notion of the Jewish and urban Silvers playing a con man, however lovable, raised questions similar to those prompted by Jack Benny's cheap persona. Would Bilko's con artistry validate or even stir up anti-Semitism? In a different American culture, the question would have had more power, but in mid-1950s America, with Jews fully entering society and anti-Semitism in rapid decline, Sergeant Bilko, especially because he was in the army, was more a source of seeing Jews as funny than a potential source of anti-Semitism. In a crucial way, the Silvers characterization was so shrewd that it took an anti-Semitic stereotype and stood it on its head. It was because Bilko, despite his name, was so clearly Jewish that Silvers stands as an important step on the way to Americans identifying Jews with humor, an identification that would be completed in the 1960s.

Soupy Sales was another Jewish comedian much beloved, especially among children. Raised in Huntington, West Virginia, Milton Supman began his career writing radio scripts and doing stand-up comedy. In 1950, he moved to Cincinnati and entered television with *Soupy's Soda Shop*, the first teenage dance program on television. A talk show followed. Sales next moved to Detroit in 1953 where he achieved great success. (In Detroit, he was known just as Soupy. The "Sales" name came from a comic named Chic Sales and was first used during a brief stay in Cleveland.) His *Lunch with Soupy Sales* was the first ABC program on Saturday morning that wasn't a cartoon.

By 1960, Sales was in Los Angeles, continuing to attract a national audience. His first Friday night show featured him as a waiter with Frank Sinatra, Sammy Davis Jr., and Trini Lopez as guests. By the time the bit is finished all of his guests had received multiple pies in the face—Sales's signature gag. He created a wonderful world for children, featuring the giant off-screen paw of White Fang and the sweeter paw of Black Tooth, the angry neighbor character, puppets such as Pookie the Lion, silent films for which he provided hilarious running commentaries, and dances such as the Soupy Shuffle and the Mouse. He joked not with an audience but with the camera operators and others in the studio. (The staff had a great time. They would devise their own jokes on Soupy. Once, when he went to the door to talk to the angry neighbor character who was always off-camera, the staff replaced the neighbor with a topless dancer exercising her art.) He laughed at the material in an infectious way that audiences found endearing.

Soupy Sales was not widely identified as a Jewish comedian, though he admires the compassion of Jewish families and traces his own sense of humor, in part, to his mother's. Sometimes that humor, which had a subversive, prankish quality, got him in trouble. Sales got suspended for a week after one of his gags backfired. On January 1, 1965, he told his young viewers to "tiptoe into the bedroom" in search of parental wallets in which they would find "green pieces of paper." He advised the viewers to mail the green paper to him. The gag was a good setup for his follow-up line: "If you send me those pieces of paper, you know what I'm gonna send you? A postcard from Puerto Rico."

Pinky Lee (born Pincus Leff) was another Jewish comedian popular with children. Lee had worked in burlesque. His trademark small checkered cap, borrowed from a child when Lee's regular hat couldn't be found before a performance, served as a sight gag; to supplement it, Lee added a checked suit. His slapstick humor, lisp, and breakneck speed were far more popular with children than critics or parents, and, in various guises, Lee kept doing children's programs on and off through the 1950s and '60s.

There were other comedians as characters on shows, such as Morey Amsterdam on *The Dick Van Dyke Show*, playing the clearly Jewish character Buddy Sorrel. Amsterdam had achieved fame with his theme song "Yuk-a-Puk," which he would play on the cello as a way to pause between jokes, a technique Henny Youngman and his violin would later popularize even more. The show, created by Carl Reiner, was a semiautobiographical effort to describe the writer's room on Sid Caesar's shows. Although profoundly muted, Buddy Sorrel and Sally Rogers, played by Rose Marie, seem modeled on Mel Brooks and Selma Diamond and Van Dyke on the less manic Reiner. Buddy's Jewishness was constantly subdued except for the episode "Buddy Sorrel—Man and Boy," in which Buddy takes long-belated bar mitzvah lessons and actually has the bar mitzvah at the end of the show. Dick Van Dyke is wearing a yarmulke, and the rabbi calls Buddy by his Hebrew name.

Another popular comic was Louis Nye, who appeared most famously as Gordon Hathaway, a man on the street on Steve Allen's program. Of the character, Nye said, "I wanted to create an amusing, eloquent, elegant, real goyish guy." Bill Dana (born William Szathmary), like Nye, also appeared on Steve Allen's show. His character's trademark means of identification, "My name Jose Jimenez," became a national catchphrase. Although Dana refrained from ethnic content, by the name and accent, he was obviously identified as a Spanish character. He dropped the character when he realized that the character was causing pain for Spanish-speaking viewers.

Of course, many of the successful Jewish radio comedians tried to make the transition to television. Some were more successful than others. Watching Ed Wynn's shows, filled with terrible puns, is not enjoyable if current comedic standards are used. Eddie Cantor's programs similarly don't hold up in part because his age prevented him from either looking or acting with the same energy that had so charmed vaudeville audiences.

Cantor does belong in one significant footnote to television history. He was on the first show that was censored. It was May 25, 1944. Cantor was scheduled to sing "We're Having a Baby, My Baby and Me." NBC censors, however, decided forty minutes before the show was to air that the lyrics might offend NBC executives who had invited members of the Philadelphia business community to publicize a relay link between Philadelphia and New York, and it was an audience that NBC didn't want to take a chance on offending. The officials were also concerned about the broader American audience. Cantor was used to the more sophisticated urban crowds that had enjoyed the suggestiveness of "Makin' Whoopee," a song with a euphemism for sex even in its title, or such lyrics as "If you knew Susie like I know Susie—Oh! Oh! Oh! What a girl," which vaudeville audiences understood as implying physical intimacy.

The furious Cantor claimed that time prevented him from preparing another song. The nervous censors then seemingly decided to let him sing because he began the number. However, during the broadcast the audio signal was shut off during a supposedly inappropriate exchange between Cantor and Nora Martin, the woman he was singing with. Cantor then performed what the *New York Times* called "a modified hula-hula dance," but the camera operators showed Cantor only from the waist up. (This was a dozen years before Elvis Presley's hip gyrations were shot in the same way on the *Ed Sullivan Show*).

George Burns and Gracie Allen also made the leap to television. *The George Burns and Gracie Allen Show* (1950–1958) was their successful effort to transport their famous radio program to the new medium. It relied on simple sets of the Burns and Allen household, the neighbor's house, and downstage, where George Burns would make comments about Gracie, the plot of his own show, and the people around him. This bizarre commentary, accompanied by an ever present cigar, gently mocked the very medium being presented.

The show itself relied almost completely on the charm of the stars. The plots were thin, based as they were on classic, simple conflicts between spouses, parents and children, neighbors, and friends. The show was sometimes awkwardly filmed. The boom mike could be seen, and character movement from one setting to another seemed to elude the camera operators' ability to keep track. The program added little to television or comedic history other than to illustrate, as if such an illustration were needed, that the public genuinely liked Burns and Allen.

Groucho Marx reprised his successful radio show *You Bet Your*

Life for television (1950–1961). He grew a real mustache for the show in place of the painted-on one he wore in his films, but he continued the traditions of endless wisecracks and extended leering at attractive women. His interplay with the announcer George Fenneman, his use of celebrities as contestants, the falling duck with money for a contestant who said the secret word, and the straightforward nature of the quiz itself complemented Groucho's personality. The show, like the Marx Brothers' movies, made audiences even more comfortable with the fast delivery of one-liners and the patter of Jewish humor.

Jack Benny made a similarly successful transition to television in *The Jack Benny Program* (1950–1964). Like Burns and Allen, who played themselves, Benny played a comedian named Jack Benny. Benny, like Burns, stood in front of a curtain to make comments directly to the audience, which appreciated getting an "inside" view of a celebrity's life. That such a life was often at odds with reality didn't bother the audience. By the time of television, Burns and Allen as well as Benny were cultural icons, and their shows took advantage of this status in a cleverer way than would have been done had they been in standard situation comedies. Benny's shows were better written than Burns and Allen's. Benny was extremely generous in giving both screen time and funny lines to those around him. Such professional generosity was as evident as his character's stinginess.

Benny continued to rely on the same characters as on his radio program. For example, in the episode "The Railroad Station," there was an exchange between Benny and the character Mr. Kitzel, who spoke with a strong Yiddish accent.

KITZEL: Hello, Meestah Benneh . . .
BENNY: What are you doing here at the station?
KITZEL: I'm taking a trip to Chicago.

BENNY: Oh, you're going all the way to Chicago.
KITZEL: Yes, and I can see my wife's face now. Whew! Will she
    be surprised.
BENNY: She doesn't know you're coming?
KITZEL: She doesn't know I'm going.

But despite his fame and success, Benny was never as sharp on television as on the radio show, which had depended on getting audiences to use their imaginations creatively. The television show was forced to render real the objects and places that were more suitable to and funnier in the human imagination.

The era of Burns and Benny was coming to a close. American culture by the late 1950s was at the very beginning of a long revolution, one so sweeping that no element of the culture would be left unchanged.

Jewish stand-up comedians, outside the mainstream of American television's bland family comedies, were about to stage a comeback. The new culture would usher in a new set of audience needs, and Jewish comedians, with their cutting wit and appetite for satire, were especially well suited to meet those needs. These comedians would, in time, forever alter American comedy and American culture.

The teeming streets of the Lower East Side in New York City were filled with the raucous rhythms of immigrant life. In 1880 there were 80,000 Jews living in New York. By 1910, that number had swelled to 1,250,000. A typical block consisted of 2,781 people—and no bathtubs.

Credit: Brown Brothers

Vaudeville comedians Joe Weber (*right*) and Lew Fields specialized in physical comedy and the immensely popular but ultimately troubling use of thick Yiddish dialects.

Credit: Photofest

Pop-eyed Eddie Cantor thrilled vaudeville audiences with his high energy and clever ad-libs. Later, he was the first person ever censored on television. *Credit: Brian Gari Archives*

George Burns and Gracie Allen were the most successful team in vaudeville. Originally, Burns was supposed to be the funny one until he realized audiences loved and laughed at Gracie while they ignored his jokes. *Credit: Photofest*

anny Brice played Baby Snooks, a character that enabled her to utter words no grown-up would be free to say. Jewish audiences, often justifiably afraid to express their true feelings to those in power in the Old Country and not yet comfortable enough in America to do so, identified with Snooks.

Credit: Photofest

The children of immigrant Jews left the crowded streets and sought a community in the crowded rooms of "Borscht Belt" resorts. Here is the Stardust Room at Kutsher's Country Club.

Credit: Kutsher's Country Club

The Marx Brothers entered vaudeville at the insistence of their indomitable mother, Minnie. In this early photograph are (*left to right*) Groucho, Gummo, Harpo, and Chico. Gummo would soon be replaced by Zeppo. *Credit: Photofest*

Harpo, Chico, and Groucho carefully developed characters that mocked authority and social conventions in a way that helped an immigrant generation confront their feelings of being overwhelmed by America.

Credit: Photofest

The Three Stooges were famous for their slapstick comedy. Here Moe twists Curly's nose while an anguished Larry looks on. Later, the Stooges were among the very few comedians who mocked the Nazis. *Credit: Ronald L. Smith Collection*

Jack Benny in a characteristic pose. His cheapskate character and mastery of comic timing helped depression audiences cope with their troubles. *Credit: Photofest*

D anny Kaye was one of many Jewish comedians who entertained members of the Armed Forces. Here Kaye is en route to Berlin in 1948 and seems a bit perplexed about the intricacies of his parachute. *Credit: Photofest*

G ertrude Berg played Molly Goldberg, a warm immigrant Jewish homemaker who spoke to the wider world from her window. Here she plays to the camera. Note the Sanka Coffee flowerpot. Stars frequently did commercials for their advertisers. *Credit: Photofest*

Milton Berle's popularity made audiences want to buy their own television sets. He was famous for his outlandish costumes and his portrayal of stars, such as the singer Carmen Miranda.

Credits: (left) Ronald L. Smith Collection (below) Photofest

Henny Youngman punctuated one-liners with his violin playing. His trademark joke of "Take my wife, please" masked a deep tension between Jewish male comedians and Jewish women.

Credit: Photofest

Sid Caesar (*right*) not only was a brilliant mimic but assembled the most talented collection of writers in television history. Here, from left to right, Mel Brooks, Woody Allen, and Mel Tolkin are unpersuasive in their pleas to convince Caesar that their efforts have comedic value. *Credit: Photofest*

Buddy Hackett's unique Brooklyn-accented voice, rubber face, and pudgy frame added to his quick mind to make him one of the funniest comedians in front of live audiences.

Credit: Ronald L. Smith Collection

Jerry Lewis in *The Nutty Professor* (1963) trying with the help of science to transform himself from being awkward and nerdy to suave and confident so he could win the love of a beautiful student. Such a change mirrored Jewish attempts to become fully American.

Credit: Photofest

R odney Dangerfield, nervously pulling at his tie, didn't "get no respect," and he found that large numbers of Americans felt the same way.

Credit: Ronald L. Smith Collection

D on Rickles, dubbed "Mr. Warmth," was one of the very few comedians who could insult celebrities and audience members alike and get laughter in return.

Credit: Photofest

Jackie Mason, whose undiluted, Yiddish-inflected delivery and Jewish-saturated routines are one of the last connections to an Old World comic heritage, here combines two passions: comedy and food. *Credit: By Ronald L. Smith*

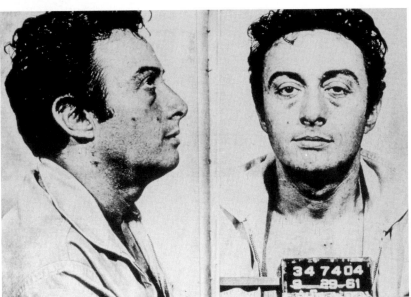

34 7404

These are the police photos of Lenny Bruce after a 1961 narcotics arrest in Philadelphia. Bruce challenged the legal limits of obscene language and explored religion and sex as acceptable subject matter for comedy. No comedic performer since Bruce has been put on trial for obscenity.

Credit: Ronald L. Smith Collection

Mort Sahl, using a darting, jazz-like delivery, let comedy relax in a sweater but be more seriously connected to the outer world through the newspapers that he used for material.   *Credit: Photofest*

Shelley Berman led a brilliant exploration into the neurotic underside of American life. Known, along with Bruce and Sahl, as a "sick comic," Berman showed that comedy could handle troubling and profound subjects without surrendering the humor.

Credit: Ronald L. Smith Collection

A pained Woody Allen in the theatrical production of *Play It Again, Sam* (1969). Allen, the clearest comedic guide to the changing romantic relationships in American society from the 1960s to the 1980s, never hid either his Jewishness or his troubled relationship with that Jewish identity.   *Credit: Ronald L. Smith Collection*

M el Brooks in *Blazing Saddles* (1974) portraying what surely is the funniest Yiddish-speaking Indian chief in cinematic history. Beginning with this film, Brooks mastered the spoof, following it up with *Young Frankenstein, Silent Movie, High Anxiety, History of the World: Part I, Spaceballs*, and others.   *Credit: Photofest*

Andy Kaufman, more performance artist than comedian, is here playing at Carnegie Hall. Kaufman explored the pain of always having to portray characters, and, in doing do, risking the identity of the real person underneath.

Credit: Photofest

Joan Rivers was a major breakthrough for women comedians. Her success at subverting the role assigned to women who did stand-up paved the way for many other women to enter comedy.

Credit: Photofest

Roseanne, whose proud, working-class character provided a voice for millions of television viewers, mocked husbands and questioned the traditional place of women in society.

Credit: Photofest

The cast of *Seinfield* included, from left to right, Michael Richards (Kramer), Jason Alexander (George), Jerry Seinfeld (Jerry), and Julia Louis-Dreyfus (Elaine). The "show about nothing" featured Seinfeld's clever observations and inspired writing. Seventy-six million viewers tuned in for the final episode.   *Credit: Photofest*

Adam Sandler, here in *Big Daddy* (1999), used his films to explore the difficulties of growing up. Sandler's "Chanukah Song" illustrates how at ease and proud he is about being Jewish.   *Credit: Photofest*

7

"IS THERE ANY GROUP I HAVEN'T OFFENDED?"

THE CHANGING WORLD OF STAND-UP COMEDY

Lenny Bruce paced the stage at the Basin Street West nightclub in San Francisco. It was August 1965, and Bruce was reeling from his arrest a year earlier on obscenity charges, which had led to a four-month jail sentence. In 1960, Bruce had made $108,000. Now he was broke and desperate. Hardly any club would book him for fear of being closed down by the authorities.

The small audience had come to hear a comedy legend, a man who had become a symbol of the struggle to speak freely. The people listening were patient, waiting for laughs. They wanted to like the increasingly degenerating Bruce.

Lenny Bruce was wearing his trademark car coat, and the fake cobblestone wall behind him added to the darkness of the moment. Cameras were recording the performance; Bruce couldn't stand the bright lights, and so a fast film stock was used, the grainy result perfectly capturing the performer's inner pain. Bruce was a cornered, even confused, rebel, emotionally and ideologically refusing to surrender his fighting spirit but characteristically clear-eyed about the cruel inevitability of his struggle against the authorities.

Living up to a boisterous assertion that "I'm not a comedian, I'm Lenny Bruce," he read from his trial transcript, arguing that he never said what he was charged with saying. When he sporadically went into his regular routines, Bruce left large parts out and wandered around the stage. The confused but partisan audience went in search of laughs but too rarely found the hunt successful. That audience, beatniks and hipsters, rebels and iconoclasts, small in number but large in influence, would eventually usher in a cultural revolution that would define a young generation, but in 1965, as Bruce was spiraling downward, the victor in this cultural struggle remained unclear.

Lenny Bruce's moment on the cultural stage had its origins not in the politics of the 1960s but in the complacency of the preceding decade. The 1950s had begun with tremendous promise. The aftermath of World War II had led to the greatest era of economic growth in American history. The baby boom that started in 1946 had led to a resurgence in emphasis on family life, to a need for housing, and to a tremendous increase in the number of consumers. With their newfound money and their concern for open space, better schools, new housing, and safety for their young children, families moved from the cities to the suburbs.

The seeming utopia that parents believed they were creating for their children soon revealed a troubled underside The cluster of new lifestyles led to a new American identity, but it was one in which there was great pressure to conform, to aspire to a stable marriage and children, to want a well-paying and secure job, to seek happiness from the institutions that defined the society and from the goods and services the society produced.

This bland homogeneity was comforting for many in a new generation anxious about their roles in the new America. But three groups emerged in opposition to the prevailing social vision.

The first group included adults who disdained material values, the politics of the era, the very rules of a society, or some combination of these. They sought to separate themselves from the society by deliberately violating its rules and challenging its preconceptions. J. D. Salinger in *Catcher in the Rye* and the works of Beat-generation writers exemplified these concerns. People in these groups consciously sought a place for the voices shut out of American society, especially dissenting voices of the political Left. For them, the widespread accusations and investigations of purported communists were reckless intrusions into the private political values of citizens. They disdained Sen. Joseph R. McCarthy, who charged that many government officials and others were communists or had communist connections. The anticommunism of the era culminated in the 1953 execution of Julius and Ethel Rosenberg for passing military information to Soviet agents. There was worldwide protest against the executions, with some claiming the Rosenbergs innocent and others objecting to the severity of the punishment. The accusations went beyond the entertainment community. Many intellectuals—professors, journalists, and others—were suspected of communist leanings.

The second group troubled by the new culture included teenagers who disliked the parental pressures on them to conform. They found rock and roll an especially powerful voice with which to express their anxieties.

The third group lacked power to rebel. They were those who, in spite of the successful economy, remained poor. African Americans, in particular, remained locked out of much of the success because of widespread discrimination. The increasing economic gap between rich and poor was a glaring symbol of what separated the American Dream from reality. It is, of course, precisely such separations between the officially accepted version of reality and the actual reality that feed comedians.

There were some Jewish comedians who found audiences among the satisfied suburbanites and successful urban professionals. These comedians aimed their humor especially at Jewish audiences and Gentiles attracted to warm, ethnic stories.

Sam Levenson and Myron Cohen, in particular, remained close to the Jewish community, drawing nourishment from its culture, feeling especially comfortable with Jewish audiences, living as much in the world of Yiddish as English.

Levenson's humor was warm and nostalgic. He did not mock the Jewish family but offered it as a model of what families could be. Nor did he mock Yiddish by doing dialect comedy, but used the American English of his contemporaries.

Levenson was proud of not challenging the premises of a middle-class life. He loved to talk about raising children, but his mother was his best subject. He told of his mother shopping:

"How much are these cucumbers?"

"Two for five."

"And how much is this one?"

"Three cents."

"Okay. I'll take the other one."

Once she took young Sammy shopping for a tie. They went to the tie man, and Mama agreed, to Sammy's shock, to pay the fifty cents the man asked. The man was astonished because Mama Levenson always argued about the price. On the way home, Mama said, "Sammy, you are wondering why your mother paid the fifty cents without a word. Well, you are young yet . . . I never liked that man. I'm getting even. Tonight he will kill himself because he didn't ask me for a dollar."

He would tell stories of her pride in being able to feed any unexpected company. To do this, she kept a pot full of chicken legs always cooking on the stove. The family was unable to afford whole chickens, but the legs were readily available. One day, Uncle Louis and Aunt Lena and their eleven children dropped in unannounced. Mama Levenson was in a panic. She simply didn't have enough legs ready. Her honor was at stake. Hastily, she called her own children into the bedroom and told them, "Children, do me a favor. Say you don't like chicken." The children, of course, were understanding and sympathetic. They went back in and dutifully refused all the chicken when the visiting relatives offered to share. Finally, it was time for dessert. The same problem arose, but this time Mama Levenson didn't have to call the children into the bedroom. Instead, at the table, she announced to one and all, "Now, all the children who wouldn't eat the chicken don't get any dessert."

Myron Cohen started telling jokes to sell his garment goods to customers. By 1948, his success and the encouragement of others prompted him to head for the Catskills and Miami. His stories, like Levenson's, were warmly anecdotal. They might depend on a punch line, but they were not just jokes. Although Cohen spoke without a trace of an accent, he used Jewish and other accents constantly in his act. His warmth, genuine charm, and inoffensive material made him popular in nightclubs and on television.

He'd talk, for instance, of sitting on a plane next to a woman who was wearing a huge diamond.

"Excuse me," Cohen would say in a soft Yiddish accent. "I'm not trying to be forward, but that is a beautiful diamond."

"It's called the Klopman diamond. It's like the Hope Diamond. It comes with a curse."

"What's the curse?"

"Klopman."

Cohen would encourage his audience to substitute any name they wished in retelling the story.

He'd even joke gently about infidelity, such as when a man comes home and smells cigar smoke. He searches throughout the apartment until he sees a man in the shower.

"What are you doing here?" the man asks.

"I'm voting" is the answer.

Because his audiences were often elderly, and were comfortable with him, he could even joke about death, but he did it cleverly. "An undertaker calls a man whose mother-in-law has died. 'About your mother-in-law, should we embalm her, cremate her, or bury her?' He says, 'Do all three. Don't take chances.'"

Despite their success, Levenson and Cohen, along with Gertrude Berg, marked the end of a Jewish comedic era. Their need for the protective warmth they found in Jewish life, their closeness to the Jewish community, and their clearly being more comfortable in a Jewish than in a Gentile world were characteristics of humorists whose time was about to end.

Many Jewish comedians strayed from Myron Cohen's deliberate injection of Yiddish accents or Sam Levenson's nostalgic vision of Jewish immigrant life and spoke as Americans to Americans. They had various degrees of attachment to the Jewish community and various feelings about the relation of their Jewishness to their comedy, but, as a group, they both adapted to and challenged the new America.

The new American pressure to conform combined with the loss of the traditional Jewish comic identity to produce some confusion among Jewish comedians of the era. Some of them were unsure whether or how their Jewishness contributed to their comedy. Others found it easy simply to separate their Jewish from their comedic identities. Many straddled the line just as many American Jews did.

Many Jewish comedians found success as nightclub acts, especially in the then newly popular Las Vegas. Joe E. Lewis was the most popular nightclub comedian of the 1940s, and he was famous for joking about the nightclub environment itself. Drinking became central to his act. He held a glass as he ventured into song parody or one-liners. ("I know more old drunks than I know old doctors," he often said.) He began his act by holding up the glass and announcing, "It's post time." Then he might attack the audience. "You'll notice that I'm doing a very fast show. I'm cutting out all the laughs. These jokes may not sound like much to you, but your laughs don't sound like much to me either." He'd then go into some one-liners, such as "a race track is where the windows clean the people" and some stories.

Lewis's career is also important in emphasizing an unpleasant underbelly—its connection to organized crime. In 1927, Lewis was working in Chicago at the Green Mill, a club that was under the control of gangsters. Lewis was earning $650 a week. Another club offered Lewis $1000 a week to perform. After Lewis signed a contract, the owners of the Green Mill hired three men to attack him. Lewis was pistol-whipped, and his throat was slashed from ear to ear. Left for dead, Lewis struggled out of his hotel room into the hallway. He was hospitalized for six weeks, and his voice was changed forever (resulting in a raspy, slow delivery).

Jack E. Leonard, known to friends as "Fat Jack," earned his nickname by carrying more than three hundred pounds on his frame. Starting out in Chicago, Leonard showed up in New York with old and weak material. Leonard, angry at unamused audiences, confrontational as many comedians were, surer of his own talents than the audiences' judgments, began to insult those around him. Soon the occasional insults became absorbed into his new onstage identity as a mumbling sprayer of insults. He'd look at someone in the audience and say, "I always wanted to know how long a man can live without brains. Would you mind telling us your age?" He once told Perry Como, "You have a very fine voice. Too bad it's in Bing Crosby's throat." Once, on Ed Sullivan's show, Leonard turned to the host and said, "Don't worry, Ed. Someday you'll find yourself, and you'll be terribly disappointed. There's nothing wrong with you that reincarnation won't cure."

It is the rare performer who can make a huge success from insult comedy. Besides Fat Jack Leonard, only Don Rickles made a career of it. Leonard's awkward appearance, his weight, his bald head, and his black glasses made his appearance itself funny, and the seeming incongruity of a man looking like that mumbling insults was also funny.

Other Jewish nightclub comedians would find later fame in television. Larry Storch, for example, won fame doing impressions of such people as Jack Benny before becoming nationally known for his role as Corporal Agarn on *F-Troop*. Phil Foster worked in the Catskills and nightclubs for many years until he became well known on *Laverne and Shirley*. Jan Murray told typical wife, gambling, and other jokes as well as deliberately silly puns ("How about a tissue?" "Tissue, I don't even know you") prior to fame on a variety of game shows, especially *Treasure Hunt*. Jack Carter, popular in nightclubs, made more than fifty appearances on Ed Sullivan's show. With his woolly hair and tremendous energy, his manic use of numerous facial expressions, and his gift for mimicry, Carter was a master of delivery. Joey Bishop became famous as a member of the Rat Pack along with Frank Sinatra, Peter Lawford, Dean Martin, and Sammy Davis Jr. Bishop's sad face and throwaway delivery style fitted perfectly in with nightclub audiences. He was not above kidding that audience: "This is a nice family crowd, so many middle-aged men with their daughters." Later Bishop appeared frequently on television.

The increasing pace of American life was reflected in Henny

Youngman's delivery. Youngman didn't believe in transitions or segues between jokes, and so left out the unfunny parts. He turned the whole notion of comic timing on its head by ignoring time completely. His delivery was perfect for people who didn't have the patience to relax, who wanted the payoff quickly.

Youngman's one-liners about his wife, doctors, airlines, drunks, and other parts of life endeared him to audiences. Though most of his bits were simple, corny jokes that appealed to all ages and across the social spectrum, underneath they subtly probed the anxieties of normal life. Youngman's jokes about his wife came in an era leading to an explosion in the divorce rate, clearly reflecting marital unhappiness beneath the surface.

Consider the hostility in some of the humor:

I take my wife everywhere, but she keeps finding her way back. My wife will buy anything marked down. Last year she bought an escalator. We always hold hands. If I let go, she shops. My wife told me the car wasn't running well. There was water in the carburetor. I asked where the car was, and she told me it was in the lake. My wife and I went to a hotel where we got a waterbed. My wife called it the Dead Sea. My wife is on a new diet. Coconuts and bananas. She hasn't lost weight, but can she climb a tree.

Henny Youngman's jokes about relatives and others he had to deal with were simple releases from the frustrations of contemporary life. One target of his jokes, though, was not part of normal suburban life. Youngman kidded about the homeless: "A bum told me, 'I haven't tasted food all week.' I told him, 'Don't worry, it still tastes the same.'" The fact that people found such jokes funny reflected some uneasiness about maintaining their newfound economic security.

The comic Marty Allen relied on his physical appearance to

help the comedy. Allen's wild mane of hair, his squinting eyes, and his sad voice nasally delivering his trademark introduction "Hello dere" all were part of his act. The routines were standard gags, but Allen was important in emphasizing a naturally funny appearance as part of the act. The importance of the visual appearance of the comedian is a sign of the audience's changing taste from verbal humor to a combined verbal and visual humor and from the formal to the wilder.

Buddy Hackett took up where Allen left off. His heft, his bulbous nose, his mouth at an angle, and his cheeks made him a cross between an angel and an imp. (He said of himself: "I'm not a human being. I'm a cartoon.") More emphatically, and more subtly, than Marty Allen, Buddy Hackett used his looks to promote his humor. Beyond appearance, though, it was Hackett's voice and his use of it that made him unique.

Hackett started out in the 1950s using material from his Catskill experience. His signature Chinese waiter bit straddled the line between humor and ethnic stereotyping, but he made the waiter appear smarter than the customers he served through clever use of his accent. In this sense the waiter was like the Jews, having to appear servile to those in power but in fact being cleverer than the powerful despite being foreign.

Hackett did not see himself as a specifically Jewish comedian, but as a performer working in a nonethnic comedy tradition. That tradition can be seen in his early jokes, which were about being fat and about diets he had heard about ("You'll have the nicest figure in the whole cemetery. They bury you in an envelope"), about wives ("We eat every meal out. Where does my wife get garbage?"), about his lack of education ("School. What fun I had that day"), and about his family (concerning his father: "Once he tried to teach me how to smoke in bed"). Later, Hackett transformed himself, using bluer language and getting his audience to participate. Even then, though, his barbs were gentle. "I don't do things that will give anyone pain." He saw no harm in four-letter words in a world filled with poverty and hate.

Another comic, Shecky Greene, was one of the first comedians of his era to talk directly about his Jewishness openly onstage as he described his background. "I use everything in my own life," he said. "Everything is autobiographical." He started talking about being Jewish "when everyone said don't do it. I had a little rebellion in me. I had pride in what I am."

However much the audience enjoyed Shecky Greene's performance (and he was wildly popular with Las Vegas audiences), his sense of accomplishment is revealing of how many comedians feel about their very successful, widely admired, and much envied profession: "I never liked it. I was always depressed. I used to walk off the stage, and I'd say, 'What happened?' It wasn't a happy experience." He adds, "I'm sorry I never finished my education. We gave up a lot of things."

Alan King was the voice of the put-upon suburbanite talking back, taking on the powerful institutions that shaped the living environment—but steering clear of political institutions. His was a laughter of reconciliation. In laughing at what was annoying, King relied on the Yiddish foundations of Jewish humor, on the use of humor to make us accept what is beyond our power to change. He was aggrieved by family members, airlines, plumbers, decorators, doctors, lawyers, and so on. King walked the line between exasperation and a loss of control over his rage, but he always remained in control. He was a model of the good suburban citizen, letting loose his anxieties but not letting the anger undermine either his ability to function or his fundamental belief in the rightness of the system. King was a perfect comic for middle America. He dressed for the part as well, looking every bit the prosperous American with his cigar and his suit and vest.

Elsewhere in the society, though, tremors of a cultural earthquake had begun to shake the placid surface of American society. The Beats began writing poetry and novels attacking the ideological foundations of America and exploring alternative modes of consciousness and experience. The questioning of the society soon found its comedic voices as well. These new comedians—filled with sarcasm, social satire, outrage, offense, and anger—so challenged the preconceptions of the suburban dream that they were labeled "sick."

By 1953, Mort Sahl had decided to be a comedian, but he was poor (he slept in the back of a 1936 Buick) and couldn't afford to look like a comedian, that is, to wear a tuxedo. His girlfriend suggested he approach the Hungry i (for intellectual) in the North Beach area of San Francisco. The Hungry i was a small club (eighty-three seats) run by Enrico Banducci, a beret-wearing, kindly owner. Until Sahl walked in, Banducci had hired only musicians and singers. Feeling sorry for the thin comic, who looked to the owner as though he were suffering from malnutrition, Banducci decided to take a chance essentially on the basis of one joke. Sahl had described the popular Eisenhower jacket and then suggested a McCarthy jacket, with an extra zipper over the mouth. Banducci hadn't thought Sahl was all that funny, but he offered him seventy-five dollars a week, believing he was helping the young man and that "he can't hurt the place." Banducci then gave Sahl twenty dollars to get some food. Banducci recalls also telling Sahl to take off his tie and coat.

Sahl did, and then proceeded to change stand-up comedy. He did more than just alter the look that comedians had. He also changed both the delivery and, most important, the subject matter of mainstream comedy. Sahl had been deeply influenced by jazz, and the music's free association made its way into Sahl's speech rhythms. A mainstream comedian structured jokes by stating a premise, then identifying the setup, and finally delivering a punch line. The form was structured. Henny Youngman might do one-liners and Shecky Greene might tell longer stories, but the sound and rhythm of those comedians were smooth.

In total contrast, audiences had to pay attention to Sahl. He'd shift subjects suddenly. Darting thoughts, not always obviously connected logically to what had just been said, were given voice. His words had wings, and they always flew where he wanted them to go. His was a technique that would soon be adapted by many other young comedians, including Lenny Bruce and Woody Allen.

Sahl was not packaged. He wasn't smooth. Sometimes audiences weren't sure when and whether to laugh. Sahl, reflexively or on purpose, developed a clever prompt. His laugh, a slight bark, signaled that an intentionally funny observation had been made.

Sahl often walked onstage carrying a newspaper. This seemingly simple prop was an extraordinary comedic landmark. The usual model was a comedian in control but succeeding by meeting the audience's deepest emotional needs. Sahl turned that on its head. He remained in control but offered the revolutionary notion that political and social needs transcended the private needs of audience members. The focus on community and politics, deeply embedded in Jewish life, not only was transformed into suitable material for comedy but also became the central focus of the act.

Sahl's ability to walk the thin line between challenging and alienating the audience was the secret to his success. He enjoyed shocking the beliefs of his own audience—whomever they were. (His trademark saying was, "Is there any group I haven't offended?") He tempered his self-confessed offenses with cleverness and humor, so that audiences laughed even as they were outraged. Also, Sahl avoided alienating audiences by consistently refusing to use profanity. So clean was Sahl that Lenny Bruce would clean up his own act whenever Sahl was in the audience.

Even without profanity, though, he could puncture the cher-
ished presuppositions of his audience. Playing to liberal audiences
for whom racial equality was a sacred goal, Sahl could say, "I went
to my dressing room between shows and an attorney for the
NAACP was waiting for me. He wanted to know why I don't have
any Negroes in my act." He also became famous for shockingly
antifemale remarks, such as this one: "A woman's place is in the
stove." His line about the death penalty also became famous: "I'm
for capital punishment. You've got to execute people. How else are
they going to learn?"

One famous Sahl routine involved a group of robbers. They
write a holdup note that reads: "Give us all your money and act
normal." The cashier reads the note, writes on it, and hands it
back: "What do you mean by normal? Define your terms."
Another routine recounted "a course at Cal called Statistical
Analysis. And there was a guy in the course who used to make up
all his computations and he never used Sigma. He used his own
initials. 'Cause he was the standard deviation." It was not surprising that Sahl appealed to college audiences, and he often performed on campuses, essentially founding a new venue for
comedians. He also was the first comedian to put his routines on
a phonograph record, which further spread his popularity.

Sahl become most famous for his political commentary. He
directly took on the House Un-American Activities Committee
(HUAC): "Every time the Russians throw an American in jail,
HUAC retaliates—by throwing an American in jail." He'd also
pack an unhappiness with the entire political system into a single
line: "I'm not so much interested in politics as I am in overthrow-
ing the government." About one favorite target, Richard Nixon,
Sahl would dryly note: "He's been on the cover of every magazine
except *True*."

Such words were simply not traditionally spoken in public. It was this conspiratorial sense—that Mort Sahl would say openly what others said behind closed doors or even words that they dared not utter at all, or had not the wit to formulate—that made him so appealing. *Time* called him "a sort of Will Rogers with fangs," but Sahl was a cultural prophet as well, giving voice to the anxieties of the age, the unspoken horrors of nuclear weapons, the emerging sexual revolution, the racial divide, and the sense of being controlled by the government.

He did not, however, speak of his own Jewishness. Like Buddy Hackett, Sahl saw himself as an American observer and did not consciously draw on his Jewish heritage for his act. Of course, the very notion of social satire was deeply rooted in East European Jewish life.

Sahl attracted audiences, media attention, and followers. One of them was a young man named Lenny Bruce who would come in, watch Sahl, and tell Enrico Banducci that he, too, wanted to be a social satirist.

Bruce has become comedy's public martyr, making it difficult to assess him simply as someone out to get laughs. Some younger comedy fans, reared on the Bruce legend, are shocked to discover that when they listen to him they don't find him funny, but those who saw Bruce in his prime, like the writer Norman Podhoretz, recall him as hilarious. Bruce mixed the social satire and delivery he had learned from Sahl, the dirty language he had used for years as he worked in strip clubs, his own interest in religion, drug experimentation, and an idealist's distaste for hypocrisy into a brew that was too intoxicating for many in the society.

Bruce's mother, most often known professionally as Sally Marr, was not, to put it mildly, a typical Jewish homemaker. Divorced, struggling to be a comic herself, Marr took the adolescent Bruce to a burlesque house, let him read sexually explicit magazines, and frequently left him on his own.

Born Sadie Kitchenberg, Marr had, at age twelve, been a contestant in a beauty contest judged by Rudolph Valentino. She was offered a job on the basis of her provocative performance, but her father refused to let her accept it. She began dancing, winning a variety of contests, giving dance lessons, and always looking to perform.

During World War II, with her son Lenny off in the navy and her husband long gone, Marr worked in bars as an emcee. Audiences responded well to her slightly off-color jokes, and eventually she moved on to larger comedy clubs. When her career waned, Marr transferred her show business ambitions to her son, becoming Lenny's coach and number-one fan, in the tradition of Sadie Berle and Minnie Marx.

Lenny Bruce began performing stand-up work in burlesque houses and dives after getting out of the navy. His first break came on Arthur Godfrey's *Talent Scouts* television show. On April 18, 1949, Bruce tied for first place doing imitations of Katharine Hepburn and James Cagney as well as portraying a Bavarian mimic doing Cagney and Bogart. But while the publicity resulted in some work, Bruce couldn't escape the small strip clubs, where male customers tolerated the comics as they waited for the strippers.

In a way, strip clubs were crucial for the creation of Lenny Bruce as a comedian, for in those clubs Bruce was expected to use sexually charged language and obscenities. He was hardly the only person to use foul language in these clubs, but he learned how best to use obscenity to get laughs.

Bruce's attachment to this world was more than just professional; he even married a stripper named Honey Harlowe. Together, they began a life marked both by a strong bond and by dissolute behavior. They used drugs and believed in sexual experimentation and an open marriage. Bruce also exhibited some odd behaviors. He was once arrested for pretending to be a priest who was raising money for lepers.

Over time, Bruce began to evolve his special brand of humor. He became deliberately provocative about sexual matters: "My mother-in-law broke up my marriage. My wife came home and found us in bed together." He also began to explore his own feelings toward language itself. In an antique store, Bruce and his wife bought an old record titled "Bake dat Chicken Pie." The song had the word *nigger* in it repeated several times. Bruce began to sing the song onstage. He knew it was offensive, but he said if the word were repeated often enough it would lose its meaning and its sting.

Unlike Sahl, Bruce was not political. He was, in a way, a good American: "I don't dig communism. Capitalism is the best. Communism is like one big phone company," he said. But Bruce did become increasingly interested in religion. His wife was Catholic, and Bruce kept asking questions about her faith. He also started to use Yiddish expressions in his act, not caring who did or did not understand them. He talked a lot about Jews. Some of the humor was deliberately shocking. In one bit, using a salesman's voice, Bruce would say: "Here's a Volkswagen pickup truck that was just used slightly during the war carrying the people back and forth to the furnaces." He would hold up a paper with the headline "Six Million Jews Found Alive in Argentina." The shock of such "jokes" came not only from the inappropriateness of joking about the Holocaust, but also from the fact that very few people even discussed it at all. Bruce's provocative joking forced Americans to recall what had already been discarded as forgotten history or simply repressed.

One of Bruce's most famous routines stemmed from his view of what it means to be Jewish. He structured the routine as a guide to who or what is Jewish and who or what is not Jewish, though Bruce used the offensive word "goyish" to define the non-Jewish. However, his distinctions were unusual: "I'm Jewish. Count Basie's Jewish. Ray Charles is Jewish. Eddie Cantor is goyish . . . Hadassah, Jewish. Marine corps—heavy goyim, dangerous. Pumpernickel is Jewish, and, as you know, white bread is very goyish."

In eradicating religious reality, Bruce anticipated where the culture was going. For him, being Jewish did not mean belonging to a religious group, but instead having a particular approach to life; being Jewish did not mean belonging to an ethnic group, but instead having a particular tone and attitude. Bruce's "Jews" were urban and hip, whatever their actual identity, while his "goyim" were too unhip for his taste, whether or not they were actually Jewish.

In looking for a comic persona, Bruce evolved through several guises. He could be a normal comic, doing impressions, telling jokes. But in performance he also became a social critic, a therapist, a preacher. (His first movement in *The Lenny Bruce Performance Film* is to offer a priest's blessing.) The writer and critic Nat Hentoff saw him confronting his audience's deepest "defenses and self-evasions." Hentoff suggests that "Bruce, in sum, continually puts his audiences on trial, a judge and prosecutor in one."

Bruce had learned a lesson well in the strip joints. He saw in the slow removal of clothes a metaphor for the stripping of the false layers that cover the true soul. He wanted to remove the layers that society, language, religion, and our own selves put on truth. In stripping away hypocrisy, Bruce sought the naked reality underneath. He wanted his audience to face their unadorned selves.

Bruce's comedy, his lifestyle, and his personality eventually led to a confrontation with authorities. On September 29, 1961, Bruce was playing the Red Hill in New Jersey and stayed over in Philadelphia. He attended a private party and may have offended an important guest there. The next morning the police broke his motel room door and arrested Bruce on a narcotics charge. A bail bondsman (or a lawyer, depending on who is telling the story) asked Bruce for ten thousand dollars in payoffs to get out of his mess. Instead, Bruce went to the press, naming the bondsman and the judge who wanted the bribe. Five days later, on October 4, Bruce was arrested in San Francisco. There were no complaining customers, but Bruce was considered to have performed an obscene act. On October 5, 1962, he was arrested in Hollywood for using the word *schmuck*.

Bruce believed, with justification, that he was arrested so frequently because he had annoyed powerful people throughout the legal community. Certainly, other comedians used more obscenities in their acts than Bruce did. (B. S. Pully was famous for threatening to urinate on audience members.) Still, it was Bruce who violated the tacit understandings of the era that dirty language would be uttered only in small nightclubs. Few people in show business were willing to take a chance on him. The major exception was Steve Allen, who invited Bruce onto television several times.

Opposition to Bruce's public obscenity was not limited to those in power. Many mainstream comedians were also troubled. Jack Carter told the *New York Sunday News* in 1961: "I think the guy should be stopped by the union from working. . . . The sick comic's embarrassing to the business. He gets up there mouthing four-letter words of filth as if no one had ever heard them before. . . . His act is nothing more than unprofessional rambling."

Bruce believed that he was specifically persecuted because of what he saw as his exposure of the hypocrisy of the Roman Catholic Church. Another part of the understanding of the era was that attacks on religion were not permitted. Bruce ignored this rule with abandon. His unflattering Father Flotsky character, his mocking use of Christian gestures (like making a cross), and his attacks on Catholic wealth made him an obvious target. In one famous Bruce bit about Christ and Moses returning to Earth, the two venture into St. Patrick's Cathedral in New York and watch Cardinal Spellman. Bruce notes that Christ is confused by the splendor of the cardinal's comments "because his route took him through Spanish Harlem and he was wondering what the forty Puerto Ricans were doing living in one room when this guy [the cardinal] had a ring on that was worth eight grand." Bruce would add, "More and more people are drifting away from the Church and back to God every day."

It remains unclear to what extent Bruce's explicit Jewishness played a part in his being a target. On the one hand, America was becoming more tolerant. However, in a culture where the Rosenberg trial made some people suspicious of Jews, at a time when many in power were beginning to see a real challenge to mainstream values, at a time when the Catholic Church had not yet proclaimed that Jews were communally innocent in the killing of Christ, it didn't help Bruce to be so overtly Jewish, or, more precisely, a certain type of Jew. The warm Jewish immigrants and the successful suburbanites were welcome, but the Jews who angrily questioned the society were much more the residual recipients of a previous generation's dislike of Jews.

Bruce's continuing arrests, most significantly his obscenity arrest in New York on April 4, 1964, ruined him. Writers and intellectuals supported him. Norman Podhoretz, for example, went so far as to speak to the district attorney about the charge. By October, Bruce had been found guilty and sentenced to four months in jail. He appealed and was free for the time being, but he knew that if he couldn't work in New York, he wouldn't be able to work anywhere. Club owners were afraid of being shut down.

Legally bankrupt by October 1965, Bruce could barely get any bookings. When he did, his sad face, his obsession with the letter of the law, if not the power behind it, as being on his side, and his refusal to do an act doomed his reception. He had become a symbol of the fight for the right to use explicit language in comedy acts instead of a comedian himself.

Bruce was working on his appeal when he died on August 3, 1966, the victim of a drug overdose. And in fact, eighteen months after his death, the New York State Supreme Court reversed his conviction. No comedian has since been put on trial for the obscene use of language.

Beyond being a comedy martyr, Lenny Bruce was also a guide to the struggle for a modern American Jewish identity. The mainstream comedians of the time were increasingly accepted by American culture and felt very American. They didn't, at least openly, express a struggle between keeping a Jewish identity and an American identity. They had accepted the established model of assimilation for minority groups in a society; they were Jews in private and Americans in public, comfortable in their suburban synagogues and their urban jobs.

But not everyone was at ease. Bruce and many other Jews of his generation felt caught between an American and a Jewish identity, uncomfortable in either one. Such a position was related to but different from the feeling of an earlier Jewish generation. The Marx Brothers had tried to get through the barred door. Bruce was let in, didn't like what he saw, but didn't like what he had left behind either. Bruce played out in public the anguish of many American Jews, some of whom did not recognize their confusion and many of whom were unable or unwilling to express it openly.

Lenny Bruce was not the only comedian to challenge religion. Tom Lehrer began singing comic songs around the Harvard campus in 1950. By 1953, his album *The Songs of Tom Lehrer* was produced. Although his work started out as simple satire, as he developed as a songwriter, Lehrer wrote and performed comic songs that were savage, honest, and telling.

He mocked National Brotherhood Week ("Oh, the Protestants hate the Catholics / And the Catholics hate the Protestants / And the Hindus hate the Moslems / And everybody hates the Jews"), the ex-Nazi rocket scientist Wernher von Braun ("'Once the rockets are up, who cares where they come down? That's not my department,' says Wernher von Braun"), and much else. He praised smut. He wrote antimilitary songs, including "So Long, Mom," a preparatory anthem for World War III. Lehrer, a cultural but not a religious Jew, did not directly write about his own Jewishness or throw in Yiddish phrases. Still, his material had contents that some would have considered as offensive as Bruce's had been. Even at a distance, his talent with language matched an honesty in examining the culture.

There were other Jewish performers who used music to present their comedy. Allan Sherman had had a particularly unhappy childhood. His parents were divorced, and his mother moved frequently and introduced the young boy to a string of male "uncles" who came to visit. After college, he tried to be a stand-up comic. His mother showed up drunk for his first performance. Sherman and a partner later developed the popular television game show *I've Got a Secret*, but his own interest in performing didn't die.

Sherman began to write parodies of popular songs, inevitably making them particularly Jewish. Harpo Marx, Steve Allen, Jerry Lewis, and Jack Benny were among those who urged him to put the songs on a record album. When copyright problems prevented him from using the tunes, executives at Warner Brothers suggested that Sherman use music in the public domain. He did, and his album *My Son the Folk Singer* was a big hit. Singing to the tune of "The Battle Hymn of the Republic," Sherman told about Harry Lewis, a garment worker in the employ of a man named Irving Roth. Lewis, Sherman sings, died while "trampling through the warehouse where the drapes of Roth were stored." "Hello Muddah, Hello Faddah," Sherman's biggest hit, was written in the form of a child writing home from summer camp. Sherman's recounting all the horrors of this supposed sanctuary for wealthy, suburban children illustrates his own insecure, even fearful, sense of American society and the place of Jews in such a society. "There was a time when I couldn't find roots because I was ashamed to look where they were," he once recalled. "When you are running around Madison Avenue. . . . you carefully avoid mentioning your grandfather the ladies' coat presser. . . . You cover up the old roots because something in your own upbringing has convinced you that they are weeds."

Jackie Mason was one important comedian who straddled the line between the lounge comics and the sick ones. Mason was born in Sheboygan, Wisconsin, but luckily for his comedy future, the family soon moved to the Lower East Side. Like his father and three older brothers, Jacob Maza (as he was then known) studied to become a rabbi. But he also became interested in performing comedy. The popular Barry Gray radio show was broadcast from the nearby Chandler's Restaurant. One night, young Yakov Maza was in the audience, and someone sent a note up to Gray: "There's a comedian named Maza in the audience." Gray stumbled over the name. In a fateful moment, Maza shouted out, "Mason." In one moment, he had found his new name.

Still not "Jackie Mason" just yet, Maza was ordained as a rabbi in 1958. For three years he led congregations in Weldon, North Carolina, and Latrobe, Pennsylvania. But the desire to do comedy was overpowering. He knew he was a rabbi simply to please his father, and so he quit—though without telling his father of his decision.

Mason didn't tell dirty jokes like Bruce. His politics were not like Sahl's. His psychological humor, based on his own therapy, was funny but not as pointed as Woody Allen's would be. His Jewish warmth was not Myron Cohen's or Sam Levenson's; indeed, Mason sometimes almost mocked the old-style comedic sensibilities: "Money is not important," he'd proclaim, "Love is important. Fortunately, I love money."

Falling between the comedic cracks, Mason created a unique identity. It started with the Jewish accent. "I was told my first day in show business that I should lose my accent," he recalled. "When I was about to go on the Steve Allen show, I got a telegram from the William Morris Agency begging me to take elocution lessons. 'This is okay for the mountains, but . . . '" In fact, the Yiddish-inflected accent became Mason's trademark, a part of his persona as indispensable as Jack Benny's violin or Mort Sahl's newspaper. The voice fitted the comedian, and, more important, it fitted the material; indeed, it made funny material sound even funnier.

Much of Mason's act was standard self-deprecatory stuff, such as "All my life, I've had trouble with my back. I can't get it off the bed," or standard lounge material, such as "A man only wants one thing from a woman, companionship. I'm talking about a very old man." But gradually, Mason began to speak openly about his Jewishness, especially about the differences between Jews and Gentiles, and did so in a way that was far less provocative than Bruce though provocative enough for audiences to feel avant-garde. He did paranoid jokes clearly rooted in Jewish life: "When I went to a football game, every time the players went into a huddle, I thought they were talking about me." Or "A Jew could never be a mugger cause a mugger has to say 'Give me your money or I'll kill you.' . . . A Jew cannot say, 'I'll kill you.' A Jew would have to say, 'Listen, you don't have to give me all your money . . . maybe you got a few dollars now, a few dollars later. There are Jewish muggers . . . but they're not called muggers. They're called lawyers." Mason became the Jew that Gentiles came to in order to find out about being Jewish.

A significant turning point in Mason's career occurred on October 18, 1964, when he appeared on Ed Sullivan's television show.

After Mason began his act, the White House called CBS to request part of the show's time for a speech. Sullivan and his producers agreed, and, having to signal Mason, they stood offstage and held up two fingers, indicating that Mason should conclude his act in two minutes. Mason, not knowing what was going on, seeing the movement as a distraction both to him and to the audience, reacted. "Everybody's showing me fingers. Who should I talk to? Let me show you my fingers." He put his hand to his nose, wiggled his fingers, and began a series of odd utterances. "I finally became a hit, I can't finish the show." He then pleaded with the audience, "Listen here, listen here." Mason then muttered a weird self-criticism: "I'm afraid to be a hit. I do good, I'm wiped out." Also inexplicably, Mason added, "Ed, I want to thank you very much, whatever you did for my career."

Mason then swiped his hand across the air, pointing with his index finger and said, "Now I want to show you a finger. Here's a finger to you, and a finger to him." He gave a final gesture, pointing with his finger, and dashed off the stage.

Sullivan believed this last gesture was obscene. It is hard to tell if it was a typical Yiddish mannerism or a very American rude gesture or somewhere in between. Whatever was really going on in Mason's mind, the act interrupted his career for two decades. Mason was seen as a troublemaker, and his career plummeted.

Eventually, impressed by Dick Shawn's one-man show, Mason saw an approach right for him—to write and perform a Broadway show. At first hearing, it sounds odd. Broadway audiences are generally used to eye-filling scenery and expensive costumes, extravagant musical pieces or profound and moving drama. Mason was essentially offering only himself. Nonetheless, *The World According To Me* became a big hit in the 1980s, and Mason remains a major star to this day.

While Jackie Mason was being accused of making an obscene

gesture, a significant group of Jewish women comedians was also pushing the limits of decency, in word as well as gesture.

Marie Alvarez (who, despite her name, was Jewish) would put on a curly blonde wig and work at stag parties. Starting in the early 1940s, she delivered one dirty joke after the next, taking delight in shocking the male audience. Alvarez continued to work even as she got older, remaining outside any wider recognition that would have come with records or television appearances.

Belle Barth appeared in vaudeville and in the Catskills, doing imitations and evolving a sweet exterior that provided good armor against audience members who were disturbed by her risqué stories. Married five times, the former Annabelle Salzman spoke in direct, earthy language to them: "I always say the most difficult thing for a woman to do is try to act naive—on the first night of her second marriage." She frequently used Yiddish. "There's only two Yiddish words you need to know. *Gelt* and *schmuck*. If a man has no *gelt*, he is." Barth was sometimes arrested for obscenity, but she was less confrontational than Lenny Bruce. When she knew the police were in the audience, she toned down her act.

Rusty Warren was not as overtly Jewish as Belle Barth, and her songs were more risqué than her patter. She would talk with the audience, and, like a wise aunt, sprinkle advice and her own brand of wisdom. She included observations about sexual relations, where it was the women who did the enjoying but also the worrying: "Saturday night's the night all the girls go out to sow their wild oats, and Sunday morning they pray for a crop failure."

Whereas Mort Sahl and Lenny Bruce used San Francisco as a springboard, and many others used New York, another comic tradition was arising in Chicago: improvisational theater.

The roots of improvisational theater can be traced directly back to the Italian *commedia dell'arte*, in which traveling performers gave public shows from the mid-1500s. The public popularity of such theater attracted the attention in the 1920s of a Chicago theater educator, Viola Spolin, who believed that teaching theater to children could best be accomplished through games. Spolin (who was Jewish) eventually became the supervisor of drama for the Works Progress Administration during the New Deal, where she started many improvisational theater groups for adults. Improvisational theater is a communal effort, as actors band together to perform in front of an outside audience and make up the characters and the dialogue as they go along. In many ways, this art form echoes the traditional Jewish community, which relied on mutual support in the face of a hostile outside society. Indeed, the very idea of improvising has a Jewish sensibility, coming up constantly with new survival strategies for dealing with that society.

Viola Spolin's son, Paul Sills, had been a student at the University of Chicago. In June 1953, he and David Shepherd founded the Playwrights Theatre Club. The club attracted a circle of other students and friends—all of whom were interested in theater and in improvisation—including performers such as Mike Nichols (born Michael Igor Peschkowsky) and Elaine May.

Mike Nichols's improvisational routines with Elaine May (the daughter of Yiddish actor Jack Berlin) built on the Jewish comic tradition. One of their most famous routines was "Mother and Son," a Jewish psychodrama played out for an American audience, focusing on a guilt-inducing mother and a weak, dependent son, both of whom degenerate into babylike behavior. One of the best lines illustrates its comic genealogy. The mother says to the son: "I sat by that phone all day Friday, all day Saturday, and all day Sunday. Your father said to me, 'Phyllis, eat something. You'll faint.' I said, 'No, Harry. No. I don't want my mouth to be full when my son calls me.'" This is, of course, directly reminiscent of George Jessel's monologues about talking to his mother. But Nichols and May took the immigrant comic piece and transformed it by putting the mother onstage herself. Not only does she have a voice, but the focus is on her, rather than the son, as in Jessel's case. Such a transformation can be seen in two conflicting ways. The inclusion of the mother onstage reflects an increase in the power and influence of women in society. But the Nichols and May piece was also a sign of the changing perceptions of Jewish mothers from warm and kind (like Molly Goldberg) into hectoring and intrusive. The troubling question is whether the two changes are intertwined, whether the warm Jewish mother was deprived by marriage and family expectations from finding her true self, turning bitter and needy in the process.

This overpowering Jewish mother, exemplified in Philip Roth's work, and the Jewish American Princess became ethnic stereotypes that have not disappeared and remain profoundly troubling. Jessel's mama remained funny precisely because she was not present, and her onstage son could remain in control. May's presence changed the center of power in the relationship. When Nichols defends his not calling her, May replies: "Someday, someday, Arthur, you'll get married, and you'll have children of your own, and, honey, when you do, I only pray that they make you suffer. That's a mother's prayer." He says he already feels awful. She responds: "Oh, honey, if I could believe that, I'd be the happiest mother in the world."

By performing this exchange on Broadway and on television, Nichols and May transformed a typical Jewish routine and made it apply to a contemporary American situation: the increasing tension between young people and their parents, a tension that by the end of the decade would develop into a widespread social phenomenon.

Jerry Stiller, Anne Meara, David Steinberg, Avery Schreiber, and Joan Rivers were among the other performers working with Paul Sills in Chicago in the 1950s. In 1959, Sills reorganized the group as the Second City.

Shelley Berman was one of the most successful of the group's members. Born in Chicago, Berman had worked as a comedy writer for Steve Allen in New York, where he met Mark Gordon (one of Sills's associates), who thought Berman would fit in well in the improv group. It was, in some ways, an odd choice, since Berman was not associated with the University of Chicago; was, at nearly thirty, older than the other members; and, even more important, had been involved with professional comedy, not an attractive credit to this antiestablishment crowd.

At first, Berman went against the emerging improvisational etiquette and tried for laughs instead of focusing on the situation and the action. This did not go over well with the other performers, and Berman learned a valuable lesson: "When you're going to just go for the laughs, you're sealing off all possibilities for exploring anything richer."

Berman's insight was crucial in the development of a comedy that was more serious than the standard comedy of the day. "It is far more than going out and getting laughter," Berman notes. "The moment of performed humor requires humor as an ingredient not as a result. You need the extremes of emotion. Laughter is one extreme."

Berman's first important success came with a routine called "The Morning after the Night Before." Alone onstage, Berman intuitively found the perfect idea: to mime the use of a telephone. But, unlike George Jessel, Berman found that the telephone did not put him in touch with a kind and funny world. In a culture increasingly populated by people who felt alienated, Berman's telephone was the thin connection between the fragile self and the pitiless society.

In "The Morning after the Night Before," Berman plays a man who has drunk too much and who calls the host of the party he attended the previous evening. Slowly unveiling the damage he inflicted, the hungover character tries to apologize: "How did I break a window? I see. Were you very fond of that cat? It's lucky the only thing I threw through the window was a cat. Oh. She's a very good sport, your mother."

Berman's humor came in part from his personality. He was a comic perfectionist, a trait he considered simply a prerequisite to living, and so he found unprofessional behavior disturbing— whether it was on airlines, at the telephone company, or in other places. Berman's voice and his face were perfect outer representations of an inner angst. (*Time*'s observation about his face was that it was "like a hastily sculpted meatball.")

Berman's fame quickly spread. He appeared on numerous television shows and was the first comedian to perform at Carnegie Hall. His 1960 album, *Inside Shelley Berman,* was the first comedy album to sell a million copies. His second album, *Outside Shelley Berman,* included one of his greatest bits, "Franz Kafka on the Telephone," in which Berman played the famous Czech writer struggling against a contemporary bureaucracy, the phone company.

One reason Shelley Berman's kind of comedy worked (and his bit about the author of *The Trial* is a perfect example of this) was that in 1950s America he had a more educated audience than in previous generations.

Neuroses were among the concepts that audiences understood. Berman's own neurotic personality gave audiences emotional permission to speak about topics that the culture had asked them to repress and sublimate into communally acceptable activities. In this sense, Berman joined with Bruce, who gave the freedom to speak their feelings in direct language, and with Sahl, who gave the freedom to talk about political leaders.

And Berman caught the era perfectly. As the economic insecurities of the depression receded and economic successes gave people more money and free time, as World War II receded in memory and gave people a chance to examine their own society and their own selves, Berman's humor turned inward.

Despite their great fame and enormous talents, the immense success of Mort Sahl and Shelley Berman would not last. The culture itself was changing. The baby boomers were reaching adolescence, yearning for respect and an identity separate from their parents. The society around them deeply influenced their personal search. A war was growing in Southeast Asia, a war to which either they or many of their peers would be sent. It was a time, after the assassination of John F. Kennedy, when idealism suffered a rapid fall. It was a moment when the inherent unfairness of segregation became morally unbearable to larger numbers of people. It was a time when drugs, once identified with the criminal underworld, the lower classes, and parts of the entertainment industry, became a symbol of countercultural identity.

Finally, it was a time of changing sexual attitudes and behavior. The baby boomers flooded college campuses in the mid-1960s, and, relieved from parental authority, lured by the philosophy of free love, driven by the same hormones that had driven every young generation, having access to (not always used) birth control information and devices, and feeling cynical about their own futures and that of the United States, the young generation led the sexual revolution.

Mostly the young looked to musicians, such as Bob Dylan, to express their feelings, but comedians emerged to speak for them as well.

In the mid-1960s, Berman's neuroses were still a perfect lens through which to see life, but audiences now wanted the neuroses to be not about the institutions their parents fought but about the sexual revolution they were enjoyably fighting. Those audiences were not interested in stories of Franz Kafka's telephone calls; they would have liked jokes about Franz Kafka's love life. Berman's sensibility, however, did not match the loosening of the culture. For that, audiences turned to Mel Brooks and Woody Allen.

After Sid Caesar's last show went off the air, Mel Brooks teamed up with his fellow writer Carl Reiner to invent and perform skits at parties. In one skit, Brooks claimed to be 2,000 years old. Steve Allen was at the party and, always appreciative of new talent, suggested that the two make a record out of the skit. He helped them book time in a studio. A group of friends was invited over in order to simulate a party, and Brooks and Reiner recorded the now classic album *The 2000-Year-Old Man*.

Stanley Ralph Ross was among those present. Ross, a writer and actor, recalls: "It was a big studio, a recording studio where they usually have an orchestra. Instead of an orchestra, it was just the two guys up on stage. They had chairs and coffee and juice. That was it. They just went on. Carl had some cards for asking the questions. I don't think Mel had an idea of what Carl was going to say to him. I don't know if Mel had ever seen them."

The 2,000-year-old man spoke with a Yiddish accent and was an amalgam of immigrant Jewish humor and Borscht Belt humor. Brooks made his creation contemporary by the wildness of responses. The 2,000-year-old man responded to questions not as he would in a carefully phrased vaudeville skit but in an explosion of ideas freed from the mind's censor.

Reiner was the straight man, cleverly asking questions that would prompt Brooks's imagination. Reiner asks, "Who was the person who discovered the female?"

Brooks answers: "Bernie . . . One morning he got up smiling . . . He went into such a story. It was hundreds of years. I still blush."

Brooks tells of hiring six men to help him make Jewish stars. They each had a point, but "We would make two a day because of the accidents."

He offers the traditional Jewish parental lament: "I have over forty-two thousand children, and not one comes to visit me."

"When I became [the 2,000-year-old man]," Brooks later said,

"I could hear 5,000 years of Jews pouring through me. Look at Jewish history. Unrelieved lamenting would be intolerable . . . so, for every ten Jews beating their breasts, God designated one to be crazy and amuse the breast beaters! By the time I was five I knew I was that one."

Brooks's wild antics offered a symbolic release of tensions. He represented the repressed feelings of the culture, and his antics, childlike in a way like Jerry Lewis, were nonthreatening. By reverting to such behavior, rather than, say, being antic by challenging power, Brooks provided a safe outlet for the loosening of repressed feelings. He would, a decade later, go to the next step and put his wild character on film.

Mel Brooks was not the only one of Sid Caesar's former writers to become a comedy legend.

Woody Allen was well known in the comedy business for his writing, but he increasingly wanted to perform. Allen studied Sahl's and Berman's easygoing styles, the rhythms of their language, and their general informality. His material, however, was not as improvised as theirs. His routines were carefully thought out. There was not a wasted word or movement; Allen delivered brilliant commentary in a way that only seemed improvisational. The effect was devastatingly funny.

In 1960, he got an audition at the Blue Angel. By 1961 he was appearing in Greenwich Village, and by 1962 he was touring college campuses.

Allen had been particularly influenced by Mort Sahl's delivery. Sahl had altered the whole rhythm of a joke, and Allen saw in the free-form delivery a way to harness and express the surreal images he wanted to string together into a comic narrative. Sahl's free association and conversational delivery gave Allen his comedic form. Shelley Berman's use of neurosis as an acceptable subject of comedy was grafted onto Allen's own interest in sex, providing

Allen with all the equipment he needed to display the results of his brilliance.

Allen's genius lay in transformation. Sometimes this came out as satire, but much more significantly Allen took standard comedy and simply coupled it with a contemporary sensibility. Allen made audiences see images not from suburban life but from the imagination. In some respects, he harnessed the joys that radio audiences found in creating their own images. No audience members had ridden with a live moose on their fender, but, with Allen's suggestive language, the imagination could create such a mental picture. He borrowed from Sahl's and Berman's intellectualism, but uniquely saw intellectuals as inferior in confronting a very tough world. He took Henny Youngman's wife jokes and turned them into jokes about sex.

Most particularly, though, Allen found the voice of alienation. "I am at two with myself," he'd say. Like Jack Benny, Allen mocked himself; however, his weakness was not stinginess but a lust combined with an inadequate ability to satisfy himself. Like Shelley Berman, he talked about neurotic behavior, but his neurosis involved personal tales of his own psychoanalytic experiences. His incompetence with mechanical gadgets, a useful metaphor for all the accoutrements of modern life, became crucial to the character he invented.

That character perfectly matched Allen's own appearance. His thin, sad face, his red hair and black-framed glasses, and his body that could almost hide behind the microphone stand all gave credence to the words he uttered.

His political comments were brief; both he and his audience found political expression increasingly outside comedy. He would say lines such as "I was working on a nonfiction version of the *Warren Report*," but such lines were outside the persona and so withered. Like Mort Sahl, Allen made it clear that women were the enemy, but Sahl's political lens was replaced by one of sexual frustration. Allen would deliver such lines as "Sex is a beautiful thing between two people. Between five, it's fantastic."

Like many Jewish comics, Allen joked about his family. He told the story of how two men kidnapped him. The kidnappers then sent a ransom note to his father. But his father didn't read the mail regularly. When his parents realize he's gone, "they snap into action immediately. They rent out my room."

Allen frequently told tales of family members who were less than kindly. One popular bit doubled as a way to find out how much time he had left in his performance. He would pause halfway through his act and pull out a pocket watch. "Pardon me a moment while I check the time . . . I don't know if you can see this, but it's a very handsome watch. Has marble inlay. My grandfather [pause]—on his deathbed—[pause] sold me this watch."

Sometimes, Allen took on institutional Judaism, as in his story of getting offered the chance to do a vodka ad and asking his rabbi about the morality of promoting liquor. In the story, the rabbi sharply counsels against Allen doing the ad, and so Allen refuses. One day, however, he discovers the hypocritical rabbi on TV doing the commercial. In another routine, Allen talks about being married by a rabbi who was "very Reform—a Nazi" whose wife cooked such dishes as "chicken Himmler."

Allen found no comfort in Judaism as a religion. Indeed, he has often expressed a wistful regret that he was not granted the gift of faith. But, even though expressing some repellent images of Jewish life, Allen was caught in the reality of his own Jewishness. He grafted a more American lust onto the traditional Jewish loser, but even then the schlemiel intruded by making the would-be lover inadequate. And if Allen rejected many strains of Jewishness, he did absorb its intellectuality, making frequent allusions to philosophers and thinkers. Even here, though, Allen's interest in thinkers is different from a Jewish thirst for learning. His intellectual heroes are existential thinkers or philosophers, not Jewish sages.

Allen, though, does identify with the Jew as a victim and as someone justifiably paranoid about the world. In one routine, an elevator recording hurls anti-Semitic insults at him. In another, an ad agency hires him so that they have more minorities on their staff: "I was the show Jew of the agency. I tried to look Jewish desperately. Used to read my memos from right to left all the time. They fired me finally because I took off too many Jewish holidays."

The Jews, separated from others by religion, diet, dress, and much else, were, for Allen, a metaphor of his own feelings of anxiety. He found his model for alienation in the Jewish experience as the weak outsider, the group exiled for two thousand years, constantly having to worry about physical attack and lesser forms of hatred. He saw other ways to express and explore such feelings—the dark films of Ingmar Bergman, the pessimistic philosophies of many thinkers—but Jewishness was particularly potent precisely because Allen was so frequently identified as a Jewish comedian by others and because, by fate or plan, he had been born a Jew.

By making Jews the heroes of the alienated, Allen succeeded in making Jews more acceptable, even more attractive. As Vivian Gornick so precisely put it in a *Village Voice* article: "What was most striking about Allen's humor . . . is that this Jewish anxiety at the center of his wit touched something alive in America at the moment and went out beyond us. . . . It made Jews of gentiles. . . . It meshed so perfectly with the deepest undercurrents of feeling in the national life that it made outsiders of us all."

It was this stance that gave Allen a sense of power and made being Jewish meaningful to his audience. In one routine called "Down South," three men in white sheets kidnap Allen. The Klansmen prepare to hang him, and, facing death, he says: "Sud-

denly my whole life passed before my eyes. I saw myself as a kid
. . . swimmin' at the swimmin' hole and fishin' and fryin' up a mess
o' catfish, goin' down to the general store and gettin' a piece of
gingham for Emmy Lou. And I realize it's not my life." Allen, that
is, at this crucial moment realizes that his is not a normal "American" life. And not only does he talk the Klansmen out of hanging
him, but he also sells them Israel bonds. At bottom he is a proud
Jew, but his Jewishness comes from an existential condition of vic-
timhood, not from traditional religious beliefs or behaviors.

The wider Jewish community, though, did not always appreciate
Allen's particular sense of Jewishness. Like writers such as Philip
Roth, Allen would be accused of self-hatred. In both cases,
though, the satirical attacks were on the way that Jewishness was
expressed in American Jewish life. Allen saw in an increasingly
comfortable American suburban Jewish life a removal from the
alienated anxiety that had in some crucial way defined Jews and
offered them a unique identity. It was not Jewishness that he
attacked, but the way Jews had navigated in American culture. He
used the alienation he had learned from being Jewish to express his
alienation from the Jewishness he saw around him, exemplified by
his parents, whose "values in life are God and carpeting."

Soon, though, Woody Allen was ready to jump from the comic
stage onto the big screen. He would define the very idea of a Jewish comic filmmaker.

IV

THE YEARS
OF TRIUMPH
1965–PRESENT

8

"I NEED THE EGGS"

JEWISH COMIC FILMMAKERS

For those who confused Woody Allen with his comedy character, his film career might have seemed odd. A director, after all, couldn't afford to be a neurotic schlemiel. The real Allen, though, was a lot more competent than the character he played. Allen's confidence and control were essential in building his film career, since moviemaking is such a complicated team endeavor. Sometimes Allen found himself in situations that would have made his stand-up persona faint. Part of the first film he directed, *Take the Money and Run,* was filmed on location inside San Quentin prison. San Quentin then held four thousand prisoners, men who, Allen later told Dick Cavett, "hadn't seen a woman in years, much less a fair-skinned Jew." Indeed, the guards warned Allen, "If you're held hostage, we'll do everything we can to get you out short of opening the gates." The prisoners, though, were cooperative and pleasant.

Throughout his film career, Allen has dealt again and again with the issue of confused identity. "I have frequently been accused of being a self-hating Jew," Allen once wrote, "and while it's true I am Jewish and I don't like myself very much, it's not because of my persuasion." He gives a similar line to his character in *Deconstructing Harry*, and John Baxter in a recent biography asserts that Allen incorporates no Jewish elements in his personal life.

Allen knows himself, and he may certainly be right about his own makeup, but his characters, such as Harry Block, omit an important way in which their Jewishness is defined. They see being Jewish as belonging to a religious group when they don't accept religious views, or belonging to a particular ethnic group when they feel alienated from other members of that group, starting with their family. They don't, however, see being Jewish as inescapably belonging to a minority group with the particular psychological strains caused by their membership in that group and the pattern of thinking that ultimately emerges from such an emotional location. Allen's characters are not Jewish by religion or ethnicity but by their Jewish consciousness and temperament.

Of course, in his stand-up days Allen did display something close to such a Jewish temperament by seeing Jews as the symbol of all alienated people. To some extent this continues into his films. This temperament changed, though, among Jews themselves. Before their wide acceptance into American life, Jews felt considerable alienation as victims; this was a temperament Allen could find congenial. However, just as Allen's parents' generation sought acceptance and just as his own was getting it, the alienation decreased. Allen's characters, though, were uncomfortable with this new Jewish identity. They retained a Jewish consciousness in an alien land filled with hostile gadgets and unreachable, strange, or unfaithful women. Their identity crisis would be played out in Allen's films.

American Jews found in Allen's films a mirror of the enormous strains they faced in defining their new identity. After all, Jews as Jews are the chosen people and therefore of extraordinary historical importance whereas Jews as Americans are ordinary and even statistically insignificant. Jews living in a Jewish world can often rely on a shared history and a shared fate, on shared familial and cultural references, and even a shared consciousness. Jews living in an American world have a limited shared history, sometimes conflicting familial and cultural references, especially when those references are to Christian experiences and holidays, and they lack a shared consciousness. Even those Jews who have succeeded— becoming good citizens, economically successful, and socially integrated—often feel caught between two conflicting worlds.

Additionally, the very acceptance by American society carried its own problems. American Jews were increasingly free to pursue their dreams to the limits of their formidable skills. They were enshrined in much of the American consciousness as models of sobriety, intelligence, and humor, as good neighbors and ultimately as good marriage partners. This success, though, inevitably triggered guilt, for their acceptance of the rhythms of a secular calendar robbed them of the sense of living in Jewish time. Their parents or grandparents who had struggled so hard, whose sense of *Yiddishkeit* was undiminished by the opulence of the Golden Land, were reminders of the emotional world they were leaving. They were, in a vital sense, abandoning their heritage even as America embraced them.

Woody Allen's recurring focus on themes of adultery not only reflected his own sexual tensions or an evolving sexual ethic in American life, but at its roots also reflected his sense that Jews had abandoned what he saw as a genuine Jewish consciousness for an

American life that radically and negatively transformed that consciousness. Jewish audiences could see in such adultery their own unfaithfulness to Jewish tradition.

Ironically, just as American Jews were starting in large numbers to leave their religious identity behind them, the culture began to reemphasize ethnic identity. Pushed by the civil rights movement, African Americans found in their particular culture the strength to confront social and economic inequalities. The surge of pride they displayed was infectious, and many other groups, including Jews, felt that pride, or felt they should feel it even if they didn't. Jews who identified with black efforts to achieve equality were struck by a sense of guilt, reminded of their own ethnic identity that they were trying to jettison.

Though many Jews, like Allen, tried psychotherapy, they may have really needed ethnotherapy. Like Allen's characters, they didn't understand the depth of their relationship with an ethnic heritage because they rejected the theology and practices of the religion and incorrectly believed, in doing so, that they had separated themselves from their Jewishness, not recognizing their status as Jews independent of being religious or members of a group. Like Allen's characters, they needed a clear sense of belonging and a way to integrate the seemingly rejected Jewish identity with their American identity. They too often accepted majority values about their own selves; they could be—and were—accused of self-hatred.

It is no surprise that Allen's characters prize courage, independence, and artistic achievement. All these are the goals of a person focusing on overcoming identity tensions by the audacity and brilliance of individual acts. As Allen's characters (and perhaps Allen himself) ruefully discovered, and as many secular American Jews learned, such heroic efforts still proved incapable of overcoming the powerful social forces at work. Allen's characters, sadly, never truly learn the lessons of their lives in a way that helps them overcome their anxieties.

Sometimes the characters' conflicts show up in their names. In *Bananas*, for example, the character played by Woody Allen is Fielding Mellish, a quintessentially WASP first name coupled with a clearly Jewish surname. This happens in other roles, such as Cliff Stern in *Crimes and Misdemeanors*. (Of course, the "Cliff" name is also symbolic of being on the edge.)

Allen's films also appealed to urban, secular, intellectual Gentiles, who were themselves going through an identity crisis in the mid-1970s, when Allen's success and influence were at their height. Unlike the Jews, these Gentiles were not leaving an ethnic nest for the lures of America's glittering prizes, though they were, in a crucial sense, abandoning a way of life. Their parents, shaped by World War II and the need to build a postwar America, had focused on work, family, a sense of duty and responsibility. These parents believed that a crucial part of their identity lay in sublimating their own interests to the interests of their children. Those children, though, didn't have the same sense of responsibility. As they grew, the children put their own focus on self-expression, on personal fulfillment. The focus on self led to an explosion in divorce rates, to a sprouting of the recognition and assertion of assorted rights, and, most crucially, to defining the role of life as finding and nurturing the true self. In a direct reversal of their parents' views, this new generation believed that the self was not to be repressed in order to take care of others. They found rebellion in sexual experimentation and satisfaction in feeling alienated from their government and their religious roots. They sought alternative values, and they found—or created—them.

Gentile audiences found in Woody Allen's failure to integrate a self their own failure to match a sense of responsibility with a sense of focusing on self. They identified with Jews in a profound way.

But Allen, however, would only comically represent the dilemma the generation faced. He could not offer a solution.

Of course, Allen's Gentile audience was small compared to other movie stars. The fact that the audience was primarily urban and intellectual is a hint at another reason for their attraction to Allen's films. Intellectuals are a minority group in any culture. Jews formed a natural model for them as a gifted minority group that had mastered survival.

It is an oversimplification to see Woody Allen's characters simply as unable to decide on an identity or to recognize the nature of their Jewish identity. Indeed, part of Allen's artistic strength is that his films are prisms reflecting an enormous range of audience reactions, all of which may be distorted. But it is useful to see identity tensions as a central struggle for the characters in his films. Such difficulties can be seen, for example, in Allen's attempt to create serious films as opposed to comedies, to focus on art rather than commerce. Those tensions can be seen in the very earliest of his films.

Take the Money and Run (1969) is a strung-together series of visual and verbal bits loosely connected by a plot that focuses on perhaps the world's most incompetent criminal, Virgil Starkwell, played by Allen. Using a documentary style, Allen retells Starkwell's life. Even here, Allen muses on acceptance and assimilation such as when the narrator notes of Starkwell: "He wants nothing more than to belong, if only to a street gang."

Starkwell is imprisoned after a bungled bank robbery that included an illegible holdup note the teller at a bank reads as "I have a gub." In prison, Starkwell willingly undergoes an experiment in order to have his sentence reduced. One effect of the experiment is that "for several hours he is turned into a rabbi." The line is accompanied by an obvious shot: Allen in Hasidic garb. Eventually finding love, Starkwell is nevertheless unable to restrain himself from a criminal life and, at the end, is still trying to escape prison. Indeed, all Starkwell wants to do is escape—from himself, from his disapproving parents, from a society that can't find a place for him. In a famous scene, his parents hide behind Groucho masks, covering not just their faces but also their real selves. Trapped in an uncaring world, with an identity he can't grasp, Virgil, naturally, tries to find redemption with love, a redemption that is denied him. Indeed, in the original version of the film the couple is killed at the end of the movie.

Bananas (1971) involves a product tester who gets caught up in a South American revolution. Like *Take the Money and Run*, the film was basically a string of gags. A soldier is tortured by the playing of *The Naughty Marionette*. Howard Cosell provides live coverage, not of a sporting event, but of an assassination and of the Allen character's wedding night. Wielding language like Groucho Marx, Allen, as his own lawyer, complains: "This trial is a travesty. It's a travesty of a mockery of a sham of a mockery of a travesty of two mockeries of a sham." Again, Allen mocks intellectuals; in one scene he starts to hide behind a copy of *Commentary* when a woman is being mugged on a subway. And, again, his parents wear masks. A ridiculous red beard covers his identity as a nebbish; with this ludicrous disguise he appears to his ex-girlfriend as an exciting lover.

Allen's next film, *Sleeper* (1973), took the Allen character completely away from his New York life. Allen was growing in his ability to master parody, to mesh gags with a real story, and to avoid jokes that read better on the page than they appear on screen. *Sleeper*, set two hundred years in the future, does contain an assortment of classic Allen gags and lines, such as when his character, Miles Monroe, professes his lack of heroism by announcing that he was once beaten up by Quakers. He asserts that he believes in "sex and death—two things that come once in my life, but at least after death, you're not nauseous." Allen would take up similar themes in his next film, the less explicitly titled *Love and Death* (1975).

But it was *Annie Hall* (1977) that was Allen's breakthrough film, a shift in his work from a focus on sheer comedy to a concern with a particular character: a male, Jewish, secular intellectual living in New York City. Allen finally places his character in a more realistic setting, includes clear autobiographical elements, and, most important, doesn't slide from gag to gag but apportions them out, focusing more on human relationships than on jokes. Allen does take on such typical targets as schooling ("Those who can't do, teach. And those who can't teach, teach gym. And of course those who couldn't do anything . . . were assigned to our school") and Jewish intellectual life ("I've heard that *Commentary* and *Dissent* merged and formed *Dysentery*"), and he even drew on his best stand-up lines from his nightclub work ("I was thrown out of there during my freshman year for cheating on my metaphysics final. You know, I looked within the soul of the boy sitting next to me"). But at the film's center is a story of a New York Jew in love with a midwestern WASP. Allen's character, Alvy Singer, desperately wants to be accepted by Annie Hall's family—by America—but repeatedly can't avoid thinking of himself as Jewish and thinking that everyone else perceives him that way. Praising the ham at a dinner, Alvy suddenly sees himself as he thinks Annie's family sees him: as a Hasidic Jew. The American mask has been removed to reveal the core Jew underneath, a Jew whose external humor has been replaced by a haunting pathos.

Some Jewish audiences believed Allen bordered on self-hatred, but in fact Allen was being bold in putting his Jewishness directly in front of American audiences. In this, it is instructive to contrast Allen with a writer that Jewish audiences much more widely admired—Neil Simon—and to see how little overtly Jewish content was in Simon's plays and movies. Allen didn't smuggle his content in; he loudly proclaimed his Jewishness. However troubled his relationship to that Jewishness might have been, he refused to hide it.

American audiences loved *Annie Hall*; it won several Academy Awards, including Best Picture, because of its penetrating view of the status of modern romance. But if American audiences wanted to be told that love, finally, conquers all, Allen's bittersweet films left them with a more realistic message: love gets lost, love doesn't prevent lusting after others, love dies. For all the romance that Allen put in his films, for all the redemption seemingly offered by beautiful WASP women, in the end romantic love can't cure anhedonia either. (*Anhedonia* is the inability to experience pleasure and was the working title of the movie.) At the film's conclusion, Annie Hall leaves Alvy to move to California to live with Tony Lacey, a record producer. In real life, the Lacey character represents Warren Beatty, the actress Diane Keaton's love interest after she ended her relationship with Allen. Alvy sums up his feelings by invoking an old joke and then using it to make a poignant observation about Annie and about us:

> I realized what a terrific person she was . . . and I thought of that old joke . . . this guy goes to a psychiatrist and says, "Doc, my brother's crazy. He thinks he's a chicken." And the doctor says "Well, why don't you turn him in?" And the guy says, "I would, but I need the eggs." . . . I guess that's pretty much how I feel about relationships. You know they're totally irrational and crazy and absurd . . . but I guess we keep going through it because most of us need the eggs.

Manhattan (1979) again focused on failed relationships. Americans in the 1970s needed both to laugh at the idea of divorce or simply breaking up and the lures of adultery, and to get some form of artistic permission to separate because of the longings of the human heart. Isaac Davis, Allen's character, again justifies the power of sexual urges over the rational. "The brain," Isaac says, "is the most overrated organ." In Allen's films romantic love stands in opposition to Judaism, which is identified with stifling family life and repressed sexuality, and to Jews who are outsiders to the more serene world of WASP emotional calm and beauty. Indeed, *Annie Hall* and *Manhattan* turn WASP women into more than attractive sexual partners. They become the metaphors for acceptance.

Zelig (1983) is the most crucial of all Allen's movies in understanding the struggle to find a real self. The film is presented as a documentary about a man named Leonard Zelig who, in the 1920s, had the uncanny ability to change into the identity of those he was around. (Allen may have based Zelig on a famous Jewish impostor of the era named Stephen Jacob Weinberg, who seemed able to pass himself off as all kinds of officials, even if he didn't physically change appearance.) Zelig is the son of a Yiddish actor and was bullied by anti-Semites. He has an "unstable makeup." He wants to be accepted. As Zelig says, "It's safe . . . to be like the others. I want to be liked." His chameleon-like quality allows him to protect "himself by becoming whoever he's around." He notes, "I go to such extreme lengths to blend in" and "My whole life's been a lie." Once again, as in other films, family life is a disaster. Using Groucho-like patter, Zelig says, "My brother beat me. My sister beat me. My father beat my sister and my brother and me. My mother beat my father and my sister and me and my brother. The neighbors beat our family. People down the block beat the neighbors and our family." Appropriately, it is a beautiful WASP, Dr. Eudora Fletcher, who tries to save him.

There are a variety of ways to interpret Zelig. He can be seen as a person filled with fear, simply afraid to show his true self. In this sense, Allen is providing a warning to us to show courage, to not let others dictate our real beings. The film can also be understood as a political warning against dictators (Zelig is seen as part of Hitler's entourage) or being overwhelmed by the outside culture. It also works as a comment on a celebrity-hungry culture, one that worships people it doesn't really know for skills that are not worth worshiping.

Those interpretations would have been stronger, however, if they weren't confused by Zelig's obvious Jewishness. Indeed, Allen writes about the centrality of such an interpretation in words that are spoken by the writer Irving Howe in the film: "When I think about it, it seems to me that his story reflected a lot of the Jewish experience in America, the great urge to push in and to find one's place and then to assimilate into the culture. I mean he wanted to assimilate like crazy." Zelig is in this sense the model Allen character.

The film's technical effects are extraordinary. Placing Zelig alongside famous figures, such as F. Scott Fitzgerald, Fanny Brice, and Josephine Baker, was seamless and seemed utterly natural. However, placing Zelig in the past robs the character of relevance to the current American condition. In fact, Zelig is anachronistic. He fits Howe's comments perfectly, but those comments described only Jews who had lived in America decades after Zelig's purported fame. Had the film been set in the present, Allen would, in an ultimate way, have confronted the identity confusion he had indirectly dealt with in other films.

Moreover, Zelig never fully resolves his dilemma. As the last spoken words of the film assert, "It was the love of one woman that changed his life." But redemptive love depends on continuing devotion, a sentiment that Allen's characters found profoundly difficult to maintain. True love helps form and releases the true self in both partners. True love would have brought Zelig his real identity; instead, the romantic love simply reduces his anxiety.

Allen's characters in such films as *Hannah and Her Sisters* (1986) continue to make the mistake of seeking to end identity confusion through romantic love. In *Hannah*, some characters are attracted to people who are not their marital partners. Others are just searching for the right person.

Allen plays Mickey, Hannah's ex-husband. He does try some nonromantic alternatives to solve his identity crisis. At one point he seeks to escape his Jewishness completely by converting to Catholicism, but poor Mickey is trapped in his profoundly Jewish understanding of the world: he prepares for his new life by purchasing Wonder Bread and mayonnaise. The religious search, which includes an inquiry about Hare Krishna as well, proves fruitless, though, unusually, *Hannah and Her Sisters* ends with almost all the characters actually happy, again providing a misleading "solution" to the problem of Jewish identity.

In *Crimes and Misdemeanors* (1989), the moral collapse of the culture, and more particularly Jewish culture, is dramatically played out. Judah Rosenthal, an ophthalmologist played by Martin Landau, arranges the murder of his mistress. Only a patient, a rabbi named Ben, retains a traditional sense of morality, but Ben is going blind. Allen is reflecting sadly that Judaism as a moral force has lost its way. This is crucial, for without a moral base, Judaism cannot form the basis of a modern identity. Allen unfortunately does not further explore how such a moral vision can shape a contemporary life.

By *Deconstructing Harry* (1997), the Allen character's efforts to integrate identity completely fall apart. The sexual behavior and language of the characters, always restrained in previous movies, become blunt and profane, as though all controls have disappeared. Harry, more specifically than other characters, rejects worshiping God. His sister and brother-in-law are deeply religious and accuse him of belittling Jews in his stories. He reacts heatedly to them, saying, "Tradition is the illusion of permanence." He saves special venom for organized religion, including Jews who identify specifically as Jews. "They're clubs . . . They foster the concept of the other . . . so you know clearly who you should hate."

Not much works for Harry. On his way to get an award, Harry is shocked when a friend dies in the backseat of the car. He finds fleeting relief with prostitutes, but he loses his girlfriend to his own friend, who, in a symbolic visit to Hell, is the Devil. Once again, romance is presented as the answer (Allen tells his young son, "We don't know if there is a God, but there are women"), but it, too, eventually fails. Finally, for Harry (and for Allen), art is all that is left, and even that cannot conquer death. Not even a scene at the Red Apple Rest, the real-life roadside diner for generations of Catskill entertainers, can provide comfort. This invocation of comedy's past serves only to reveal a self that seeks to capture the past because the present reality is so fractured. The irony of Woody Allen is that he can be uncomfortable with tradition and nostalgic at the same time.

In some recent films, such as *Celebrity* (1998) and *Sweet and Lowdown* (1999), Allen uses surrogates to play the parts that he once did, but the themes remain the same. In *Celebrity*, for example, Allen goes back to the notion that "everything is show business." *Sweet and Lowdown*, on the other hand, is about a fictional jazz guitarist named Emmett Ray. It is impossible to resist interpreting the film, at least in part, as an autobiographical fable. Emmett is a musical genius who is misunderstood. He is self-absorbed, doing whatever he wants because he believes his gift gives him permission, even the right, to do so. An intriguing autobiographical element of the film centers around Hattie, the woman Emmett loves, a woman who cannot speak. It is possible to interpret Hattie as a stand-in for Soon-Yi, Allen's wife, who grew up speaking another language and who some accuse of being not an appropriate match for Allen. If such an interpretation is plausible, the film shows Allen's poignant justification of his love for Soon-Yi. Such a justification is particularly moving because in the film Emmett, finally realizing how much he loves Hattie, goes back to her only to discover that she's already married and the mother of a child.

Small-Time Crooks (2000) was Allen's comically successful attempt to return to his roots. The main character is a grown-up version of Virgil Starkwell. Allen has thus come full circle, and the film has many early Allen touches, among them allusions to the Marx Brothers (the wife of Allen's character is nicknamed "Frenchy," the nickname the Marx Brothers gave their father, and a harp is prominently placed in a room) and attacks on high culture. But though very similar to his early films, *Small-Time Crooks* was released at a time when Woody Allen's audience had greatly shrunk since the days of *Annie Hall* and *Manhattan*. To many Americans, Allen himself was more interesting as tabloid fodder than as cinematic auteur. He alludes to that fate by starting the movie with a shot of him reading a newspaper with a story about the sportscaster Marv Albert, who was also involved in a sex scandal, as was the actor Hugh Grant, who plays a major part in the film. (Scandal-ridden Sean Penn had been cast as the lead in *Sweet and Lowdown*.)

But, however much Allen's success has dimmed, his overall achievement is monumental. Whether he is a seeker or a self-hater, a genius or a gagman, his work, more than anyone else's, successfully tracks the footprints of a prominent urban psyche of the 1970s and 1980s.

Mel Brooks was Woody Allen's great rival for the title of the best and funniest writer, director, and star of the era. Initially, Brooks struggled with his film career. His years with Sid Caesar over, his record career with Carl Reiner having waned, his work on television interrupted, Brooks considered a story he had written called "Springtime for Hitler." He pondered trying to write a novel, which might in time be a film. As Brooks wrote, though, the substantial dialogue and quick succession of scenes made a film more appropriate.

The story was about a less than moral theatrical producer who, after selling considerably more than 100 percent of the shares in a play to romantically starved women, planned to put on a show that will deliberately fail.

The main character is confident of failure when he finds a musical about Hitler, but in a culture unable to distinguish between a horrifying, immoral production and a clever parody, the show actually succeeds, leaving the producer and his partner in financial trouble.

For Brooks, the tale was a parable of Jewish life, a series of failures, but which, in America, becomes suddenly successful. Brooks also liked the fact that the script shocked audiences and attacked Germans; he liked mocking those who had attacked Jews.

Brooks took his script, then titled *Springtime for Hitler*, to all the major studios, but they found dancing Nazis considerably less humorous than he did. Independent producers were no more hospitable. Then Brooks met the producer Sidney Glazier.

Glazier sipped some coffee while the enthusiastic Brooks began to tell the story. When Brooks described the "Springtime for Hitler" production number, Glazier laughed so hard he fell on the floor. Glazier convinced Brooks to direct the film, found additional funding, and soon *The Producers* (1968), as the film was renamed, was made.

Zero Mostel plays Max Bialystock, the film's main character. Mostel and Brooks had consistently clashing egos, and some critics found Mostel physically inappropriate as a producer capable of seducing older women. But Mostel is overwhelming, perfect for Brooks's crude, outrageous, and extreme humor.

Brooks's exuberant story is, at its heart, not so much a send-up of Broadway or greed or anti-Semites or an unperceptive culture. Rather, *The Producers* is the story of a relationship between two men. Max and Leo Bloom, an accountant played by Gene Wilder, are from different generations yet develop a trust and even a love for each other. Since this is a theme that will exist in later Brooks films as well, it is important to recognize it as a crucial emotional touchstone. One possibility for his focus on male relationships was suggested by Brooks himself: "Maybe in having the male characters in my movies find each other, I'm expressing the longing I feel to find my father and be close to him." (Brooks's father died when Brooks was two and a half.) There is, in addition, another way to look at the male relationships in Brooks's films: the two males can be seen as parts of the same person struggling to find a way to live together. In the case of Bialystock and Bloom, both are Jewish, though one is the assertive insider and the other the passive outsider. (It is no wonder that Brooks took the outsider Bloom's name from James Joyce's Jewish character in *Ulysses*.) The assertive side "wins" in trying to trick the public, but both sides are eventually punished. Seen this way, *The Producers* is American society "punishing" Brooks for his overt Jewishness and, insofar as it can be distinguished from that Jewishness, his brashness. But the Jewish dilemma is still complicated, because the passive approach also brings poor results.

Brooks was upset that some critics considered *The Producers* a work of low art, if it was art at all. Eventually, Brooks would triumphantly prove his critics wrong when the Broadway musical of *The Producers* set a record by winning twelve Tony Awards in 2001. At the time, though, all the determined Brooks could do was direct a great movie, and so he turned to a work he had read as a child. The Russian novel *The Twelve Chairs* had been filmed before. (One version, titled *It's in the Bag*, starred Fred Allen and Jack Benny.) The plot involves three men in search of family jewels hidden in one of the dozen chairs in a set. Ippolit, a former noble, and Ostap, a handsome con man, team up to track down the jewels, while Father Fyodor, the family priest, competes with them. As in *The Producers*, the hunt for money brings together two very different men who ultimately forge a bond that endures even as the hunt for the jewels ends in a surprise. Brooks again gets to explore a favorite theme, that only love and friendship, not greed, can form the basis of a worthwhile life, using the Russia from which his family escaped as a backdrop. Ostap has a chance at one point to let Ippolit drown and seek all the jewels himself. Instead, Ostap saves the drowning man and then even gives the shivering man a much needed coat. Mel Brooks has a small part as Ippolit's former servant who misses his old life. *The Twelve Chairs* is technically much more sophisticated than *The Producers*, and many critics who didn't like the earlier film liked this one. Yet, *The Twelve Chairs* (1970) was not a commercial success, though it did make money because it had cost so little to produce.

It took Brooks four years before his next film was made and released, but the wait proved worthwhile. *Blazing Saddles* (1974) was Brooks's great breakthrough with audiences.

Blazing Saddles is Brooks's first clear spoof. Finding this form was crucial. A spoof pokes fun at social, artistic, and other conventions. It is not, and does not wish to be, as serious as is its conceptual relative, satire. Nor does it follow the original as closely as does its other relative, the parody.

Spoofing recognizable people, genres, and social conventions is meant not so much to attack them, the way satire does, as to pay a compliment to their influence. Spoofs, like much other humor, provide a simple release from the anxieties of life. Spoofs do not call for a transformation of what is spoofed. A spoof, that is, is a pure form of therapy, not the complex form offered by Woody Allen.

Crucially, the spoof as a form fits perfectly into Brooks's attempt to integrate a Jewish and an American identity. A spoof connects two related subjects, the object of the spoof and the spoof itself. This is analogous to America, the object, and Jews, those who do the spoofing. Such spoofing allows Jews to mock the wider society, as they traditionally did, without seriously attempting to undermine it, and spoofing also allows Jews to have enough irony so as not to be absorbed by America. Brooks offers a Jewish identity that renders Jews as permanently partial insiders and partial outsiders. However tenuous, such an identity perpetuates a unique Jewishness while being connected to a wider Americanism.

Blazing Saddles was not an original Brooks creation. Andrew Bergman had written a story called *Tex-X* about a black sheriff in the West. Brooks played off the already-created material and changed it according to his own vision—unloosing wildly comic bits into the world Bergman had created. When, after two years, the film was completed, Brooks screened it for the executives at Warner Brothers. The executives were silent at the first joke; Brooks recalls the moment as one of the worst of his life. And the laughter never came. In fact, the people in the screening room did not find the film humorous in the least. Brooks wanted to cancel the sneak preview scheduled for that night. But, instead of the expected disaster, the audience burst into waves of laughter. *Blazing Saddles* became a huge hit, and not just in New York and Los Angeles.

Clearly, one attraction of the film is the close relationship between the white gunslinger, played by Gene Wilder, and the black sheriff, played by Cleavon Little. The bad guys are presented not only as anti-Semites but also as racists. Adults are again seen as immature. Brooks has brief roles as Governor Lepetomaine (named after an actor whose fame rested on his extraordinary ability to use his rump as a trumpet) and a Yiddish-speaking Sioux chief. Brooks does not provide a translation of the Yiddish, partly because he assumed that a Sioux chief speaking Yiddish was funny all by itself. Still, what he said is important. At one point, for instance, the braves come upon a black family, the child of whom would later grow up to be the sheriff. Brooks says to let them alone: "Zeit nisht meshugge. Loz em gaien . . . Abee gezint." The translation is "Don't be crazy. Let them go . . . As long as we are all healthy." Even in Yiddish, perhaps especially in Yiddish, what the film critic Andrew Sarris calls Brooks's "emotional generosity" comes through.

Brooks expressed surprise at the film's attractions for middle America, but his good humor and plea for tolerance resonated in 1974 when the film was released. What Brooks intuitively grasped was that most Americans, especially the young Americans drawn to his films, saw themselves as some form of minority, even if that minority resided in their very youth. His audience members believed that they were outsiders, and Brooks's inclusive message made them feel welcome. Also, Brooks's message was the opposite of Allen's: anxiety about entering the society can be overcome.

Brooks's humor was considerably different from Allen's in another respect as well. Brooks was repeatedly accused of vulgarity. The most famous scene in the film, a symphony of cowboy flatulence around a campfire, drew heated criticism. This genuinely surprised Brooks, who knew what made people laugh. Interestingly, even his defense of the scene draws on the image of minority status: "Farts are a repressed minority. The mouth gets to say all kinds of things, but the other place is supposed to keep quiet." In another comment, he said, "Shakespeare said hold the mirror up to life; I held it a little behind and below."

Most of Brooks's films after *Blazing Saddles* were less successful. It is hard to tell how much of Brooks is in *Young Frankenstein* (1974) since Gene Wilder had the original idea for the film and wrote the screenplay. It was Wilder who came up with the idea of having Dr. Frankenstein and the monster sing "Puttin' on the Ritz" wearing top hat and tails.

However credit for the film is apportioned, the symbolism beyond the spoof in *Young Frankenstein* is revealing. Surely, in a story about what society sees as a monster and rejects, Brooks—ever sensitive to Jewish suffering—saw a reflection of the Jews' all-too-frequent status in history. Indeed, at one point, scientists are charged with an ancient anti-Semitic slur: "All they really want is to rule the world." The experiment in making the "monster" human can, in this sense, be seen as "civilizing" Jews. Like Allen, Brooks believes the success depends on love. In this sense, he, too, in this film takes an easy answer to the complex nature of identity in society.

Silent Movie (1976) showed Brooks's conceptual daring, though poor box-office receipts suggest that audiences were unwilling to accept the experiment in returning to an old pretalking comedy form. *High Anxiety* (1977) continues another Brooks theme, spoofing moviemaking itself, in particular the films of Alfred Hitchcock. In one scene, Brooks plays a psychiatrist called upon to use explicit language in a speech to his peers. He sees, however, some young girls in the audience and resorts to childish euphemisms instead of the planned explicitness. The prissiness illustrates the limit of Brooks's vulgarity; he does not use any nudity or excessive profanity. He actually has a prudish side when it comes to protecting innocence. Just as Shelley Berman reached a line and would not cross it but Woody Allen did, so Mel Brooks reached a line and would not cross it, though later performers, such as Howard Stern, did.

In another scene, spoofing *The Birds*, Brooks is attacked by an enormous number of pigeons that deposit waste on him. (Ray Berwick, who had trained thousands of birds for the original film, was hired by Brooks to train the pigeons.) Again it is vulgar, but with prepubescent limits. Brooks is, in a sense, like an older brother to Jerry Lewis—not nine or ten, but not thirteen either.

Brooks's next movie was *History of the World, Part I* (1981), a series of historical vignettes. Brooks appears as Moses carrying three tablets with fifteen commandments and calling out that God wants all these fifteen obeyed. He drops one of the tablets and immediately adapts by altering the required number to ten. Later in the film we see Moses parting the Red Sea. In fact, Moses is being robbed, and the sea mistakenly parts as he raises his hands in response to the thief's demand. At another point, Brooks plays a waiter working at the Last Supper. "Does everyone want soup?" he asks, and "Are you all together, or is it separate checks?"

There is also a classic musical number based loosely on the Spanish Inquisition. Jews are being tortured to get them to convert. When they don't, nuns enter, strip to reveal swimsuits, and do synchronized swimming. The smitten Jews jump in the water to be with them. It is an interesting scene—Jews could resist religious persecution, but the attractiveness of the Christian culture exemplified by beautiful women was too enticing to resist.

In one sense, of course, Brooks is just making anti-Semites so pathetic, so subject to ridicule, that they hold no mythological power. He reduces them to ridiculous figures. Still, the need to hold them up to such ridicule indicates a lingering anger. "I think that, unconsciously, there's an outrage there," Brooks says. "I may be angry at God, or at the world, for that. And I'm sure a lot of my comedy is based on anger and hostility. Growing up in Williamsburg, I learned to clothe it in comedy to spare myself problems—like a punch in the face."

To Be or Not to Be (1983) was, of course, a remake of the 1942 Ernst Lubitsch film starring Jack Benny. (In a bow to the comic, a street in the remake is called "Kubelski," which is a variant of Benny's family name.) Although the film is well done, it does not provide a rationale for its existence when the original is still widely available. Still, it gives Brooks a direct chance to attack Nazis, serving both his continuing emotional need and his desire to make a more serious film.

That desire continued in his next film. *Life Stinks* (1991) was an attempt to deal with homelessness, with the guilt of success, and with love. It is the story of a wealthy man who accepts a bet to survive as a homeless person for thirty days. The brutality of such a life is made clear. Eventually, the character leads other homeless people to fight the powerful. He realizes that "it's good to be alive. There are so many things you can't do when you're dead." The film ends with the character's money and home restored and with him embarking on his honeymoon.

Brooks's film career waned as audiences found comedians willing to start where Brooks had taken humor but go to places where Brooks wouldn't. In addition, the spoof has built-in limitations: There are only so many well-liked and recognizable genres.

The anxiety-ridden heroes of Woody Allen's films focus on death and finding moments of love. Such heroes fitted perfectly in the culture of the 1960s and 1970s, but, as the culture changed, other anxieties emerged, particularly an anxiety about success. There was also continuing interest in the shifting rules of contemporary romance.

Albert Brooks brilliantly captured these concerns in his films. Brooks is the son of the comedian Harry Einstein and the actress-singer Thelma Leeds. He was originally named Albert Einstein, but, unsurprisingly, changed the name. (When asked why, he responded, "Do I even have to answer?") He first had an act as a completely inept ventriloquist and soon created other bits. He was developing a modestly successful stand-up career until one night in Boston in 1974. The singer Leo Sayer, also on the bill, used to come onstage in a clown suit, and that evening people from his record company filled the audience, all wearing clown outfits. Brooks, who had never felt fear, was overwhelmed by it. He did the performance but then stopped being a stand-up comic. Even when Lorne Michaels invited him to host *Saturday Night Live*, Brooks declined.

Brooks acted in such films as *Taxi Driver* and then began to make movies. His first film, *Real Life* (1979), was produced in 1979. It was a mock documentary about an American family, a parody of a PBS series. The humor was subtle and clever, too subtle for a general audience. Indeed, Brooks, who is widely considered by his peers to be one of the funniest comedians, has had box office problems all through his career.

His next film was *Modern Romance* (1981). Brooks plays a film editor named Robert Cole who wants to stay with a woman named Mary Harvard but is afraid that somewhere there is a perfect woman for him. He finds himself in a romantic dilemma: He thinks he must leave his girlfriend, Mary, to find that perfect woman but in doing so he will lose a wonderful relationship. As an epilogue makes clear, their relationship will always be one marked by coming together and breaking apart. In *Lost in America* (1985), Brooks is an advertising executive who loses his job and convinces his wife that they should buy a Winnebago and roam America, trying to find themselves. It takes no longer than a trip to Las Vegas for the plan to fall apart. He is, indeed, lost, but his loss is that he can't survive outside a middle-class life. *Defending Your Life* (1991) is a fantasy about how our souls must defend their existence, in particular their ability to overcome anxiety or else be returned to Earth to try again. Only the pursuit of a woman he loves convinces the prosecutor who has tried his case that he has overcome his fears and can move on to the next level. *Mother* (1996) is about a man who moves back in with his mother to pick up the pieces of his life. *The Muse* (1999) is an exceptionally clever film about a screenwriter who meets a woman he believes is a muse who can help him through a creatively dry period. Various writers and directors (such as Rob Reiner, Martin Scorsese, and James Cameron) have also used the Muse, who never does the writing but only inspires. Sharon Stone plays the spoiled Muse perfectly.

Perhaps Brooks's existence as a cult and peer favorite rather than a popular success may be due to his subject matter and his refusal to engage in the sort of simple and increasingly crude and personal physical comedy that is becoming popular. The internal struggle of Brooks's protagonists was about finding a self, but the struggle remained inside.

This is all the more so because none of Brooks's characters have Jewish names, express their Jewishness verbally, or seem to have ethnic struggles. The ethnic debate played out so directly in Woody Allen's and Mel Brooks's films has been submerged so much that the identity struggle is no longer understood by enough of the audience. Far from being the eternal outsider, Brooks plays almost archetypal insiders who momentarily find themselves adrift. His characters lack the outsider, minority identity struggling with reconciling that identity with the wider culture.

This lack of Jewishness in the characters is particularly sad in *The Muse* because a Jewish character would have made the film into a useful metaphor about American Jewish life. The protagonist uses a beautiful woman as inspiration; he does not see her as an object of temptation. Had the character been explicitly Jewish, this distinction could have provided a suggestion about how Jews should view America. That is, instead of being tempted by its lures, America could be seen as a muse to develop Jewishness in creative ways.

Billy Crystal's film *Mr. Saturday Night* (1992), which Crystal wrote, directed, produced, and starred in, had the opposite problem. The film follows the life of Buddy Young Jr., a Jewish comedian, a user, a self-centered comic who insults audiences, a man perpetually cruel to those who are closest to him, his wife, daughter, and especially his brother. His career parallels that of many famous Jewish comedians. He starts out by lip-synching songs, as Jerry Lewis did. He has a variety show like Sid Caesar or Red Buttons with the same pressures. Like Jackie Mason, he gets into trouble with Ed Sullivan.

Crystal's film is not just funny; it's courageous in presenting a psychologically acute but ultimately unflattering portrait of a comedian. Perhaps for that very reason, though, audiences struggled with the film. They were used to, and wanted, their comedian heroes to be wild and funny but not cruel.

More crucially, though, Buddy Young Jr. had no struggles with which they could identify. If Albert Brooks had taken the Jewish side out of the identity struggle between being Jewish and being American, Crystal had taken the American side out. Buddy certainly wants success in America. But behind the scenes, he is close to his mother and marries a Jewish woman. There is a professional struggle with which audiences might identify, but no personal identity struggle with which they could.

Although explicitly Jewish comedy sometimes struggled to emerge on the movie screen, it found its greatest success on television and in stand-up. Perhaps the big screen favored broader, physical comedy and not the warm, intimate, verbal comedy typically offered by Jews. When, however, Jewish comedians came into American homes through the smaller television screen or spoke directly to audiences in clubs, concert halls, or campuses, they were embraced not just by critics or urban audiences but also by large numbers of ordinary Americans.

9

MASTERS OF
THEIR DOMAIN

─────────

COMEDY ALL OVER THE PLACE

Jacob Cohen had a difficult road to being a star; he came by his anxieties honestly. When Jacob was a child, his parents had separated; his father, a former vaudeville performer, left the family. Weighted down by an appearance that was less than classically handsome, young Jacob had deep feelings of self-doubt. At fifteen he began writing jokes as a way to overcome his unhappiness. At nineteen, he tried comedy under the name Jack Roy, earning twelve dollars a week plus room and board. Cohen struggled for almost a decade but finally quit to sell paint and siding. His major failure was in defining a distinct comic persona.

However, unable to rid himself of the urge to tell jokes, Cohen used his years selling paint to write part-time for others such as Joan Rivers and Jackie Mason.

Desperate to return, he started out with a new name thought up by a club owner named George McFadden.

Rodney Dangerfield was born.

Slowly, over time, Dangerfield developed the brilliant persona of a man who "don't get no respect." The grammatical error was obviously on purpose. The Dangerfield character was not educated, just an ordinary working stiff struggling to succeed in a world that rewarded attractiveness and intelligence. The character was perfect for several reasons. It fitted Dangerfield's appearance: the Eddie Cantor eyes popping from his head, the thick body, the deep bags under his eyes, the flop sweat, and the nervous tics. Dangerfield also used a new kind of delivery. The Catskill tummlers were swift, delivering lines with clear beats. Mort Sahl and Woody Allen had been more jazzlike, drifting from subject to subject, though Allen's material was more fully prepared. Dangerfield couldn't use these deliveries because they didn't fit the character. Instead, he presented himself as extremely nervous. The anguish came out not only in the bulge of the eyes or the pull of the tie, but also in the rhythm of the voice.

Dangerfield also found a character that audiences could empathize with even if they also laughed at him. The feeling of not being respected was widely held in an achievement-oriented society, and here was someone who got even less respect than they did. Dangerfield complained that his mother refrained from breast-feeding him: "She told me she liked me as a friend." He connected this parental lack of respect to his own lack of self-respect: "I was an ugly kid . . . My mother had morning sickness after I was born." He mocked his wife's appearance and her extravagance: "My wife ran after the garbage truck this morning. Too bad they waved her off." He would joke that she gave tips at a tollbooth.

Like Woody Allen, Dangerfield was both brilliant and careful as he wrote jokes. He didn't usually ad-lib. Instead, he would spend an extraordinary amount of time preparing. He was one of the cleverest of those comedians who wrote their own jokes. "We were so poor in my neighborhood the rainbow was in black and white . . . I was an ugly baby. When the doctor cut the cord, he hung himself." Such were the funny lines that made Dangerfield's stand-up career.

Dangerfield worked on records, in clubs, on television, and eventually in movies. Unlike Woody Allen, Mel Brooks, Albert Brooks, and Billy Crystal, who did their comedy primarily in their films, Dangerfield exemplified the comedians who would enter all comedy venues.

When Dangerfield eventually entered films, starring in such movies as *Caddyshack*, *Easy Money*, and, perhaps his best, *Back to School*, he took on a new role because the films attracted young audiences. In those movies, Dangerfield often portrayed a character who was simultaneously successful in society while capable of mocking its conventions. He was playing the part of a loving adult, giving young people permission to laugh at the society while telling them that it was their very ability to laugh that would lead them to success in the society. That was just the message his young audiences wanted to hear: They were allowed to have fun and doing so wouldn't endanger their future.

Not all Jewish comedians were as successful as Dangerfield in migrating from one venue to another. In particular, some found the journey between stand-up in clubs and television a difficult one. Shecky Greene, for example, was a huge success in Las Vegas, but less so on television. "I never had the feeling for television," he explained. "I am in control of myself on the stage. I am not in control in a TV studio. I've got a director. I've got a producer telling me 'no.' I've got a guy behind the desk. On stage, I was the director, the producer, the writer. I work off the audience. I couldn't look at the camera and work. I had to work to an audience."

Jackie Mason had some success as a stand-up until the Ed Sullivan incident but not afterward, although he starred on television in *Chicken Soup*, a situation comedy in which he played a Jewish man who enters a relationship with a Gentile woman. The television critic and humor writer Marvin Kitman, looking back at the show, says Mason was "a gefilte fish out of water" and notes that the show was a too typical example of how the media mistreated Jewish subjects.

If Dangerfield turned his anxieties inward, Don Rickles turned them outward, attacking those who caused him grief, pushing into the territory of insult humor explored earlier by Fat Jack Leonard. If Dangerfield was the American Jewish psyche blaming itself for its troubles, Rickles was the American Jewish psyche blaming everyone else. He was the Jewish hostility to anti-Semitism finally allowed to speak and doing so with a barely controlled anger and a barking outrage. Rickles had been in the navy during World War II, studied at the Academy of Dramatic Arts, sold life insurance, tried acting, and was a failure as a stand-up comedian, focusing on doing impressions. Rickles began ad-libbing and noticed that his responses were getting laughs. Many comedians talk with audience members, but Rickles changed the nature of the dialogue. He was working in strip joints, and the tough audience liked it when he began to yell at them. Whereas Jack Leonard had been nonconfrontational even as he insulted, Rickles was much more direct. He became famous for taking on everyone, most significantly Frank Sinatra in 1956: "Your voice is gone. It's all over for you. You're making a fool of yourself. You've got to find some other work." Sinatra laughed. Other celebrities came under attack and enjoyed it. He said of Bob Hope that "when he was in Vietnam, they were shooting at him from both sides." He also singled out Bob

Newhart: "Bob Newhart is a stammering idiot, and his wife is a former hooker from Bayonne." He was very popular on *The Tonight Show*; Johnny Carson dubbed him "Mr. Warmth."

Rickles became famous—and infamous—for using ethnic and other personal insults. In his first album, *Hello Dummy*, he offers some typical comments: Seeing a woman wearing a fur coat, he says, "You're either a Jew, lady, or an old beaver in heat." He's not done, though. "That was a good one, right, queer? Look. The Italian guy. Oil all over the table." He later turns to an African American. "We need blacks—so we can have cotton in the drugstore."

These kinds of jokes drew criticism, of course. But Rickles succeeded because audiences knew he was kidding and meant no harm, though the words themselves cut deeply.

Most Jewish comedians would not follow in Rickles's footsteps. Jewish comedians might be neurotics, satirists, or observers. They were more than willing to deflate the powerful and the celebrated. But the history of their people made Jewish comedians reluctant to mock minorities. Instead, they relied on more traditional Jewish strategies such as a focus on language, as Norm Crosby exemplified.

Crosby's malapropisms came in an effort to find a new way to do comedy.

I was looking for something unique. I was working clubs around Boston, doing charitable events. The man who owned the Latin Quarter in New York saw me and said he enjoyed my work. He offered me a week there. At the time I was working like every other comedian. I realized I couldn't do that material. Every subject matter had been done. Every premise had been taken. I thought of presenting the material differently.

When I started, though, the audiences didn't know the differences between the words. When I'd say, "The Etruscans vanquished the Trojans and pushed them out of Trojia down the Agamemnon Valley which led to the Connecticut Valley," they'd sit there and look at me and say, "Oh yeah I learned that in school." But I stayed with it.

Crosby's success with mangled English seemed destined to invite competitors. Crosby, though, notes that "the industry protects you. It becomes your thing. People would say new comics were copying me."

Younger comedians came along to speak to a new generation.

Robert Klein found a niche as a young, hip observer of youth and the grim realities of growing up in the 1950s, moaning about the indignities of adolescence in suburbia. He also edged into Lenny Bruce territory, taking on subjects his contemporaries did not want to, especially Jewish subjects. He mocked anti-Semites and their beliefs. Kurt Waldheim, former secretary-general of the United Nations who was accused of having a Nazi past but who denied it, was a target: "The proceeds from tonight's show are going to the Kurt Waldheim Fund. We're sending Kurt to the Harry Lorraine Memory Institute to try to remember five years of his life . . . 'It vas 1941. I vas in Vienna. I vas drinking a cup of cafe mit sclage. Suddenly it vas 1946.'" One famous piece was about the rigors of ordering kosher food on an airline as Klein gives voice to the plane's personnel: "Will the Jew who ordered the kosher meal please make himself known to flight attendant Vicki? Will the Jew . . . may I see your genitalia, sir? We have the Jew here." Klein was also clever in seeing how suburban life robbed people of real experience.

Robert Klein was crucial in another way. He explored nostalgia. Before him, nostalgia among Jewish comedians was about immigrant life, loving mamas, and family support. The disappearance of this nostalgia in the comedians of the 1950s and '60s led to an unmet need. Jews had often found emotional nourishment in a triumphant ancestry, a proud and defiant spirit of survival, and an embracing family and community. All of these rapidly diminished in the New World, trampled by the need to fit in, to be truly and unambiguously American.

Realizing that his nostalgic impulses couldn't take him all the way back to immigrant life, Klein found a new use for nostalgia. He explored his own adolescence and the cultural icons of that era. He looked to a mythical personal American past, not a mythical communal Jewish past. In doing so, he was participating in and expanding the acculturating process being undertaken by American Jews. He, like they, was taking attitudes from that Jewish past and transplanting them in America's fertile soil. Suddenly, warm, personal immigrant grandparents were replaced by heroes from baseball and the mass media.

David Steinberg had studied religion (his father, at one time, had been a rabbi). He had been particularly successful at Second City in Chicago and then began to do stand-up. Steinberg explored some of the sexual frontier pioneered by Woody Allen. He told jokes about religion and parents and other typical subjects, sometimes combining them: "My parents were intelligent, enlightened people. They accepted me exactly for what I was—a punishment from God." His religious explorations are what got him in trouble. In 1969, on the Smothers Brothers' program, Steinberg was scheduled to deliver a comic sermon on Solomon and Jonah. Steinberg included such lines as "And the Gentiles, as is their wont from time to time, threw the Jew overboard." CBS officials considered the routine "irreverent and offensive" and asked that the piece be deleted. There is a dispute about what happened next, but one step was clear: CBS eventually canceled the show. Ironically, Steinberg's clean style and good looks would come into fashion a generation after he entered show business. He was a forerunner of people such as Jerry Seinfeld and others Steve Allen called "cute Jewish guys."

All of these comedians were a prelude to a new generation of Jewish comedians, comedians who had grown up in a very different America than their parents had.

Life in the fifties had included a rigid social order, a sense of place for most Americans (but a sense of alienation for others), and a basic faith in society and in the future. The raw events of the 1960s and 1970s changed all that. The war in Vietnam; disagreements about how best to achieve racial justice; the assassinations of John Kennedy, Robert Kennedy, and Martin Luther King Jr.; and the invention of the pill were among the events that changed the culture. The loss of faith in the government and an increase in premarital and extramarital sex led to an increasing focus on the self, on the need for a personal identity and on the search for personal happiness. The search by men and women for individuality and the refusal to accept any longer an intolerable reality for the sake of an institution rather than for the self led to an explosion in the rate of divorces, children born outside traditional marriages, drug use in search of a higher or at least alternative consciousness, and in other factors that made America in the 1980s and beyond unrecognizable from three decades earlier.

The new Jewish comedians thus existed in a very different American environment from their ancestors. The early-twentieth-century immigrants struggled to become acculturated and to adjust to the strangeness of the language, to the rough-and-tumble of urban life, and the peculiar manners and morals of their adopted homeland. Their children, born in the United States, had to fight anti-Semitism, help Israel, and continue seeking full integration into American life. By the next generation, the battle for acceptance had been won, and these Jews moved to suburbia where they had good jobs and sent their children to the best schools. By the beginning of the 1980s, though, a new reality entered American life. Acculturation had been so successful, and antipathy toward Jews so reduced, that the new struggle in organized American Jewish life became survival. Intermarriage between Jews and Gentiles had been virtually nonexistent at the beginning of the century, and the rate was just 3 percent before World War II. By 1965, the rate had grown to 17 percent. Between 1966 and 1972, the rate jumped to 32 percent. In the 1990 National Jewish Population Survey, it was estimated that since 1985, 52 percent of Jews had married an unconverted Gentile partner. The new generation of American Jews, like all Americans, also began to divorce in numbers comparable to other Americans.

There were other demographic changes that also influenced Jewish comedy. The 1980s were an era of political if not cultural conservatism. Indeed, the Reagan years witnessed the emergence of what could be considered two broad cultures in America: one more traditional, often rooted in religion, and the other more secular. The battle between these two, over language and subject matter, was particularly crucial for comedians. The Jewish comedians no longer had a Jewish self, but represented a wide variety of selves along an American Jewish continuum. The clearest way to see contemporary Jewish comedians is to see them as representing the different ways in which Jews have entered American culture, changed it, and were changed by it.

In was in such a world that a new generation of Jewish comedians emerged. Many of them, unsurprisingly, followed the neurotic humor explored by Shelley Berman and Woody Allen.

Richard Lewis went into comedy after his father, a caterer, died. Lewis had graduated from Ohio State and went home to New Jersey to enter advertising. Bored, he began to put jokes in the ads he wrote. Soon he was hanging out at a comedy club, the Improv, listening to the comedian David Brenner. (Brenner would eventually loan Lewis one thousand dollars so that Lewis could quit all his part-time jobs and make an effort to become a comedian.) Lewis began to write jokes that he sold to comedians who worked in the Borscht Belt. Eventually, he tried stand-up himself and, slowly, his comedy character emerged. It was a comedy of personal and family pain, as though his neuroses were genetic but funny: "Our favorite party game was 'Pin the Blame on the Donkey.' I tell my mother that our blood type is negative. Very negative." He would bring a huge amount of notes onstage, pages of a yellow legal pad taped one to another and appended with new material. Like many Jewish comedians, Lewis went after his mother as the cause of his anguish ("Her Yiddish name is 'I'm tawwking to you'") and after his family ("We went to see *Les Miserables*. I thought it was gonna be like a play about one of my family's seders.") Lewis dug deeply, if fictionally, into his presumably anxiety-ridden childhood: "My only childhood pet, a collie named Phil, committed suicide because of my mother. I mean, she would toss Phil a bone and say, 'Don't fetch it. See what I care.'" Poor Phil eventually "shot himself with a handgun that he whittled out of a biscuit." Lewis is Woody Allen for an audience reared on family jokes rather than existentialism or Ingmar Bergman.

Woody Allen also influenced Garry Shandling, who first saw the comedian on *Hot Dog*, a children's television program. Shandling began his professional career by writing for television. He also began doing stand-up. His first series, *It's Garry Shandling's Show*, found a devoted but limited audience. But its follow-up, *The Larry Sanders Show,* received extraordinary critical praise for its inside show business feel, its self-deprecatory, pitiless look at the characters behind a late-night talk show, and its never less than brilliant writing. In *Larry Sanders*, Shandling sought to blur the distinctions between reality and show business. He deliberately attempted to hop back and forth between the real Garry Shandling and the fictional person Larry Sanders. The effort to create such a confused self, that is, became a perfect reflection not just of how celebrities live but also of how American Jews live: having to run from one identity to another, leaping from the real Jewish self to the self that had to perform in American culture. Shandling produces a vision of American Jewish life that can lead only to exhaustion. The juggling of identities can be done, but the price is enormous and the result one of constant tension and anxiety. Whereas Shandling's Larry Sanders character carefully avoids disclosing his obviously Jewish identity, the show did deal with Jewish issues, such as in an episode in which Larry's sidekick decides to wear a yarmulke on the air.

Bob Goldthwait took the child that Jerry Lewis had nurtured and turned him into a late-1980s full-blown neurotic kid, with a dark sense of humor: "My father's turning over in his grave. He wasn't quite dead when we buried him." Gilbert Gottfried combined a perpetual squint with a shout at once filled with adult outrage but also with a childish whine. He, too, often went for the outrageous: "I went up to Jackie Kennedy at a party and figured I'd try to break the ice by getting a little conversation going. So I said, 'Do you remember where you were and what you were doing when you heard that Kennedy was shot?'"

Pee-Wee Herman (born Paul Reubens) was a childlike performer who eventually starred in several films and hosted a children's program before an arrest for public lewdness. Reubens explored the annoying child—the direct descendant of Jerry Lewis's juvenile character—and mixed in contemporary aspects such as gender confusion. The odd character by definition couldn't develop, and so the Pee-Wee fad eventually faded.

One of the most interesting of this new generation of neurotic Jewish comics worked primarily in animation. The premise of the animated show *Dr. Katz, Professional Comedian*, was unique: Dr.

Katz, given voice by Jonathan Katz, is a therapist who treats patients who are themselves comedians. This premise provided the opportunity to explore comic neuroses and simultaneously gave an outlet to numerous well-known and lesser-known comedians. The show is a perfect metaphor for the role of the Jewish comedian in American society. The comedians have been elevated to crucial importance. They are talented and eager to help, but their ability to solve the real problems of society is limited. Their acceptance of this new social role as the custodians of an audience's mental health is not completely satisfying because they, like Dr. Katz, are all too familiar with the emptiness of their own lives and relationships. "The creation of Dr. Katz had more to do with my range as an actor than almost anything else," Katz recalls. "I remember being in therapy and thinking to myself hearing my shrink say his third 'hmmm' that 'I could do that.' The fact that he's Jewish is just a coincidence."

Besides the neurotic comics, Jewish comedians also explored other areas, especially satire and political humor. Al Franken, who explored both, says, "A large part of the reason that I went into comedy was that my dad loved it so much." He also notes, "The fact that Jews really revere comedy was part of the reason I chose it. Humor is respected in Jewish life. Even rabbis try to be funny."

Franken started doing stand-up in college and eventually got a job writing for *Saturday Night Live,* specializing in political satire. Later he developed a series of characters such as Stuart Smalley and in doing so satirized the entire self-help movement. He says, however, that although Stuart was silly, there was also something serious and important about him.

I go to Al-Anon which is for family members and friends of alcoholics. By going to those meetings I learned that I could learn stuff from people who at first blush didn't seem smart. At

Al-Anon meetings, I learned a lot from people who at first seemed like idiots. That gave me the idea to create a character that also at first seemed like an idiot but who really had some wisdom or at least some courage that you could learn from.

After leaving *Saturday Night Live*, Franken turned to political humor. This, too, came out of his childhood, when his family would watch the news while eating dinner. Franken was especially successful with books such as *Rush Limbaugh Is a Big Fat Idiot and Other Observations*. Franken remains a rarity of Jewish comedians who specialize in social satire. He is carrying on the traditions of political commentary pioneered by Lenny Bruce and Mort Sahl, traditions that few of his contemporaries are interested in exploring. Franken, though, didn't, in most public appearances, follow Bruce's use of explicit language.

Andy Kaufman was also a satirist of sorts. Before his death from lung cancer at age thirty-five, Andy Kaufman won the admiration of other comedians for daring to explore the edges of what an audience would accept. Most comedians wanted success and audience approval and did their best to please an audience. Kaufman, of course, wanted to be successful, he wanted to make audiences laugh, but he wanted to do it in very nontraditional ways. He wanted audiences to explore the very nature of humor with him.

Bob Zmuda, who would eventually write a biography of Kaufman and help produce *Man on the Moon*, a film about the comedian's life, recalls when he first saw Kaufman at Catch a Rising Star, a comedy club in Manhattan. A variety of then unknown comedians performed. (They included, among others, Jay Leno, Richard Lewis, Richard Belzer, and Elayne Boosler.) Between performances, club owner Budd Friedman would get up to introduce the next comic. Each time, an odd young man with a strange accent demanded to be let onstage. The man and Friedman would go back and forth. As the evening neared its end, Friedman introduced the "visitor from afar," Andy Kaufman.

Kaufman, wide-eyed, with a high-pitched voice and vague accent, began doing terrible imitations of Archie Bunker, Ed Sullivan, and Richard Nixon. The act was so bad that audience members began to laugh at this "comedian." Then Kaufman announced he was going to do "de Elbis Presley." The audience groaned. Then Kaufman combed his hair, raised his collar, put on a spangled jacket, set his lips at a perfect angle for an Elvis sneer, and turned around. He began singing. As Zmuda notes, "My jaw dropped. This was no impression, this *was* Elvis."

In the middle of a comedy club, Kaufman was doing what has since become known as performance art; the humor emerged from the whole unusual experience, from the entirety of the performance, not from the packaged jokes offered by all the other comedians.

Another example of his unusual approach occurred on October 11, 1975, during the premiere episode of *Saturday Night Live*. After the first sketches, Kaufman went onstage, gave his faintly weird smile, and started a record on the phonograph by his side. The theme song from *Mighty Mouse*, a cartoon show, began to play. Kaufman swayed to the music, not saying a word, until the famous refrain came on. With "Here I come to save the day," Kaufman began to lip-synch to the song. When the refrain ended, Kaufman ceased his lip-synching, only to do it again when the refrain returned. Kaufman himself never said one word. However daring such antics were, the *Saturday Night Live* audience later voted in a call-in ballot to have him removed from the show.

Kaufman's most famous performance was his April 26, 1979, performance at Carnegie Hall. The performance itself was wild. He told the audience about growing up and telling his Grandma Pearl that he would one day play Carnegie Hall and that when he did she would have the best seat. He then introduced his Grandma Pearl, flown all the way in from Florida. The little old lady walked out onstage. Kaufman then had some movers bring in her couch, which had been specially flown in as well. The couch was put at the edge of the stage. After watching the entire performance from the couch, Grandma Pearl came back up to take a bow. Grandma then took off her wig and threw it into the audience. The makeup came off. The audience could finally see that "Grandma" was in fact Robin Williams. Kaufman then hired buses to take his audience to the New York School of Printing for milk and cookies. Once there, Kaufman invited the crowd to come the next day to the Staten Island Ferry. Three hundred people showed up at one the next afternoon. Kaufman performed—and bought everyone ice cream.

Kaufman's character with the funny accent eventually became known as Foreign Man. He was later given a name on the situation comedy *Taxi*—Latka Gravas. (The first name is a Jewish food, a potato pancake.) The other actors on the sitcom found him unusual. He showed up late, didn't socialize with the others, and would stay in character even while people tried to talk to him before or after the filming.

Kaufman also developed a character named Tony Clifton, who was his alter ego. Clifton, with his dark glasses, thick face, and mustache was a semitalented lounge singer. He was the opposite of Foreign Man; he was confident, even arrogant; he was active in confronting the audience; he smoked and cursed and gambled. Based partially on Richard Belzer, once a belligerent emcee at Catch a Rising Star, the character annoyed not only fans but some of Kaufman's costars and friends as well.

Kaufman, like many performers of his generation, did not explicitly present himself as Jewish. His roots, however, become clear when seen against the backdrop of those Jewish comedians who came before him. Jerry Lewis was one clear influence, from the lip-synching to *The Nutty Professor*. Foreign Man and Tony Clifton were almost exact analogues to Julius Kelp and Buddy Love. It is this comparison that opens up an understanding of Kaufman's place. Both Lewis and Kaufman had portrayed transformational characters who had been frightened outsiders into characters who were confident insiders. The transformation, of course, was a metaphor for what had happened to Jews in America.

Jews had broken through the boundaries of American life; they had, with great success, assimilated into a foreign culture. The Marx Brothers had been the first to explore those boundaries comically. By the time such an exploration reached Kaufman it had been transformed from a searching out of how far immigrants could enter American society into how far a comedian could go. The boundaries were from comedy not society, precisely because the social boundaries had already been crossed.

Kaufman probed the most elemental of questions; he wanted us to ask not only which part of us is the real self, but also, much more radically, whether we have a real self. Kaufman has a unique and deeply disturbing answer to the identity questions of American Jews, and, by extension, to everyone. Jews aren't really cute immigrants like Latka. They aren't arrogant success stories like Tony Clifton. They may have to wrestle to prove their mettle, but they're not even genuine wrestlers. In Andy Kaufman's vision, a Jewish identity in America is completely extinguished and is covered up by a series of interchangeable masks. There are hints of such a view in the Marx Brothers, who emphasized their own interchangeability in key sequences such as the mirror scene in *Duck Soup*, though for them there was a real Jewish self underneath that the majority culture wanted to cover. By Kaufman's time, the real self, covered up for so long, no longer existed. The heat and exhaustion caused by having to wear masks in America melted the faces under the masks. Kaufman's pained, deliberately noncomedic struggles were a cry from the heart that audiences didn't understand.

Kaufman may have confused audiences, but he never used explicit language. Others did, however. By the late 1980s and especially the 1990s, the blue material that had been restricted to strip clubs and Las Vegas was prominent in most comedy clubs. This was partly the result of the enormous popularity of several comedians (among them George Carlin, Richard Pryor, and Eddie Murphy) whose routines were as profane as they were hysterical. Some Jewish comedians had also contributed to this trend.

Richard Belzer carried the Rickles approach further. Audiences were far less sure than they had been of Rickles that Belzer was not serious. Belzer came from a difficult family life, and he kept being kicked out of schools. "God expelled me from Hebrew school—personally," he said. Still, he knew he was funny even as he was getting kicked out. Discharged from the army, Belzer struggled with his despair. Finally, in 1971, he won a part on *The Groove Tube*, an underground movie that achieved a cult following. He then entered stand-up. He became well known among comedians for his work at Catch a Rising Star, where, jazzlike, his mind would wander from subject to subject, and where he browbeat audiences. Later, after a bout with cancer, Belzer entered television with great success, starring first on *Homicide* and then on *Law and Order: Special Victims Unit*.

Belzer explicitly sees himself as carrying on a Jewish tradition of employing social satire.

I consider myself a badchen. Badchens would be in the shtetl. They would shmooze with the bride's family and the groom's family. Then, after the ceremony, they'd get up on a table for two hours or more and they would make fun of everybody there.

They were scandalous, filled with gossip. They'd say things like "The butcher's fooling around with the goat man's daughter." Also, they were very dirty, even vicious. Their essence was to expose and make fun of things in their society. The badchen's society was the shtetl. We expand to include the whole society.

Howard Stern, like Belzer, is as much a performance artist as a comedian. The comedy comes from the overall high-wire act of listening to radio (or watching on television) to see what Stern will do next. The humor comes from going to the edge of the boundaries of decency, of personal intrusion, of appropriate subject matter. Stern, a self-styled shock jock, sometimes tries to walk some very tight ropes between being outrageous and being cruel and between being daring and being embarrassing. Soon after the singer Selena was shot, Stern played gunshot sound effects when talking about Hispanic music. He claimed Rodney King deserved to be beaten and Magic Johnson deserved to be infected with HIV. On television a male guest was literally caught with his pants down. Stern entices numerous women to bare various body parts.

Many people find Stern so offensive they won't tune in to his show, but he has more than 18 million radio listeners and more than 40 million television viewers. He clearly speaks to and for a significant segment of the culture. Stern says and does what his audience members might like to say and do but are restrained by the legal and social controls of society. In this sense, he is a safety valve, a release for the audience; Stern's detractors might also see him providing his listeners a model for what most in the society deem inappropriate social behavior. Stern's social satire is different from a Lenny Bruce or Al Franken. Stern seems less to enjoy mocking social conventions than to act as though he is ignorant of them. His asking any question that comes to his mind, giving voice to any thought, no matter how outrageous, might be seen as a frontal assault on political correctness. But such behavior can also be seen as a perverse innocence, a curiosity refusing to be fettered by the mores of a prevailing culture. Stern's is an unleashed id unrepressed by socially approved feelings. His is an attack on society's right to censor the honest feelings of the individual.

Also like Andy Kaufman and Jerry Lewis, Stern reportedly has two sides. One part of him is supposed to be the kind family man who loves his daughters, who only reluctantly separated from his wife, to whom he had been faithful, even if the fidelity was tested by daily, public temptation. He used his wife to demean himself, as Jack Benny would have had he been on radio in the late 1980s and 1990s. As Stern wrote in *Private Parts*: "Dr. Kinsey reported that two minutes was the average duration for a man to achieve orgasm while lovemaking, and that's about how long it takes me. Of course, I'm including the time it takes for Alison and me to walk up the stairs and get to the bedroom." The other part of Stern is his image as the bad boy of radio, the thrill-seeking host who never has an unuttered dirty thought. Stern, too, is interested in boundaries. It is not an accident that he once described himself incorrectly as only half-Jewish. Although he suggested such a claim was made to forestall anti-Semitism, it is just as possible to see it as a genuine struggle to search for his real self.

Stern crucially differs from Kaufman and Lewis, though, in one vital aspect. Instead of playing parts, Stern is always Howard Stern. It is "Howard Stern" who is both characters. Defining which, if either, is "real" is difficult. Stern himself has often said the radio personality is the real him, though such an assertion may be part of the deliberate and commercially successful effort to blur the two. In this sense, Stern's comic ancestors were Jack Benny and George Burns, who used their real names but created comic alter egos in their programs. It may not be an accident that, just as Benny and Burns were most successful on radio, so, too, is Stern. It is his natural medium. Stern's quick tongue, his ability to interrogate, and sometimes browbeat or ridicule, his guests, and his rich, explicit language all work best in a verbal medium, one in which his strengths are not diffused by supplementary senses.

There was, as could be expected, a reaction to what many Americans perceived as a disturbing coarsening of the culture. They did not see a new generation with different experiences having a different sense of the comic. Instead, they saw a decline in moral standards and behavior illustrated by behavior previously considered wrong (such as adultery or bearing a child out of wedlock). This behavior, it was asserted, was reflected in the media in such a way as to offer at the very least approval and at the very worst a goad to others to emulate that dangerous behavior. Some even thought the media were the leading cheerleaders of the purported moral laxity. Some evangelical Christians and Orthodox Jews took the lead in such a reaction. It was politically reflected in the election of Ronald Reagan as president in 1980 and 1984.

Layered on top of the social changes and the reaction to them was a major shift of power in the world. With the end of the cold war, Americans found new justification for the concentration on self that had begun in the 1970s. Such a focus was now clearly allowable because there was no enemy forcing a focus on the wider world.

A new comedic figure emerged in such a world: the young, cute more than handsome, nonneurotic, clean Jewish male who spoke of personal lives rather than social problems, who made small observations and not large pronouncements. The rise of the observational comics was profoundly affected by social changes and the new economy. The social world of the breakup of marriages and families, the increasing focus on self rather than on community or social issues, the rise of ethnicity as superseding an overarching American identity, and the quickened images of life presented by television (and by many illegal drugs) all added to an enormous increase in the discontinuities of life. The center didn't hold, and the amazing array of stimuli confused many people. They found it easier to focus on the small matters of life.

The audience embrace of these fresh-faced Jewish comedians with their seemingly innocent, sweet smiles was a reaction to the perceived coarsening of the culture. It is no accident, for example, that Jerry Seinfeld and Paul Reiser were extraordinarily clean comedians. They represented a desire on the part of a large segment of the audience to retreat, in part, from the hard edges of contemporary comedy.

The galloping economy was also crucial. In order for comedians to make observations, there had to be a presumption that the items that were the subjects of observation were widely available. People had to have money, they had to spend money, and there had to be adequate technology to build enough new objects so that comedians would have new materials. The technology-driven economy of the 1990s produced a wide variety of products that allowed for observation. It was a long way from Shelley Berman's simple telephone.

Observational humor had its own innate rules. Its purpose was to help people deal with the dislocations of social life. To do that, observational humor used irony, a sort of humor in which the opposite of what is said is meant. Subverting the obvious meaning and finding the real meaning underneath subtly made it seem that the social discontinuities of the era (and the economic struggles of the late 1970s and the 1980s) had a deeper meaning underneath, a real one.

The cuteness and the Jewishness of these performers were also important. They appeared clean-cut, very far from Howard Stern's long hair or Richard Belzer's dark sunglasses. The physical attractiveness was standard television fare; people had to look good on the tube to be stars. Otherwise, they were members of the supporting cast. But the Jewishness was also crucial. As they always had, American audiences saw Jews as having survived the hardships they were currently encountering. In the 1990s, Americans desperately felt a loss of family and community. They found Jewish comedians especially attractive because those comedians represented in their minds the basic family and communal values in Jewish life, values that were deeply prized in a seemingly disintegrating society. These young Jewish men were crucially different from the models provided by earlier Jewish comedians. By the 1990s the Jewish family member who provided leadership and a model was not the *Yiddische* mama but the cute son. Americans saw such a son as a good marriage catch, a good son-in-law, a friendly, funny, nice guy. The son took care of the parents.

This variant should not erase the fundamental connection between the *Yiddische* mama and the son. All Jewish comedy presupposed a belief in family and community. Even in the complaints about a spouse or sibling or child, audiences could hear the underlying love, the unbroken attachment they so wished to find in their own lives. So, once again, it was time to turn to the Jews to provide answers to the survival concerns of the culture.

David Brenner grafted his observations onto the smooth delivery of the many lounge and television comedians who had come before him. Whereas others explored the borders of acceptable language, or pondered the suddenly not very mysterious aspects of sexual relationships, Brenner stuck with clean language and common subjects: "I think the funniest fans of all have to be golf fans. I mean that's a great sport. The guy hits the ball and then all the fans follow him. Could you see that like in baseball? A guy gets a hit, 'Okay everyone, first base. Come on.'" Using his rich South Philadelphia experiences as a background, Brenner told stories that never resorted to coarseness even when he'd describe the rough neighborhood he grew up in: "I went to a bar once and said, 'What do you have on ice?' The bartender said, 'You wouldn't know him.'"

Brenner's extraordinary rise was interrupted by the failure of a talk show he hosted and family problems. He came back, though, with an approach that would have been unthinkable to an earlier generation of Jewish comedians. On February 19, 2000, Brenner starred in an HBO comedy special. For most of the performance, Brenner did a smooth, funny series of routines. Then, near the end of the program he began speaking of the woman he loved. He announced that he intended to get married. In fact, he intended to get married then and there. The bride came out. A rabbi on wires flew through the air. Brenner laughed as he recalled the scene: "The rabbi was scared. He hadn't had a chance to rehearse because it was the Sabbath. We didn't tell anyone. We wanted it to be a complete surprise." It was impossible to imagine Jack Benny or George Burns having a Jewish wedding onstage—and it was a sign of how far Jewish comedians had come.

Jerry Seinfeld's television universe was, like one of Brenner's routines, filled with small observations. Seinfeld had been attracted to comedy early. When he was eight, he saw a comedian on Ed Sullivan's show. The act, and the audience's appreciative laughter, provided a shock of recognition for the young boy. He knew he wanted to make people laugh. He began to watch endless hours of television, searching out the comedians, observing their manners and material. Despite his inauspicious debut at Catch a Rising Star, Seinfeld continued to perform onstage. He did well in New York, but Seinfeld never confused activity with achievement. He was working but not getting ahead. So he moved to Los Angeles where he landed a brief role on the situation comedy *Benson*.

He began to develop his early trademark lines such as "If I'm the best man, why is she marrying him?" He talked about a detergent commercial in which a woman brags that she could remove bloodstains. Seinfeld noted, "If you get a T-shirt with bloodstains, maybe laundry is not your problem now."

Seinfeld was a skillful writer. He carefully constructed his jokes and refused to use obscene language. "I made rules that I wouldn't use profanity because it was a more interesting game for me to try and do certain material or certain subjects without going over the line." He knew swearing released anger, but he wasn't so much angry as bemused or frustrated, with relief coming through cleverness and close observation.

In November 1988, Seinfeld went to see Larry David, widely admired among comedians for his quick mind and writing abilities but hampered in his career by self-admitted neuroses, shyness, and a willingness to confront what he frequently considered an under-appreciative audience by yelling at them or walking offstage.

Seinfeld had been speaking with NBC about starting a television show but didn't know what the series would be about. Sharing a taxi back to the West Side in New York, the two stopped at a grocery store. As they walked the aisles, they joked about the products they saw. David suddenly said, "See, this is what the show would be." Seinfeld immediately grasped the idea of finding humor in everyday activities.

They continued to talk about the show, and during ten electric minutes at the Westway Diner on Ninth Avenue they jointly came up with the initial idea for what, after some evolution, would later become one of the most successful sitcoms in television history: Describe the experiences during which comedians gather material for their performances. Jerry would play a stand-up comedian seeking material that would then be seen performed in an act at the end.

Seinfeld and David went to see Warren Littlefield, president of entertainment at NBC. Contrary to legend, though, David did not present their idea as "a show about nothing." Instead, he suggested that the humor would come from conversations more than situations. The standard story line would be much less important. Littlefield didn't like it, and David, outraged at what he saw as corporate comedic myopia, told Littlefield exactly how he felt. But one executive in the room, Rick Ludwin, offered to put up the funding for a pilot. The rest has become part of the legend of television.

Seinfeld's story was part of a long and happy saga of Jewish comedians finding a congenial home on American television. Many of them, however, succeeded only after a long struggle.

On his television show, Seinfeld dealt with several intimate subjects, including masturbation; the winner of a contest to refrain was to be known—in words that became a national catchphrase—as the "master of his domain." Always, though, the subjects in the show were handled with deftness. "It's funny," he said, "to be delicate with something that's explosive." It's hard to find another comedy manifesto more at odds with that of Howard Stern. This choice was crucial. Just as Jewish vaudevillians and later comics had used code words to include Jewish material while appearing to be completely within an American tradition, Seinfeld and David used code words to include very adult material while their language remained completely clean.

Seinfeld's appeal was as someone who was, in Carl Reiner's words, "sweet and funny." Reiner saw the combination as rare. However, Seinfeld's television success depended on more than a cute smile, a well-wrought line, and clean observational humor. That combination had worked well in the clubs, but on 1990s television more was needed. Had Seinfeld simply translated his act onto the screen, the show would not have been as successful.

The success came from the grafting of the sweet and funny real Jerry Seinfeld with the selfish and self-absorbed television Jerry Seinfeld. Jerry and his friends—George (Jason Alexander), Elaine

(Julia Louis-Dreyfus), and Kramer (Michael Richards)— cheated, lied, and used each other for their own ends. Despite these traits, however, the characters remained lovable, and the four remained friends. Seinfeld's universe, that is, is cynical and unsentimental. It is filled with small failures.

The depressive George, the emotionally distant Jerry, the self-centered Elaine, and the perpetually failing Kramer may seem to be odd characters. The relationship among characters, though, goes right back to Jack Benny. Benny let his audience laugh at him, and in doing so they laughed at those parts of themselves they recognized and perhaps felt guilty about. The young audiences that watched *Seinfeld* got the same kind of emotional release. Laughing at the self-absorbed characters provided a profound letting go of tensions collected from confronting those same characteristics they found in themselves. In the '30s, Benny's audiences were forced to be cheap and wanted someone who could simultaneously make them laugh about that cheapness while giving them permission to keep being cheap. In the '90s, the *Seinfeld* audience wanted to focus on their own self-interests, and they, too, wanted to laugh about it while being given emotional permission to continue.

Comparisons to the Benny show don't stop there. Like that show, *Seinfeld* has much more dialogue than other contemporary shows (its scripts were as long as seventy pages, about twenty pages longer than other scripts). The excess of language betrays a nervousness, a distinctly urban and distinctly Jewish approach to dealing with anxiety. Seinfeld, like Benny, is the main character, though he often lets himself be the straight man while the other characters crack jokes around him.

The characters in the show are unable to commit to a stable romantic relationship. Jerry, for example, is a perfectionist, always finding flaws in the women he meets. The profound Jewish sensibility of the show provides such a relationship phobia with another dimension. The characters' inability to commit to a partner or to maturity itself is a metaphor for their inability to commit to an identity. The long-standing tension between Jewish and American identities is partially overcome in *Seinfeld* by having the characters not choose at all, by refusing to be grown up enough to have to choose. Whereas Woody Allen struggled to define his identity, the *Seinfeld* characters avoid any such conflict. They don't see the value in their parents' struggles. They don't see the intellectual or artistic challenges in constructing an identity. They want comfort, not confusion.

Jerry does finally say that he's Jewish—to a priest in a confessional where he's gone to complain about a dentist who became Jewish just for the jokes. The Jewish identity is peripheral, however. It does not define him. As he tells the priest, he is not offended by the dentist as a Jew but as a comedian. It is as a comedian that he sees life, though with a Jewish comedian's sensibility: clear-eyed observations about life, a sense of annoyance at having to deal with life's petty travails, and as someone smaller than others. This last point is important. Seinfeld once wrote, "As a kid I was small for my age, and when you're small, you like small things. In fact, that's what a joke is, a crystallized observation, a small precision-crafted nugget of truth." Many Jewish comedians are small or were small as children. This physical characteristic might be considered the source of a psychological feeling of being without power, of having to rely on humor to protect themselves—very much like the Jews in history. Seinfeld's view renders size unimportant as a psychological impediment; indeed, it is valuable as a way to see truth and an unusual explanation of jokes as particularly Jewish constructions.

Still, though Seinfeld named his show after himself, he could have called it *Jerry*. He deliberately used his very Jewish-sounding last name. Jerry Seinfeld was at home in America. He—and the networks—felt no need to hide his Jewishness and felt no embarrassment at displaying it.

Seinfeld's cynicism ran deep. The family comedies of the 1950s and 1960s had given way to the social comedies or comedies in which coworkers substituted for traditional families. In both of these the morality passed on by the family continued to be transmitted through other means. By the late 1980s and early 1990s the gruesomely dysfunctional family shows that appeared were almost gleeful in their mockery of such values.

Seinfeld found a way to express that same moral anarchy in a different way. The amoral perpetual adolescents of *Seinfeld* not only found comfort in each other's company but also believed their views were justified by the sober realities of a cynical world. They tried to do good deeds. Jerry and George decided to visit a boy who had to live in a bubble. The boy fights with George over a game of Trivial Pursuit and asks George's girlfriend to strip. That, too, is *Seinfeld*'s universe: a world in which good deeds always backfire and, therefore, a world in which it is crucial to forge a separate peace with a few friends. It is all right, maybe even moral, not to want to grow up in such a world. The purported amorality of adolescence is, rather, its own bubble, its protection against having to join the hypocritical adult world. This was a message that Americans found congenial—and, with Seinfeld's comic touches, funny. But *Seinfeld* had a message that was ultimately subtler than just a justification of amorality. There was a recognition of legitimate adult responsibility, though that responsibility was seen as an obligation for the future, an obligation the characters were not yet prepared for. For example, in one famous episode, Jerry's parents visit him and intrude when he and his girlfriend are kissing. Jerry, a loving son, insists they remain even after they offer to leave. Several days later, Jerry and the young woman are watching *Schindler's List*. Their frustrated lust bubbles over during the film, and they start kissing in the theater. The adolescent sexual urges trump the appropriate adult response to others' suffering and the obligation to be concerned about it.

The world of *Seinfeld* was one in which the characters relied on each other to justify their existence but recognized that eventually they would have to become adults. The series finale, with its punishment in jail for their refusal to help an overweight man who is being carjacked, was a clever final chapter, for after that purgation they would presumably have grown up. When they did, the show could not go on because they would be so different.

Larry David surely deserves an enormous amount of credit for the show's success. It was his neurotic slant, his hard-to-believe but real experiences that formed the basis for many plot lines, and his writing abilities that formed the perfect complement to Jerry Seinfeld's extraordinary skills as a writer and performer.

The irony of *Seinfeld* is that it prided itself as being a show about nothing, but it was really a complex guide to the deepest needs of the American mind.

Paul Reiser, like Jerry Seinfeld, was a clean, observational comedian. Any anxiety was tempered and transformed, in a direct line from Alan King, into a concern for what's troublesome. There was no disillusionment in him or Seinfeld. They seemed calm, ready to take on life, even if the life was irksome.

Reiser found success in much the same way Seinfeld did. In his situation comedy, *Mad about You*, which debuted in 1992, Reiser shrewdly reversed a George-and-Gracie approach to comedy. Instead of his television wife (played by Helen Hunt) being perpetually confused and Reiser playing a loving and bemused partner, Reiser took the Gracie part. It was a clever device, deftly avoiding accusations of demeaning women and taking advantage of the basic comedy structure that had worked for so many decades for Burns and Allen while allowing for quick and realistic dialogue.

Reiser was a traditionalist in another way. In his show and his books, he sought to define the tiny gestures members of a couple need to make for a happy marriage. Reiser wasn't the sort of Jewish comedian who needed therapy, or the Jewish comedian who became a communal mental therapist but who also needed therapy. He became a sane comedy-therapist providing humorous hints for marital contentment. He dealt head-on with the assignment of household chores, ways to deal with eccentric relatives, and the bothersome habits of a spouse that gnaw at emotional satisfaction. His response to the dissolution of a stable self and the chaos of society was, armed with humor, to retreat to traditional marriage. His charming model for American husbands, though, worked more because of the humor than the effectiveness of the model. Despite this emphasis on family, Reiser studiously avoided giving his character, Paul Buchman, a clearly Jewish identity.

In contrast to Reiser's character, Jon Stewart is deliberately and overtly Jewish, injecting his identity into a large amount of his material as the host of *The Daily Show*. Stewart attended William and Mary, where his Jewish identity was forged in part by encountering "boys with eight first names, which also happened to be the names of Confederate generals, but who went by 'Trip.'" Once, at the Friars Club Comedy Festival, Stewart saw a group of famous comedians. He stood still, planning to go talk to them. Suddenly, though, they were headed toward him; he was standing by the elevator. Jerry Lewis was speaking about a tiny club in which "people were packed so tight, you couldn't do *this* without hitting somebody." As Lewis said "*this*," he stretched his arms out. His fist connected with Jon Stewart. Stewart went down. The elevator opened and, ignoring poor Stewart, the comedians walked inside.

Despite such an introduction to his heroes, Stewart plunged onward. He got his start at the Bitter End in New York. He hosted a show on MTV and appeared on *The Larry Sanders Show* before becoming the host on *The Daily Show.* Stewart's observations are different from Seinfeld's and Reiser's—more political and often laced with social satire. Of course, Stewart appears on cable, a more hospitable environment for such humor.

But, content aside, Stewart's appeal is utterly similar to that of others in this group of young Jewish comedians. He looks like a sweet, ordinary guy viewers would love to have over to dinner. He's safe, witty, one of the audience who somehow managed to lead a successful comedian's life.

Rob Reiner, Carl Reiner's son, costarred in the trailblazing television series *All in the Family* and has directed many successful films, including such comedies as *This Is Spinal Tap* and *When Harry Met Sally. . . ,* but, despite his clear comic gifts, he has generally refrained from acting in movies (except in small parts) and from writing a distinctly personal comic film.

Ben Stiller and Adam Sandler also belong in the group of sweet Jewish comedians, but unlike the television and club comedians and unlike Billy Crystal, their sweetness rests alongside a cruder humor; they inhabit the space between Seinfeld and Stern.

Stiller, the son of Jerry Stiller and Anne Meara, grew up around television. By his teens, Stiller was borrowing his father's super-8 camera and making parodies of popular films. Stiller was eventually hired as a writer for *Saturday Night Live.* He also created a television show that ran opposite *60 Minutes* and predictably failed. In films such as *There's Something about Mary*, *Meet the Parents*, and *Keeping the Faith*, Stiller created a coherent character—a rabbi no less—in the last film.

Adam Sandler's scatological references are a far cry from Seinfeld's hygienically clean act, and his silly voices and fraternity antics make some critics wince. Nevertheless, Sandler has found a crucial spot in the comedy of his generation. His films are about the anxiety of growing up, about the need to reconcile with family, and about taking responsibility. In *Billy Madison,* for example, Sandler's father is wealthy and powerful. He forces his son to go through school again, grade by grade. This premise allows Sandler to act like a child but also to grow up. By the end of the film, Billy becomes a teacher and reconciles with his father.

The Waterboy is Sandler's most perfect realization of what he wants to say about the pain of being young. Bobby Boucher, the main character, is thirty-one, a sexual innocent who lives with his manipulative but loving mother and has a serious problem controlling his temper.

Rodney Dangerfield's comic character can resort to sorrow and self-mockery when he doesn't get respect. Adam Sandler's character wants to release his anger more violently. Bobby's intensity, his innocence, his unfair treatment by the world, and his final triumph make him, as the movie explicitly suggests, an inspiration to the plain, charmless, and uncool.

Sandler has developed an alternate strategy to transform the self. Jerry Lewis's professor used knowledge and science to make the transformation, only to realize finally that the original self was the better one. Andy Kaufman believed that in trying to create a new self the real one was irreparably corroded. But Sandler believes the old self can provide the fuel (made up of an unusual compound of romantic innocence and seething anger) to create a new self, a self that finds family reconciliation and love and gets abundant social recognition.

Part of Sandler's character comes from his Jewish heritage. The emphasis on family and family reconciliation so prominent in Sandler's films is embedded in Jewish life. Sandler, famously proud of being Jewish, draws on those traditions to recognize not just what his Jewish generation needed but also what all young people of the generation needed. Indeed, part of his movement toward maturity is precisely his willingness to embrace an identity that transcends his individual self. Sandler's bold identification as a Jew is most prominent in a novelty number. His Hanukkah song, first performed on *Saturday Night Live*, has become an ethnic anthem with its cataloging of well-known Jews.

The open pride and the public declaration of Jewishness in such a song would have embarrassed earlier Jewish generations. Sandler, though, is right at home. He, like his generation, doesn't have to or want to hide being Jewish or feel any shame either. In this sense, there is a great irony. The earlier generations had a much more intimate relationship with their Jewishness; it enveloped and penetrated them. Yet, with all that, they were (often justifiably) reluctant to express their identity in a public forum. This new generation, with far more tenuous Jewish connections, has been freed to express just such an identity.

In part they could do this because, unlike their grandparents, the Jewish aspect of their identity often shared the sense of identity with alternate means of self-identification. This allowed the inheritance of Jewish values to influence other parts of the identity and vice versa.

Their situation perfectly reflected the lives of all American Jews—just as they are fully accepted into the culture they are increasingly unconcerned about the communal effects of interfaith marriages or assimilation. American life has been so comfortable for them that they have lost their true identities. Andy Kaufman was wrong, though. Although the inner identity eroded, a new one developed in its place, an identity that was a true graft. The future of American Jews and Jewish comedians will in part be determined by how they finally balance their American and Jewish identities. It is Adam Sandler, perched precariously between an identity of the past and one of the future who represents this dilemma for the current generation.

10

KOSHER
AT LAST

JEWISH WOMEN COMEDIANS

She was still struggling for recognition as a comedian. Billed as "Pepper January—Comedy with Spice," she faced a hostile audience. The raucous men seated at the tables had a very definite set of ideas about the men and women who stood in front of them to provide entertainment: the men were supposed to tell jokes, and the women were supposed to take their clothes off. Here, though, was this thin, loud woman trying to tell them jokes. The audience members began booing.

Joan Molinsky needed a change. She went to see a theatrical agent named Tony Rivers, a large, handsome Native American. Rivers told Molinsky: "I can't speak to anybody today. I just put my poodle to sleep." She went back the next day, and he decided to send her on an important audition, but, he said, "I can't send you out as Joan Molinsky. You've got to change your name." She looked at him and said, "Okay, I'll be Joan Rivers."

It would take some time, but the newly named Joan Rivers would eventually become one of America's most famous comedians. As a woman, she had to overcome enormous obstacles—including a very particular view of Jewish women.

It was Jewish comedians, almost exclusively male, who had helped introduce American audiences to Jewish women and who had shaped audience perceptions of what those Jewish women were like. George Jessel, Sam Levenson, and others had talked about their *Yiddische* mamas. Buoyed by images supplied by such women comedians as Gertrude Berg, the *Yiddische* mama was sentimentally seen as warm, perhaps gently meddling, but selflessly kind. These immigrant Jewish women, or their daughters, were self-sacrificing and willing to help their children in any way, especially their sons. They most of all provided unflappable emotional support, even if such support was unmerited or unwanted. Alternative stereotypes for Jewish women, such as the Red Hot Mama embodied by Sophie Tucker, were isolated to show business and didn't outlast the particular personalities who projected them.

After World War II, Catskill humor instilled a deep hostility toward women and mothers. These new images of women included the idea of a woman who was much more financially demanding than the immigrant Jewish mother and even more emotionally suffocating in a grotesque exaggeration of the genuine motherly concern. Jewish women were presented as frigid and materialistic, lost in the kitchen and quiet in the bedroom.

What happened? Why did the image of Jewish women change, and what did the jokes about Jewish women have to say about the male Jewish comedians who told the jokes and the Jewish and Gentile, male and female, audiences that laughed?

Several crucial changes in the society were at work. The children growing up and leaving suburban homes to start families of their own were both uncomfortable leaving yet anxious to get away. They felt guilty about abandoning their loving mother but angry that those mothers wished to keep them home.

There was also increasing anxiety right after the war about sex as the *Kinsey Report* was published, birth control pills became widely available and morally acceptable, and *Playboy* became the reading material of choice for young men. Gender roles became more elastic and more difficult to comprehend. Women were increasingly perceived as a source of sexual confusion, and thus a threat, because they were no longer just future wives; they could now be playmates, lovers, or one-night stands, too. With the increasing number of these possible sexual alternative roles, men became much more anxious about how to act toward women and how to view them, and women, seeing the sudden increase in possible selves, felt liberated or anxious or both. Were they principally sexual objects, as *Playboy* proposed, or were they principally potential mates, as their parents insisted?

The male Jewish comedians who joked about women were part of the wider American culture, of course, the culture that was moving to the suburbs, but they were also living at a particular moment in American Jewish history. They were still anxious about successfully assimilating into American society, a goal that had seemed unattainable to their grandparents and obvious and easy to their grandchildren. This anxiety about being true Americans made them reject what was foreign to America.

The author Riv-Ellen Prell suggests that Jewish women represented the very tradition these Jewish male comedians were worried would retard their entrance into American society. Jewish women were quite literally the way of continuing the separate Jewish life many of these comedians longed to leave.

Some of the male Jewish comedians began telling jokes about Jewish women, jokes with a peculiar characteristic. In a normal joke there is often a winner and a loser. What made the jokes by Jewish males about Jewish females different is that there was no winner. The woman was cruel or materialistic or frigid, and the man was her victim. The fact that everyone in the joke is a loser reveals a lingering, deep anxiety.

Jewish men of that generation who had successfully assimilated were concerned that women's success might compromise their own. The comedic targets also revealed a continuing sense of insecurity. In reality, these successful male comedians were very far from earlier generations of American Jews. But they were uncomfortable with their very success. By portraying themselves as subject to feminine tyranny, male Jewish comedians maintained a sense of oppression and therefore believed themselves justified in continuing their stance of self-deprecation.

There were women comedians of the era, most famously Lucille Ball, who were not Jewish. But Jewish women had a much tougher time. The postwar pioneers, Totie Fields and Joan Rivers, met enormous resistance, and both of them justifiably felt a great deal of anger. Once she had succeeded, Totie Fields maintained a demand in her contract that there be exactly twelve coffee cups in her dressing room. A quarter-century earlier, she hadn't been able to get even one cup.

Audiences simply would not accept an assertive woman, so a female stand-up comedian had to be unthreatening. But the ability of the comedian to evoke laughter was really a way of exerting control. This, of course, was one of the reasons comedy was so attractive to Jews who had been powerless for so long. Women who did stand-up comedy, though, were not supposed to exert a comparable amount of power. Such women were branded as aggressive, a term of profound disapproval in the fifties and early sixties.

Jewish women, that is, were the "new" Jews, the unaccepted minority, the people seeking power who were not allowed to gain entrance into society, in this case the society of comedians.

The Jewish women who entered comedy, therefore, were powerless and had little support. They had no Jewish wives to belittle and, for a long while, had to be careful about attacking husbands the way the male comedians attacked their wives; at the time no one laughed at jokes about Jewish husbands.

Unable to engage normal comedic targets, Totie Fields, like other women, was stuck making fun of herself, specifically her weight. "I never let myself get over 110. I'm swollen, that's my problem. I have the same measurements as Elizabeth Taylor. Her living room is nine by twelve, and so is mine." It could be, in some ways, a depressing display of the victim doing her best to manage and even prosper in a hostile environment.

Fields eventually had a leg amputated and, characteristically, used to joke that "at least I have a leg to stand on." But this almost cruel self-mockery somehow gave her the strength to go out and perform.

Joan Rivers built on Fields's success, but Rivers was funnier, with a sharper mind and a sharper delivery. She still had to tell self-mocking jokes such as "On our wedding night, my husband said, 'Can I help you with the buttons?' I was naked at the time" or "Stagehands saw me naked. One threw up and the other turned gay." At her wedding, she claimed, "When the rabbi said, 'Do you take this woman?' sixteen guys said, 'We have.'" The loose sexual morals, though, were complemented by what she claimed was her lack of attractiveness: "I have no sex appeal. If my husband did not toss and turn in his sleep, we never would have had the kid."

Rivers's experiences at Second City were crucial. She was in conflict with the others in the group because she wanted to do jokes, and many at Second City wanted to focus on a collective effort that let humor emerge from the situation they were performing. Still, her efforts let Rivers become more comfortable in trusting the sudden outbursts that came from her own mind.

The real turning point for her, though, was in watching Lenny Bruce perform in 1962. She saw in Bruce the sort of comedy she wanted to perform, a comedy that came from personal, intimate experiences, a direct and honest approach. Rivers was not interested in the political and religious confrontations that came to dominate Bruce's material, but she was deeply impressed by his delivery style. She transformed his blunt obscenity into softer words such as *tramp* or *slut*. She also made a deliberate choice. She went for the large lower middle class; indeed, she liked to quote William Randolph Hearst: "If you write for the classes, you eat with the masses, and if you write for the masses, you eat with the classes." She spoke quickly, using a large number of one-liners, in a technique that worked so well for people such as Henny Youngman.

Rivers shrewdly mined both sides of the stereotype for material. Her persona may have been pampered and spoiled and sexually unattractive, but that persona also subtly played off a power to manipulate, and Rivers manipulated audiences brilliantly. She did this especially well in confronting the image of women that most pleased men: the satisfied housewife. She would urge the women in the audience to avoid being good housekeepers: "Don't cook. Don't clean. No man will ever make love to a woman because she waxed the linoleum—'My God, the floor's immaculate. Lie down, you hot bitch.'"

One day Rivers saw Elizabeth Taylor, long a model of perfect beauty, on the cover of *People*. Taylor had clearly put on weight, and Rivers began telling jokes about Taylor's appearance: "She has more chins than a Chinese phone book" or "I took her to McDonald's just to watch her eat and watch the numbers change." (At the time the restaurant chain took pride in listing outside each store the number of hamburgers sold by the entire company.) Attacking other celebrities soon followed. Bo Derek, also a model of perfect beauty, "studies for a pap test," or she's so stupid that "when she sees a sign that says 'Wet Floor' she does."

The lost attractiveness of Taylor and the purportedly flawed attractiveness of Derek were vital to the Rivers persona. She was mocking the male images of beauty; they either don't last or are compromised. Joan Rivers had found a way for ordinary women to fight back.

Caught in her era, Rivers delivered lines that the audience wanted, lines that today seem deprecatory to women. A fuller view, though, reveals Rivers as a sort of heroine, a woman who not only found a way to fight and win at a man's game but also subtly succeeded at subverting the rules that kept her from being allowed to use the humor her male counterparts could. She talked about herself and about women's issues, subjects that were not on the comedic radar of the era.

Joan Rivers proved that a woman could succeed, clearing a path for other women. Those women would still have to fight, and they would have to make the journey from self-mockery to self-pride. But without Joan Rivers, that journey would have been a lot more difficult.

The change from self-mockery to self-assertion came in the mid-1970s and early 1980s for a number of reasons. The general society had changed, adapting, often with difficulty, to the new roles of women. In the entertainment world a large number of comedy clubs opened, some of them owned by women. The burgeoning number of clubs and the embryonic cable television industry required an enormous number of new, cheap comedians. More women working in the society also meant women having more money to spend on leisure and a wider array of common experiences from which to draw humor.

Elayne Boosler, called "the Jackie Robinson of my generation" by Richard Lewis, emerged in this new world. Seeking to be a singer, she found herself at the Improv, first as a waitress but eventually introducing the new comics. Finally, she began to include some comic bits in those introductions. Boosler developed an easy delivery and found a comic geography located halfway between Joan Rivers and the more blatant comedians such as Roseanne who would follow her. She kept some of the fat jokes ("I'm so compulsive about losing weight, I weigh myself after I cough") but also directly fired some shots from the women's side of the gender wars: "Men don't live well by themselves. They don't even live like people. They live like bears with furniture."

Like many female comedians starting out, especially attractive ones, Boosler faced hecklers, but she was always ready. When someone called out "Take it off!" she yelled back, "I can't. I have a cold." This was a double victory. The response allowed her to assert the control a comedian needs over an audience, and it verified for the audience that she was funny without being offensive.

Boosler, though, also had an edge, a sharp social satire that could be let loose in a post–Lenny Bruce world: "The Vatican came down with a new ruling. They said no surrogate mothers . . . A good thing they didn't make this rule before Jesus was born."

Unlike Rivers's part-princess approach, Boosler played off more traditional Jewish humor, going back to stock responses from the '50s but updating them for the new era: "My brother's gay. My parents don't mind as long as he marries a doctor." As with Jewish male comedians, the Jewishness of female comedians, though varied, was much less intense than in earlier generations. There were vestiges, hints, some examples of pride, but mostly their Jewishness was just one more part of their identity. Jewish women, after all, were meeting a lot more resistance because they were women than because they were Jews.

Despite her cleverness and her ability to mix and match comedy subjects in a changing world, Boosler was still living in a male-controlled business. Once she was scheduled to perform on *The Tonight Show*. As usual, she had carefully prepared her act. The show's producers, however, decided she needed someone to write her jokes for her. The first joke she was given to perform was "I'm so ugly, I can't make a nickel on a battleship." Boosler refused to go on the show, which took enormous courage because it was the principal venue for comedic talent in the country.

While Carol Leifer was at Binghamton University studying theater, her boyfriend had a burning urge to be a stand-up comic. One evening Leifer went with him to Catch a Rising Star for the open-mike night. The boyfriend, Paul Reiser, got up onstage. Leifer was impressed, and soon she decided to audition for herself at the Comic Strip in New York City. The emcee who introduced her was Jerry Seinfeld. Like Reiser and Seinfeld, Leifer became especially good at observational humor. (It's no surprise that she later was story editor for *Seinfeld*.) Leifer herself had married a Southern Baptist and used intermarriage for humor, especially after her divorce: "I was part of a mixed marriage. I'm human; he's a Klingon."

Rita Rudner similarly worked hard to develop her persona. She went to the library, getting books and comedy recordings. Then she went to the Museum of Broadcasting to look at older television shows. Slowly, carefully, professionally, she developed those crucial first few minutes of material.

Rudner's approach was clever. She took the traditional Dumb Dora as modified by Gracie Allen and turned it on its head. Her voice, wide eyes, and innocent look prepared the audience for truly idiotic remarks. Instead, Rudner delivered clever, sharp observations. The effect was devastating. She had learned a lot not only from how George Burns had altered the idea of a dumb woman, but also from how the Marx Brothers used masks to hide a real self, how the Borscht Belt comedians had smuggled in Jewish material to their work when they entered television, and how Woody Allen could avoid typical aggressiveness and still be funny. Instead of joking about mothers, for example, she reversed the situation and talked about her father who, she claimed, was very easily distracted. He would "throw me up in the air and go answer the phone." Instead of being self-deprecating about romance, she would keep her dignity under the most trying of circumstances: "I broke up with my boyfriend because he wanted to get married. I didn't want him to." She could, though, also play off on her presentation style and do straightforward dumb jokes: "I knew so little about money I used to sign my checks, 'Love, Rita.'" She also sometimes hearkened back to Joan Rivers's spoiled girl and marriage manipulator. "I was very overprotected as a child . . . My tricycle had seven wheels. And a driver . . . Men who have a pierced ear are better prepared for marriage. They've experienced pain and bought jewelry."

Sandra Bernhard was at the other end of the self-deprecation continuum: she transformed the Jewish American Princess into a dangerous warrior. Bernhard started in stand-up in 1975 in Beverly Hills, became a manicurist, and was a great success playing Masha, an obsessed groupie in *The King of Comedy*. Bernhard was a toughened Andy Kaufman in the sense of refusing to do stand-up as regularly defined. Her act was more performance art than comedy. Tall, thin, with thick lips, she had a stage persona that worked perfectly with her wild appearance. She would deliberately find a male in the audience, pretend to be sexually attracted to him, and then verbally attack him: "I'm very attracted to you . . . and yet there's something about you that makes me want to hurt you. I'd really like to smash your face." She would perform in her underwear to mock male expectations of women. She brutally attacked prominent people, even soon after they died.

Bernhard deliberately tried to stretch the boundaries of her era just as her comedic ancestors had done in theirs. Like Andy Kaufman, she wanted the audience to expand their understanding of comedy as well. But Bernhard's exploration of sexuality and power—though endearing her to her fans—left her with less mainstream appeal.

What is striking about Jewish women who do stand-up comedy is how few there are compared to men and how fewer still have achieved wide success. The Jewish women who have achieved success in comedy have done so more usually either in motion pictures or on television. In films, women such as Barbra Streisand, Bette Midler, Goldie Hawn, and Madeline Kahn achieved remarkable success. But they were truly exceptional. Streisand and Midler were initially successful, of course, because of their incredible singing voices—and not any purported comic talent, though Streisand's natural timing and comic voice could easily be heard in *Funny Girl*, and Midler has proved her comic abilities in several films. Hawn became famous as much on the basis of her attractiveness as on her comedic skills. She had been a go-go dancer before eventually landing on *Laugh-In*, where her giggling and daffy humor made her nationally popular. Madeline Kahn was most famous for her work in Mel Brooks's films, but her other efforts, including *What's Up, Doc?* and *Paper Moon* were equally accomplished.

All four of these performers were big stars. However, because films are a collaborative activity, their efforts were part of an ensemble. Their comic voices had to be part of the whole. Despite their enormous talent, they couldn't, by definition, make any defined contribution to the story of Jewish comedians in America beyond illustrating that Jewish women could be accepted by an enormous audience both for their singing and for their comedy talents—at least as long as the comedy took place in a motion picture. It would take Jewish women in television to take the next step.

Gilda Radner was the first performer hired by Lorne Michaels for *Saturday Night Live*. On the show she developed several endearing characters, including Rhonda Weiss, a perfect Jewish American Princess; Roseanne Roseanadanna, a brash consumer correspondent; Lisa Loopner, a nerdy teenager; and many others. Radner was appealing and vulnerable, a child in an adult's body. She used her characters as a mask and a shield. She was, like Fanny Brice, Harpo Marx, and Jerry Lewis, able to display the child within, but her child wasn't naughty like Brice or in need of attention like Lewis. Her child was, at its best, sweet and innocent like Harpo.

Estelle Getty started her career in a Yiddish theater group. She tried doing stand-up in the Borscht Belt in the early 1940s, but audiences clearly did not appreciate a female comedian. Eventually, in 1985, she landed the role that made her famous, Sophia Petrillo in *The Golden Girls*. Playing a woman twenty years older than she was, Getty (whose real name was Estelle Scher Gettleman) had to undergo extensive makeup. Getty's character, supposedly driven by a disease that made her unable to restrain herself from making direct comments, was brilliantly conceived. This device, plus Getty's natural skills, allowed the character to get away with a lot and be admired for her honesty. As with the movie stars, though, Getty could not define new comedy. Bea Arthur, Getty's costar on *The Golden Girls*, came much closer. As Maude, first on *All in the Family* and then in *Maude*, Arthur came to represent the outspoken, free, modern woman. The character was revolutionary: a loud, commanding woman who stood up to any man and who was very funny. Such a breakthrough led eventually to the two most popular Jewish women comedians of the 1990s: Roseanne and Fran Drescher.

Roseanne was an outsider's outsider. She grew up in Salt Lake City, a Jewish girl in an overwhelmingly Mormon city. At age three her face became temporarily paralyzed. However difficult her home life was, though, it also gave her an introduction to comedy. Her father would scream "Comedian, comedian" whenever a comic appeared on Ed Sullivan's show. Roseanne recalls him liking women comedians and telling her that comedy "is funniest when it's about speaking up for the little man or killing sacred cows."

Roseanne's troubles, though, were not over. A car hit her when she was sixteen, first putting her into a coma and then into Utah State Hospital for eight months of psychiatric treatment. After leaving the hospital, Roseanne headed west, married, had three children, lived in a trailer, and generally led a life marked by deprivation.

Getting a job as a cocktail waitress, Roseanne soon spontaneously began entertaining customers—by insulting them. She would bring over some drinks and say, "Those drinks are gonna be six bucks, and it'll cost you three more to have me take 'em off the tray and put 'em on the table." Customers loved the joking around, and Roseanne suddenly began to see a stand-up act in her working-class life.

Already a feminist, Roseanne vowed to attack stereotypical images of women. Mockingly identifying herself as a "Domestic Goddess," she homed in on jokes attacking her husband: "My husband walks in the door one night, he says to me, 'Roseanne, don't you think it's time we sat down and had a serious talk about our sex life?' I say to him, 'You want me to turn off *Wheel of Fortune* for that?'" Or she would say, "My husband said he needed more space, so I locked him out of the house." She mocked housework: "My husband asked me if we have any cheese puffs. Like he can't go and lift that couch cushion up himself." She would even demean a woman's iconic role—as a mother—by saying: "I figure when my husband comes home from work, if the kids are still alive, then I've done my job."

Roseanne was a safe figure for women to admire. Not only was she funny but she was also not a sexual threat to the audience. Their perception of her seeming physical unattractiveness helped in part for them to identify with her but also to feel superior to her physical limitations and not be concerned that she, or someone like her, could compete with them. Her female fans were frustrated, anxious, and angry with their boyfriends and husbands. Roseanne's humor gave them an outlet to express the hostility.

Roseanne wasn't so much after jokes as she was after giving a voice to married, struggling working women who had been kept silent and submissive for so long. For them, for the women who would never be as thin as the models American advertisers and producers kept presenting as ideal, and for the women who would never be wealthy or powerful, Roseanne refused to be a victim. She refused to hide her weight or be ashamed of it or make fun of it. She refused to be trapped by her husband's expectations of what a wife should be, or society's either.

The new Jews—American women—were not going to take it anymore.

When Roseanne's act became a situation comedy show in 1988, there was a subtle change at first. During the initial season, she did the normal jokes of any situation comedy, though the jokes grew out of her stand-up persona. Roseanne knew there was more to the character and more that could be said. The producers disagreed. After that first season, Roseanne rebelled. Her instincts proved exactly correct. The show took on an edge. Here was a working-class family that didn't always resolve all its problems in thirty minutes and that had characters who were angry with life.

Here, too, was a show about working-class dignity. In one episode Roseanne had to take a job giving shampoos at a barbershop. She comes home and says, "It's a degrading job, but nobody there makes me feel like it is." It also continued to be a show that was happy to describe male frailties. When a child asks Roseanne what attractions men find looking at *Playboy*, she responds: "They actually believe those girls are looking back."

In her life and in her television appearances outside the show, Roseanne gleefully displayed her gift to shock, singing the national anthem off-key at a baseball game, going through very public divorces and fights with producers, making public confessions of prior sexual sins and child abuse, and others. This was done, though, without the humor that had marked her career, and some of her fans found her antics unappealing.

There were other accusations as well. Roseanne accumulated a lot of money playing a poor character. She had plastic surgery to enhance her appearance, surgery her loyal audience could certainly not afford. She had the money, the power, and was trying for the beauty that she once so cheerfully and successfully mocked.

Roseanne's journey, though, is significant. If oppressed women were the new Jews, Roseanne's passage from the poor outsider to the more powerful insider was an exact replica of the journey Jews had made in America. Her noisy television family has incorrectly been labeled as dysfunctional. Quite the opposite is true. Working against tremendous odds, they were supportive. They were, in fact, a modern equivalent of an immigrant family trying to make it in American society. The character Roseanne was still a struggling outsider. The real Roseanne was a powerful insider, but one who still felt like an outsider. As a symbol, she represented the increased acceptance of women, an acceptance that was not without its price, just as there had been a price for Jews in being accepted.

Personally, Roseanne's seeming exit from her struggles ended in her study of kabbalah, Jewish mysticism, and her reported interest in buying a home in Safed, Israel, the ancient home of the kabbalists. Her audience was less interested in following such a trajectory, but they had followed Roseanne a long way and, like her, found out how complicated success can be.

Fran Drescher's CBS television show called *Princesses* had just been canceled when, by accident, she spotted Jeff Sagansky, CBS's president, on a plane to Paris. Drescher ran to the small bathroom on the plane to apply makeup and fix her hair. As she stepped out she spotted him near her. Walking over, she reminded him that she had a development deal and was surprised he remembered. He told her that the character she had just played wasn't the right one for her; it didn't explore all her talents. He agreed to let her pitch an idea for a new show. Now she had to find that idea.

While in France, Drescher lived with a family and, for the first time as an adult, with children—demanding children. The two little boys had a Guatemalan nanny.

From France, Drescher went to England to visit Twiggy, the ultrathin British model who had also been on *Princesses*. Twiggy was married to Leigh Lawson and also had children. Staying with them and drawing on what she had seen in France, Drescher had an idea: take a Jewish woman from Queens and throw her into this mix as a nanny. Leigh Lawson became the model for Maxwell Sheffield, the handsome widower opposite Drescher's character.

The Nanny first appeared on CBS in 1993. Clearly, the show could have worked if the character Fran had been, say, Italian or even lower-class WASP. Fran, though, was Fran Fine, with a whine that cascaded through her sinuses, a primal urge to latch onto a Jewish doctor, a deeply embedded need to shop ("My first words . . . 'Can I take it back if I wore it?'"), a sprinkling of Yiddish, an extended Jewish family, a reflexive vulgarity, a bluntness, a wit put to sharp use, and an emotional warmth especially obvious in the emotionally vapid household in which she worked. Fran Fine was a funny stereotype, a cartoon Jew, an exaggeration, an anti-Semite's Jew from Hell. And *The Nanny* gave its Jewish opponents plenty of ammunition. One episode featured Fran's mother in synagogue pulling out a (nonkosher) bacon, lettuce, and tomato sandwich and eating it because "nobody can see us here."

The most interesting part of *The Nanny* is its very success. The Jewish American Princess wanna-be that Drescher played was attractive to audiences who could identify with her longing for love, her pride in her background, the easy comfort she found in her identity, and the fact that she always was smarter than those who opposed her. American audiences didn't look down on Fran's materialism; they wanted the same goods and services Fran did. By making the character working class, in fact, Drescher was subtly able to let the audience know that not every Jew was wealthy. Jews, just like them, were struggling in the culture, trying to win the embrace of the Maxwell Sheffields.

In this sense, she was like Jackie Mason. The voice and the Yiddish-tinged language drove some Jews batty, making them fearful of a backlash that never occurred. Indeed, like Mason, Drescher showed that Jews could be Jews and still be accepted. Without changing a bit, Fran was embraced as a Jew and as a woman. The embrace was literal on the show; eventually, Fran and Sheffield got married.

If Fran Fine annoyed more than a few Jews and women, her character indicates a wider acceptance of both. The question lingers about whether American audiences can accept Jewish women characters who are unencumbered by the stereotypes that audiences have stored for so long.

11

THE COST OF VICTORY

THE PSYCHOLOGICAL AND SOCIAL WORLD OF AMERICAN JEWISH COMEDIANS

J erry Stiller looked so small. He was sitting there, overwhelmed by his large chair, being publicly and joyfully humiliated by his friends. It was the Friars Club roast in New York, and Stiller was the victim. If Stiller felt at times a bit uncomfortable with the explicit language, he sat through it all with a smile. The obscene barbs and insults came fast and furious.

Alan King noted, "I never heard anyone in a restaurant say 'Let's eat fast. Jerry Stiller's on TV tonight.'" Jeffrey Ross stared over at Stiller and said, "Jerry Stiller has the face of a star, and the star is Lassie. His Hebrew name is Yecch." Roastmaster Jason Alexander, who had played Stiller's son in *Seinfeld*, smiled fondly at Stiller and said, "I think of you the way I think of my own real father—as an old and seemingly endless drain on my patience and my pocketbook."

Behind the jokes, of course, lay real affection. There were no signs onstage that night of the loneliness of the comedian's life, the constant judgment by audiences, peers, friends, family, and, most painfully, the comedians themselves. The camaraderie hid for a few hours the real life of many comedians.

There have been several attempts to understand the inner lives of comedians, with perhaps the most sustained study made by Samuel S. Janus. His principal findings in a 1975 study show a very sad person hiding behind the jokes. Comedians are frequently haunted by early lives characterized by "suffering, isolation, and feelings of deprivation." Such pain might have been overwhelming, but "humor offered a relief from their sufferings and a defense against inescapable panic and anxiety." In laughing they are giving voice to a protest against their lives, their families, their pain. They also empower themselves. Paul McGhee, a professor of human development, focuses on the comedian's need to control: "The need to dominate is one of the basic precursors for heightened humor development." This need to control, combined with a sense that others—parents or teachers, for example—are doing the controlling is a powerful propellant for the development of a comedic personality.

Timothy Jay, a psychologist, adds that comedians need to feel above the audience, and perhaps Jews, with a greater sense of inadequacy, feel this need more intensely. Jay points out how many more words for *ineptness* there are in Yiddish than English.

The emotional sensitivity in these comedians combined with incredible intelligence. When Janus gave IQ tests, the results were startling. The mean IQ of the comedians was 138, with some scoring above 160.

The anxieties among this smart, wounded group were so profound that 80 percent had been to some form of psychotherapy, although that figure may reflect the fact that successful comedians had the money to afford therapy and the support, even expectation, of their peers, when they entered their psychiatrists' offices. While on the couches, the comedians voiced some obvious anxieties about fleeting fame, but another recurring theme was their expectation of catastrophes—a fear that ironically served as an incentive to work ever harder.

In 1980, Janus published the results of a new study, this one of seventy-six Jewish comedians. The results were intriguing:

- Fully 92 percent of the comedians came from a working-class background.

- The comedians, virtually unanimously, were much closer to their mothers than their fathers.

- The rejection of their parents' values seemed to them the only way out for their own emotional survival. The traits the comedians identified as coming from their Jewishness, "frugality, worry, guilt, caution, and passivity," were precisely the ones they wished to get rid of by rejecting.

- Despite their sense of their Jewishness somehow restricting them from enjoying or embracing life, not one had formally left Judaism, though 80 percent of the comedians who married at least twice had at least one Gentile wife. Some had had multiple Gentile spouses.

Janus believes that for the "overwhelmingly anxious" Jewish comedians, "comedy is a defense mechanism to ward off the aggression and hostility of others. . . . The one thing they live for is acceptance. . . . There is never enough respect." Their depression abates only when they're working. And indeed, as the comedy writer Abe Burrows once suggested, "The comedian must practice his comedy in order to avoid destroying himself."

Although Janus has studied comedians for the longest period, his views are not universally accepted. Seymour Fisher and Rhoda Fisher also studied comedians and came to quite a different conclusion: "We didn't find any elevated rates of psychopathology. . . . Comics are a very sturdy group." Among the Fishers' findings:

- As children, the comedians had many responsibilities. In essence, they had to grow up quickly: "They were expected to care for themselves and to act as caretakers for their brothers and sisters." This may have provided the basis to feel a need to sustain others through laughter.

- Although the comedians were close to their mothers, the comedians also saw them as asking for too much, as being "nonnurturant." As one comedian put it, "I didn't like my mother. I *loved* her, but I didn't *like* her."

Whatever turns out to be true about the psychology of comedians, there is agreement on at least one point: It takes a lot of ego to be a successful comedian. They can't in any crucial way get support from their audience beyond the laughter and applause. How, after all, can the audience truly understand what the comedian is going through? The magic would be gone if there were total comprehension. There are insiders, of course. The comedian's agent books the comedian into places. The comedian's manager helps mold a career. The public relations person tries to get appropriate positive publicity and deal with any negative publicity. But, most of all, the comedians must rely on each other.

Realizing this early on, comedians and other entertainers created a refuge, a place where they could be with other performers.

The Friars Club grew out of a meeting of the Press Agents Association in 1904 and started operating from its early headquarters starting in 1908. The first Friars Frolic began in 1911—for which Irving Berlin wrote "Alexander's Ragtime Band." After a series of moves, the New York Friars Club relocated to its current headquarters, a five-story English Renaissance brownstone on East Fifty-fifth Street, in 1957. (A scene for *The Sunshine Boys* was shot there.) Eventually, the club opened a branch in California when Jack Benny, George Burns, and George Jessel, having had their customary dinner at the Brown Derby and trip to the fights, found one evening that the fights had ended early and they had nowhere to go.

The club grew famous for its afternoon stags, off-limits to women and waiters. Although Sophie Tucker had been roasted in 1953, women were kept out of the roasts until Phyllis Diller sneaked in dressed as a man, mustache and all. In 1988, Liza Minnelli became the first woman admitted to the Friars.

Many comedians retain incredible memories of the Friars. Eddie Cantor took a twelve-year-old Milton Berle there. Berle sat at the table with Irving Berlin, Enrico Caruso, and George M. Cohan. It was a heady moment for the young boy, and he never forgot it. Often those young visitors were astonished to hear dirty words coming out of the mouths of America's most beloved comic stars, words in ample supply at the regular roasts.

Not all memories of the Friars Roasts, though, bring smiles. On November 24, 1958, the Friars were gathered to pay tribute to Lucille Ball and Desi Arnaz. Harry Einstein was at the dais speaking. He hadn't been feeling well, but he wanted to go on with his performance. This was a comeback for him, and he wanted to impress the audience. He did. Einstein was a huge hit as he said, "You must not think that the Friars Club is an easy club to get into . . . Before a prospective candidate is even issued an application, he must first satisfy us beyond any question of a doubt that he is either a resident—or a nonresident—of the State of California. He then must be proposed by and then vouched for by at least two men—who are listed in the phone book." The routine, probably five or six minutes worth of material, lasted for ten minutes because of the laughter.

Einstein got a standing ovation. He walked back to his seat, sat down next to Milton Berle, and suddenly dropped his head onto Berle's lap.

The laughing and applause stopped suddenly. Berle called for a doctor, and Art Linkletter, the roastmaster, asked if anyone had nitro tablets for heart problems. It seemed to Linkletter that half the room came up offering tablets.

Berle, trying to reassure the crowd, turned to Tony Martin. Berle knew, of course, that a comedian could not go up there at a moment like this, and so he told Martin to sing a song. Martin had to improvise quickly. He burst into the first song that came to his mind. To Berle's horror, to the shock of the crowd, Martin began to sing "There's No Tomorrow."

Harry Einstein died at the Friars that night. As his son, Albert Brooks, put it, "The interesting thing to me was that he finished." Perhaps Einstein's incredible final performance is indicative of how much an audience can buoy a performer, of how important the audience is.

All comedians in a general way help the audience laugh at and thereby ultimately accept life's difficulties and absurdities. If Freud's psychoanalytic understanding is correct, humor helps us deal with our fears. Humor is also a form of reconciliation with a world and the people in it who never live up to the ideal we hope for. In Nietzsche's poignant summary: "A joke is an epigram on the death of a feeling."

If all comedians have such a task for all audiences, Jewish comedians have a unique relationship with Jewish audiences. These comedians have a task that goes beyond simply providing laughter. Jews were proud of the comedians for gaining acceptance in American society earlier and more widely than the general Jewish community. Jewish comedians were pioneers for American Jews; the comedians cleared a pathway to acceptance. They made Americans comfortable with Jews and Jews comfortable with Americans.

Those in the Jewish community who struggle to help America's Jews choose a Jewish identity are seeking to identify the sorts of beliefs, experiences, and actions that can contribute to that identity. Some have called for intensified Jewish education or the practice of Jewish rituals. But most American Jews, in fact, do not keep kosher or go to synagogue services regularly.

Perhaps it may be that the Jewish comedians will come to the rescue. If, after all, those comedians were the ones to help Jews deal with anxieties, and if humor among Jews is attractive within and across generations—and it is—then there remains the tantalizing possibility that those comedians can enhance the distinctive Jewish culture surviving in America. It is not an accident that the National Foundation for Jewish Culture recently initiated the Alan King Award in American Jewish Humor to offer an annual recognition of Jewish comedians.

Of course, it seems unrealistic—but not impossible—that famous Jewish comedians will make deliberate efforts to structure routines that specifically enhance Jewish continuity. More likely, the Jewish community will have to develop a much larger group of comedians who mostly work specifically in front of Jewish audiences and, using humor, help those audiences overcome the anxieties of continuing to choose a Jewish identity. Training and encouraging such comedians remains a relatively unexplored option for the Jewish community.

In keeping faith with the tradition that nurtured them, the comedians, like the community, can forge a full American Jewish identity that allows both sides to fit comfortably in one body. It is unclear whether such a connection between comedian and community will take place.

Some of the stock jokes of Jewish comedians, though, will have to be carefully tempered for a new, positive identity to be forged. It is healthy for a people to laugh at itself, to see its own foibles, to be able to laugh at its own weaknesses. Some of the humor of Jewish comedians, though, crosses the line, not so much into self-hatred as a continuing sense of inferiority.

In his very first piece of writing about his efforts, Theodor Herzl, the founder of modern Zionism, wrote: "Evil and foolish self-ridicule is one of the slavish habits which we have acquired over centuries of oppression. A free man does not regard himself as ridiculous, nor does he permit anyone to ridicule him." Herzl was trying to expunge the layers of uncertainty Jews felt living in Europe, but some of that same uncertainty continues to linger at the beginning of the twenty-first century among Jews in the United States, uncertainty about the role of being Jewish in their lives, about whether they are principally Jewish or principally not, anxiety about being different but also anxiety about being too much the same and losing the very differences about which they are ambivalent.

12

NOT THE LAST LAUGH

THE FUTURE OF
JEWISH COMEDIANS IN AMERICA

I t was exactly a week after New Year's Day, 2000. Jeffrey Ross, a young man many at the Friars Club see as their future, was between sets at Caroline's on Broadway. He walked around, surveying the crowd, and then stepped outside to breathe in some of the crisp night air. He checked with the doorman. The second show was completely sold out. The doorman had already turned away more than thirty people. Ross nodded and stared up across Broadway at the Brill Building where so much musical history had been made.

Ross had been on Letterman, Leno, and Conan. He had been in several movies and had been a hit at the roasts. He's been written about in the *New Yorker*. Still, though, he awaited the big break, the network show, the rocket to the top.

Ross went back to his small ten-by-fifteen-foot dressing room behind the kitchen. There was a sink and a bathroom, lockers for the waiters and waitresses, and a mirror. A waitress brought Ross some food and a collection of drinks. He sipped the water. Some relatives stopped by. They'd been at the first show, which had gone well, and they wanted to *kvell* before they left. Ross was sitting there talking about comedy with Rick Crom, the comedian who was the emcee. A young woman wandered in, having made a really wrong turn, and asked where the bathroom was located. Ross pointed to his own and let her use it. Later, when she saw him onstage and realized who he was, she would have a story to tell.

Crom and another comedian, Felicia Michaels, were on first. Then Ross would do forty-five minutes. A red light would come on fifteen minutes before he was scheduled to finish.

Many comedians like to be totally alone before they perform. Some have to get dressed. Some have to find a special strength, to put on their game face, to locate some ideal performance state within (alternately called being in the zone, or in flow) and lock it in place. That night Ross didn't have much time to himself, but still, when the moment came, he had to go out there and make the huge crowd laugh. The place was filled. Drinks and food were being ordered. Parts of the show were being broadcast live on the Internet. The success of the evening rested on the shoulders of Jeff Ross.

He went out, playing with the crowd. They loved him immediately, and it never let up. "I couldn't afford America On Line," he told them, "So I got Brooklyn On Line. 'You got mail, bitch.' It has Windows 98 with bars." He surveyed the culture for them.

Ross is the son of a kosher caterer, and, as he notes, "You can tell I'm Jewish as soon as I open my mouth. It's there in the attitude and the inflection." In case anyone misses this, he lets the crowd know.

Ross is one of those people who knew early on that he was funny. His friends laughed at his jokes. A visit to the Friars Club, where he played a poker game and soaked up the tradition, led him to a close identification with that institution.

It remains to be seen if Jeff Ross will be tomorrow's Seinfeld, but he is one of many young Jewish comedians struggling for success. He's done better than most—by far—but still the goal of great fame lies out there.

Wendy Liebman is another comedian who has achieved considerable success but remains just outside the inner circle of fame. Liebman has been on Letterman, Leno, and Rosie. She has won comedy competitions. She had her own HBO show. Yet, Liebman, like Ross, is not yet a household name.

She has a unique delivery that in its timing is reminiscent of Jack Benny. She sets up a line that could stand on its own, pauses, and then takes the line the audience thought it understood in a whole new way in a much softer voice. "I went to the mall because I love to shop . . . lift." "I'm flying, and there's a guy sitting next to me, and I could tell he really wanted me . . . to shut up." "For Thanksgiving last year I made a seventeen-pound turkey . . . pot pie."

Liebman has set up her own website with her schedule, reviews, and biography. She's not the only one to have done so. Rodney Dangerfield has one of the largest of the comedian websites. He's got a joke of the day, his schedule, and a large amount of other material.

There are fan websites for virtually all famous comedians, and increasingly comedians are producing their own sites to stay in contact with fans.

There is a good deal of interest in humor on the Internet. At the beginning of 2001, for example, Alta Vista listed 1,204,835 pages under "comedy," 59,170 under "comedians," 2,782,015 under "humor," and 107 under "Jewish comedians." There were 106 mailing lists about "humor" on Liszt.com. There were also 73 Usenet groups and 6 IRC channels. The millions of jokes on the 'net illustrate the attractiveness of such an outlet for comedians, and the increasing ease and portability of the Internet are clear signs that future live performances on the 'net will greatly increase.

Whereas Ross and Liebman have achieved some considerable fame, other comedians are just starting out. Karen Bergreen was a lawyer for more than four years. She has made the rounds of the clubs, getting good responses with her observational humor, been at the Aspen Festival, gotten an HBO development deal, and waits, learning and struggling. Bergreen is upbeat, but as a woman she continues to have obstacles her male counterparts don't face. Like every female comedian she's heard the line "Women aren't funny" or "We have five comedians and we already have a woman." Bergreen's initial success fuels her. Luckily, she grew up in a world in which there were an increasing number of women comics. "It never occurred to me that men were funnier," she says.

Ross, Liebman, Bergreen, and the untold legions of other comedians are needed to feed a burgeoning American entertainment industry. Indeed, entertainment is a greater American export than agriculture or cars. In some ways, it is our entertainment that is the source of American economic power and influence in the world.

The power of American entertainment is fueled in part by the nation's great technological developments. Entertainment is available in an increasing number of new ways. This creates uncertainty about the technological array in which entertainment will be delivered in the future. There are other questions that grow out of the technology, such as the ownership of rights and payment. Should, for example, an entertainer be paid extra if a live show or television show is simultaneously broadcast on the Internet?

The competition to succeed and the profusion of new media make predictions difficult beyond the obvious fact that comedy will continue to be a prized product and those who survive the intense effort to get noticed will do well.

It is also unclear what type of comedy will rise over the next several decades. Gay humor is one clear candidate for that honor. There are, however, relatively few openly gay Jewish comedians.

Jason Stuart is one of them. Stuart has traveled the comedy club and college circuit, adapting his humor for the audience. He thinks America is ready to accept openly gay comics. "It's not the audiences. It's the bookers who are unwilling."

Some of the reluctance goes back to the same reason that women comedians have had to struggle. "They're worried about a gay guy in power. They're shocked."

Stuart remains scared every time he goes out to perform. He knows firsthand the painful nature of not being accepted. He has a sister who is now Orthodox and who does not want him to be near her children. "Maybe people think we have the power to turn people gay." He twitches his nose like Samantha on *Bewitched*. "I mean, what's the selling point? 'Oh, we have no rights and everyone hates us. Please come along and join us.'"

Stuart's comments about the assignation of power to gays to turn heterosexuals into homosexuals retain a faint echo of the Middle Ages (and later), when Jews were believed to be representatives of the devil with special evil powers. It remains to be seen if audiences or bookers continue to be reluctant to let gay comedians be in charge of their emotions, to accept that gays can make them laugh. Still, Stuart is optimistic. After all, "Being different in any way creates humor," he asserts, hinting that the experience gay comedians have will allow them to create a new kind of humor that will emerge from its less-than-accepted current status.

Suze Berger, a gay Jewish woman, is in a position to evaluate how audiences receive all three groups. She suggests that her being Jewish seems more of an issue with some audiences than her being gay. There are still places she's played where some audience members hadn't met any Jews. As a woman, Berger feels almost an obligation to use rough and profane language "because we're not supposed to."

She is not conscious onstage of having a particular identity; she is just trying to be funny. Is she ever scared about having to tell audiences of her identities? No, she says. Her mind is too engaged noting what the audience is laughing at, what she's going to see, or surveying the crowd to pick out someone to speak with.

Berger notes that being gay was hip in the 1990s, but now all she sees is a call to be funny. In this way, Berger sees an increasing mainstreaming of gay humor, though she's had the startling experience of being turned down for a part because she was unwilling to cut her hair to fit the stereotypical image of a lesbian.

All of the new Jewish comedians should be seen as searching for the next chapter in an ongoing story, not as a sign that the story is ending. Indeed, if there were any doubts about the continuing vitality of Jewish comedians, such doubts were dismissed on April 19, 2001, by the opening of *The Producers*, the Broadway musical Mel Brooks created from his widely beloved motion picture. The show was an enormous critical and financial success, and its nearly $4 million in ticket sales the day after the opening set a Broadway box-office record.

The play, building on a classic strategy of Jewish humor, took the ultimate in Jewish misfortune, the most horrible event to befall modern Jewry, and laughed at it. The smile might be haunted, but it was also triumphant. Brooks was around to laugh at Hitler.

And Brooks characteristically pushed to the limits. With lines like "Open audition today for the role of Adolf Hitler. No previous experience required," *The Producers* set out to shock audiences. This didn't stop with the play, however. When Brooks accepted one of the dozen Tony Awards that *The Producers* earned, he said, in a remark that would prove controversial, "I want to thank Hitler for being such a funny guy on stage." Brooks couldn't stop the mockery, for he knew that in making fun of a man with a boundless zeal for killing Jews, he was robbing the ghost of that man of any posthumous power to intimidate Jews.

The success of *The Producers* does not, though, necessarily imply an unclouded future for Jewish comedians. Whatever particular styles of comedy or particular people succeed, Jewish comedians will have a challenge in the future. A crucial reason for their success in America was that they provided not just humor but also a special body of experiences from their Jewish heritage that met the needs of America at various points in its history. If America's future has fewer needs met specifically by Jewish experiences in history or if Jewish comedians are unable or unwilling to draw on their heritage, the unique contributions of the Jewish comedians will diminish and the Jewish comedians will blend until they are among the many American comedians who can make people laugh.

Another danger is that the great American Jewish comedic tradition will be seen as simply nostalgic rather than the foundation on which the needs of the present and future can be built. This can happen as well if ties by comedians to contemporary Jewish life wither or if that communal life is so experientially thin that it offers no sustenance, no unique comic material.

Still, whatever the future will be, whoever will become famous for a day or a lifetime, the Jewish comedians of tomorrow will have an enormous legacy, an unparalleled tradition of comedy from which to draw pride and comedic lessons.

They can look back to the immigrants, to the young George

Burns going from one vaudeville house to the next, changing names and changing acts, happy even in failure, but always searching. They can laugh at Fanny Brice playing the naughty child. They can listen to Jack Benny on the radio, using silence and timing and characters to make depression life bearable. They can fall out of their seats at the Marx Brothers, as movie audiences of the 1930s literally did. They can watch the cultural revolution coming too late for Lenny Bruce as he entered the forbidden zone of comedy and didn't get out alive. They can watch Jerry Lewis become the first Jewish comedian auteur or Woody Allen brilliantly create a character who seemed like his real self but wasn't or Mel Brooks perfect the spoof. They can watch the struggle women had to succeed, the sad, long climb, but at least a climb interrupted by a thousand laughs from the likes of Joan Rivers. They can recognize themselves in Rodney Dangerfield or the whole of Yiddish tradition in Jackie Mason. They can smile wryly at Jerry Seinfeld's observations or be amazed at Wendy Liebman's cleverness, or Jeff Ross's bold attempt to carry on the Friars' legacy.

The future Jewish comedians can take pride that their comic ancestors, working out of a Jewish tradition, were able to provide much-needed humor at crucial times in American struggles during the twentieth century. As American Jews adapted to life in their adopted land, they changed America and America changed them, and the intermingling made for an ever shifting role for those Jews and the comedians who emerged from them.

In looking back, the Jewish comedians of tomorrow will see how one people, blessed with a bountiful heritage and struggling with being accepted and with finding their place in the Golden Land, forever changed American comedy and, finally, America itself.

APPENDIX

SCHLEMIELS
AND NUDNICKS

THE SOURCES AND NATURE
OF JEWISH HUMOR

A merican audiences so reflexively identify comedy with the Jewish people that it is difficult to imagine that in the nineteenth century the Jews were considered humorless. No less a figure than Hermann Adler, chief rabbi of London, felt obligated to write an article in 1893 defending the Jews against the charge, made by such thinkers as Ernest Renan and Thomas Carlyle, that they had no sense of humor.

Indeed, for many centuries, Jews were, by and large, serious scholars, hard workers, and poor peasants who lived on one side of what appeared to be a seemingly unbreachable wall of religious separation from their neighbors. Those neighbors did not turn to the Jews for laughter, social commentary, insights about life, or much else.

The Jews lived more or less by themselves despite some economic and social mixing with their Gentile neighbors. Others identified them, and they identified themselves, by their religious views and practices and their study of sacred texts.

It is possible to find random references to laughter and humor in the Bible and in other sacred Jewish religious literature. The Talmud reflects conflicted feelings toward laughter. One rabbi in the Talmud prohibited jokes except to make fun of idol worship. Others saw humor as a way to help the community. In one famous story from Jewish literature, a rabbi approached the prophet Elijah and asked him to point out those in the marketplace who were going to be admitted to paradise. Elijah agreed to do this. He surveyed the crowd and pointed to two jesters. The rabbi was surprised because these two jesters were not noted for their religious knowledge or fervor. The rabbi asked Elijah why they would be chosen to enter paradise. Elijah responded that it was the jesters' job to bring happiness to those who are in distress, and such a job merited a place in paradise.

It is also possible to search out other elements in Jewish life that contributed to what would emerge as a Jewish sense of humor. The method of studying the Talmud, for example, might not have led to recurrent explosions of laughter, but it did teach those who used it to look at a subject from all angles, to search out hidden meanings, to tolerate ambiguity and recognize contradictions, all intellectually useful skills when applied to recognizing the comic in a person, situation, or institution. Talmud was studied employing a singsong manner, and the cadence of that study made its way into daily Yiddish and, through that, to the Jewish rhythms that would make English move to a slightly different and definitely funnier beat.

Jewish ethics provided religious and cultural approval not only for helping the poor, the weak, and the oppressed, but also for questioning political powers and even God. God was sometimes put on trial—especially by Hasidic rabbis in Eastern Europe—for allowing evil to exist in the world and for the travails that had beset the chosen people. Once, during a terrible famine in the Ukraine, the Hasidic rabbis assembled as a Rabbinical Court with God as the defendant. The rabbis listened to their leader, who was making the claim against God, and then met to deliberate. Their verdict was that God was guilty. According to Hasidic tradition, a large shipment of grain from Siberia arrived just a few days later, and the poor were then again able to buy bread.

Most significantly, there are clear forerunners of comedians from within Jewish culture. These forerunners can be seen in those who made jests during the holiday of Purim and those who entertained at Jewish weddings.

During Purim, the holiday to celebrate Queen Esther's saving Persian Jews from Haman's plan to murder them, Jews got drunk and dressed in costumes and masks. From medieval times on, the Jews performed skits and plays—called *Purimshpiels*—based on the Purim story or some other religious tale. In these *Purimshpiels*, rabbis, teachers, and even Jewish religious texts were mocked. Such a tradition gave carefully demarcated approval to confronting even the most sacred with laughter. Those who performed *Purimshpiels*, however, were not the true precursors of comedians, because to mock a religious text a person had to have intimate familiarity with it. Very few future Jewish comedians would have survived if tested on their knowledge of biblical literature or if they had to swim in the sea of Talmud.

The jesters and merrymakers who performed at Jewish weddings, though, were clearly the forerunners of Jewish comedians. The *leyts*, or jester, told jokes, satirized people, sang, and otherwise amused the guests. The *marshalik* was the master of ceremonies, organizing the event, keeping the wedding festivities moving along. The *badchan* had a particular job: to provide not just jokes but also solace to those who were troubled. Of course, these roles frequently overlapped. These comedians would do all they could to provoke laughter. For example, in Brody in the Ukraine one important wedding tradition involved hundreds of young women who accompanied the bride to the *mikveh* (the ritual bath where Jews purified themselves). A comedian would lead the group, sitting backward on a horse and singing and telling jokes for the journey. In Prerau, Czechoslovakia, the comedians made fun of the bride and groom as well as many guests by mock imitation. Some of the jesters were learned, whereas others simply made jokes.

These merrymakers did not have a high social status. Rabbis and scholars frequently disparaged them; the merrymakers were ready to sacrifice truth for a good line, and the rabbis were ready to sacrifice a good line for the truth. But the merrymakers were extremely popular with the common folk. The author Rabbi Moshe Waldoks makes an interesting comparison between these comedians and those who would later work in the Borscht Belt. The wedding guests, like those guests in the Catskill hotels, would frequently stay for the week. It became a challenge to capture the audience for the whole period rather than the twenty minutes, or even two hours, that a stand-up comedian may perform. Audiences in both cases were demanding, and the wit and skill of the comedians were put to a constant test. The stakes were higher than they might be first assumed. Weddings provided a legitimate occasion for the expression of joy, an expression severely restricted by the everyday realities of life. They were a crucial emotional release.

Despite all these ancestral contributions, though, Jewish comedians would not have existed without the emergence of a particular Eastern European Yiddish culture in the nineteenth century. It was that culture that produced the humor that journeyed to America, that nourished the imaginations of generations of Jewish comedians, and that spiritually lived on in America even as it perished in Europe in the Holocaust.

This culture developed because of specific historical circumstances stemming from the political and economic emancipation of European Jews begun at the end of the eighteenth century, especially after the French Revolution. As emerging Protestant states separated church and state, Jews began to be granted civil rights, and, as these Protestants studied Christian origins in the Hebrew Bible more and more, Jews began to be seen in a new, more positive light. There were, to be sure, controversies within European Christian circles about whether the Jews were able to enter Christian societies or whether their religion prevented that entry. The Jews themselves were divided about entering society, with some arguing that joining the society would inevitably lead to assimilation.

In Eastern Europe, the process of emancipation was much slower, but its influence on Jews was no less palpable. Their hunger for freedom gave rise to an impatience that would lead, in time, to their mass emigration. Emancipation was also crucial in affecting American political views, providing the haven and environment in which the immigrant Jews could thrive.

This emancipation led directly to a movement for Jewish enlightenment, or *haskalah*, in the nineteenth century. *Haskalah*, in practice, meant an increase in knowledge of and concern for secular subjects. This led to advocating the inclusion of secular subjects in the education of Jewish children, a desire to acquire and use the various languages of the countries where Jews lived, and, in varying degrees, a desire to see the Jewish religion adapt to modernity. In some cases, secularization went beyond traditional religion, renouncing it and looking for cultural substitutions.

The secularizing influences had profound effects for the future of Jewish comedy. Indeed, the secularization of so many Jews in

Eastern Europe ultimately provided new materials for comics who no longer were restricted to mocking rabbis or using religious texts as the source of humor. In America, a self-selection process was at work. Those Jews who emigrated to the United States were young and brave enough to leave their homes and roots, and so it was not surprising that they were more secular than their peers who stayed behind. It was not so much that America secularized them as much as they wanted to be secularized by America. The Jewish comedians who emerged to enter the general American world of show business simply could not have emerged in a tightly knit religious community untouched by the modern world.

Some effects of secularization are obvious, such as the religious impulse to "repair the world" being transformed into political and social activism to make the society better. This activism found its expression in political life, as Jews helped to organize unions, work for social reforms, and serve in other ways.

Secularization also had subtle influences, more difficult to chart. For example, a religious worldview provided a particular relationship to reality. However difficult a life might be economically or politically, religion promised a release, an alternative to the "real" world, one purer and better, one where Jews could be safe. Secularity robbed many East European Jews of that safe alternate reality. The sudden removal of such a crucial support system, combined with the persecutions and hunger the Jews faced in reality, could and did lead to depression among Jews. A substitute, or at least a supplement, for religion's warm embrace was needed, a substitute that provided a release from the real world and an escape from depression. Such a substitute had to be available to Jews, and it had to be, like God, portable. It had to emerge from their daily lives. Humor became that substitute.

Religious practices also provided concrete guidelines for the expression of the natural desire for physical pleasure. As religious practices slowly declined, but with memories of them fresh and sometimes with guilt about not observing them present, Jews felt a sexual tension more pronounced than it had been. Humor became an obvious release for that tension as well.

Secularization also meant the loss of an identity. Without a clear sense as being religious, the secularized Jews of Eastern Europe needed another way to think of themselves. Although there is some overlapping of various identities, there were discrete choices that were made. Some secular Jews, as suggested, entered political life and became revolutionaries and socialists at home or in America, where the socialism diminished over the generations but where the political impulse continued even as it diffused into different directions. Most of the heirs to this political tradition remained on the political Left, forming a core constituency both for the Democratic Party and for social movements aimed at improving society and improving human rights for people not only in the United States but also around the world. A smaller number of Jews were transformed by various factors, especially a political attachment and a dissatisfaction with the direction of American culture starting in the 1960s, and became more conservative. A still smaller element of East European Jews found their political expression by moving to the land of Israel to work for the restoration of Zion.

Besides a political identity, secular Jews had other choices. Some focused on social or economic success, seeking to put their religious energy into work and family. Finally, a large number of secular Jews searched for an identity not in politics or work but in Jewish culture, in theater and dance, in literature and the entertainment arts.

The Jewish comedians who emerged, especially in America, were instrumental in providing that secular cultural identity—not of the Jews as religious people but as funny people. Those to be listened to and admired were not rabbis but comedians. However tenuous such a cultural identity might be, however far from traditional religion, it remained distinctly Jewish for those who clung to it.

Whereas in real life these various identities—lingering or prominent religious identity plus the many secular variations—commingled with varying degrees of congeniality, it is significant that humor was beloved across the Jewish spectrum. It most profoundly met the deepest emotional needs of all the Jewish people.

Initially, the Jews' lack of economic power was largely due to their wider political powerlessness. Persecution was the most obvious result of such political powerlessness, but there were other significant effects on Jewish life. The Jews were living in the margins of their societies, neither full citizens nor completely rejected.

This life of despair has been given most frequently as the source of the Jews' humor. Indeed, the power of humor as therapy should not be overlooked. As Viktor Frankl pointed out, humor was present even in the concentration camps: "It is well known that humor, more than anything else in the human makeup, can afford an aloofness and an ability to rise above any situation, even if only for a few seconds." But the idea of "laughter through tears," of laughing as a therapeutic way to cope with poverty and persecution, doesn't get at the full relationship between humor and powerlessness. It does focus on the depression that emerges from such a situation. In that sense, humor provided Jews with an emotional safety valve, a way to continue living the lives they seemingly couldn't escape but didn't like. Humor provided a source of reconciliation between hope and reality.

Depression, though, is only one emotion engendered by powerlessness. Fear is a deeper sentiment. When anthropologists, for example, examined caves and discovered that early humans had painted fierce animals on the walls, the explanation that emerged was that in painting the animals, those cave dwellers sought, through art, to rob that which they most feared of its power. Without an artistic tradition, Jews sought other ways to control their fears. It was less the tears that provided a need for laughter than the fear of death, of violation, of humiliation, of theft, and much else. Humor provided a way to cope, a sense of control, of mocking the forces that made them afraid.

For many Jews, fear also provoked a nightmarish reaction to life, a realistic sense that, because danger was such a frequent visitor to Jewish communities, a new threat would soon hover over them, their families, and their community. The anticipatory anxiety produced by such feelings, the ability to visualize with frightening clarity the potential horrors that might be visited upon them, haunted the Eastern European Jewish mind. Even when the reality of dangers was reduced in America, the fear lingered. Woody Allen's neuroses, for example, are such feelings overlaid on contemporary American life. The neuroses were quite real to him; audiences saw the inappropriateness and that added to the humor.

Political and economic weakness was only one form of the Jews' marginalization, though. There were also feelings of psychological and religious marginalization. The psychological feelings emerged in Europe, and in America as well, from being members of a minority group. As modern ego psychologists have pointed out, members of minority groups characteristically have all the regular problems of development, but some of these are exaggerated by minority status. These problems include accepting a positive self-image, being able to make clear distinctions between the self and others, and navigating through the labyrinth of many social roles and numerous, potentially contradictory group memberships. Kurt Lewin, a leading theorist who studied the implications of being a member of a minority group, noted that the conflict between absorbed majority views and natural feelings of identification with one's minority group can promote profound feelings of ambivalence about an identity. Such ambivalence can result in self-hate and deep insecurity. The point is that such self-hatred and insecurity come not from being a member of a particular group, but from feeling uncertain about which group it is to which one really belongs. As the Jewish humor researcher Avner Ziv has noted, some Jewish comedians used a self-mocking humor to show that they were, indeed, truly members of the majority, that they were different from the other Jews who kept their distance from Gentile society. The most polite interpretation of such behavior is that these comedians sought to increase the approval of Jews by the society. A less charitable view is that the comedians were abandoning their people and seeking permission to surrender their identity. However, the opposite effect can also be observed. Jewish comedians used humor to control and even subtly mock their Gentile audiences. The Jewish comedian, in being able to provoke laughter, had control over an alien audience in a way that a Jew couldn't have control, at least through the first half of the twentieth century. The laughter gave the Jewish comedian, and by extension, American Jews, acknowledgment, acceptance, and approval.

The Jews also found their own weakness in society perplexing. When they prayed, they saw themselves as a people chosen by God to perform a holy mission of being moral exemplars for humanity. Yet, in the larger society, they were seen as religious pariahs and apostates. The gap between their destined historical role and the lives they led made them feel caught between two strikingly contra-dictory religious interpretations: that the Jews were crucially signif-icant to humanity or irrelevant. The contradictions of such dual lives led Jews to seek explanations—provided by religion—and, for the secular, ways to live in the face of those contradictions.

The feeling of being chosen was, however, crucial for religious Jews in giving them the strength to continue when reality seemed to argue for surrendering their identities. Their sense of purpose was a powerful fuel to propel them through the sorrows of the world. The secularized Jews in some way kept that same sense of Jewish uniqueness. Even without a godly mandate, they found in themselves a drive to continue in the face of overwhelming odds. They may not have identified such a drive as having derived from a sense of Jewish chosenness, but that was its source.

There was, in addition, another psychological element to the laughter. Sometimes laughter is an incongruous reaction to having survived horror. Jewish laughter, in this respect, was a release of tensions, an acknowledgment of having confronted danger and lived to tell about it. This sentiment was magnified in America because not only had Jewish immigrants lived through pogroms, but they had also actually escaped from the grasp of the anti-Semites. Harpo Marx put this best when he wrote in his autobiography, "You could laugh about the Past, because you'd been lucky enough to survive it." There is, though, a more hidden aspect to such a feeling: survivor's guilt. Laughter released such guilt, providing a bridge between feelings of despair about the past and optimism about the future.

Another crucial factor in Jewish humor was that Jewish culture emphasized language. Education, like God and humor, was portable. The haters of Jews might take land and property, but they could not rob the Jews of their learning. The Jews relied on words to convey their profound religious feelings. Jews, and later Jewish comedians, unleashed the weapon of wit because the use of all other weapons was denied to them. Language became the only available way to fight back, and later comedians used this tradition to draft language in an attempt to confront what they saw as inequities or absurdities in American political and social life. This linguistic tradition continued on, even among some of the comics who notoriously disliked schooling. Groucho Marx, for example, read for several hours a day and wrote his own autobiography. George Jessel claimed that the Jews had to learn a variety of languages and dialects because of their constant movement. This provided the background for mimicry and imitation.

Yiddish has its own special status in the creation of the comedic spirit. Written using Hebrew characters, the language had begun in the early Middle Ages when Jews started using the Old High German and Middle High German of those Gentiles around them. Eventually, Jews began to move east because of attacks made in Western European countries. The Germanic content was mixed with the Slavonic elements of the previously settled Jewish community, Yiddish, the *mama-loshen* (mother tongue) of the Eastern European Jews.

It is crucial to consider the place of Yiddish on the Jews' linguistic continuum. Jessel's comment aside, even for Jews living in Eastern Europe, there were three languages. One was the local language, such as Polish or Russian, which was needed for commercial and other forms of interaction with the Gentile society. The two languages that were vital for Jewish life were Hebrew and Yiddish. Hebrew was the sacred tongue, the language used for prayer and study, the language of the Bible and much of the Talmud. Hebrew rhythms filled the Sabbath air as Jews went each Saturday morning to read the Torah and pray. Prayer took place three times each day as well. Hebrew was elevated, the language the Jews used to speak with God. Yiddish, on the other hand, was the language Jews used to speak to one another. It was filled with earthy and colloquial elements. It was the common language of the common folk.

Because Jews lived in two (or three) languages, they were, as in their political and economic lives, caught between worlds. The relationship between these two linguistic worlds was not always friendly. Yiddish was warm and close. Hebrew was formal and, by its religious nature, at some emotional distance. The juxtaposition of the two languages was another source of humor, for it made the Jews aware of an enormous emotional distance possible in language. The shift from the serious to the common (a shadow of the shift from Hebrew to Yiddish) is a frequent linguistic device of American Jewish comics. Consider Woody Allen's line: "Not only is there no God, but try getting a plumber on weekends."

Yiddish was an extraordinarily expressive language, especially in its expansive ability to characterize human beings. It was remarkably precise when it came to describing the idiosyncrasies, strengths, and weaknesses of people and identifying character types. The fools, simpletons, tricksters, liars and braggarts, sinners, schlemiels, schlimazels, and nudnicks lived alongside the wise and the learned, the holy and the wonder-workers. The language was earthy and real at times and at other times otherworldly. Yiddish was elastic enough to encompass the entirety of life; like a mother, it gave birth to expressions that could encompass all of life, even life beyond the shtetl, the small village in which a Jew might live. Its types became the models for many of the characters that comedians would eventually create.

A select number of Yiddish words and phrases have entered English. It is important to note, though, that Yiddish didn't just enrich vocabulary. The Yiddish that entered and affected American life and American entertainment deftly offered a new attitude and new characters. For example, in Yiddish one meaning of the word *schlep* is to pull or drag some object. It connotes a difficulty. In English, a person might say, "I carried the grocery bags for two blocks." Invoking Yiddish's more expressive term and saying "I schlepped the grocery bags for two blocks" is not merely a substitution of words. The Yiddish enhances the factual information contained in the sentence by saying that the carrying was difficult. It adds to the emotional information conveyed by expressing some anguish at having to carry the bags. Because the word *schlep* sounds funny (and a lot funnier than *carry*), there is an element of humor to the sentence. Finally, these last two elements—of emotional information and humor—are fused so that the difficult effort is modified by humor, signifying that the task, however trying, has been emotionally accepted. This ability to multiply the meaning of expressions and simultaneously inject humor has made Yiddish important for all comedians and, finally, for all Americans interested in wringing out all the possibilities of the language they use.

Leo Rosten, whose book *The Joys of Yiddish* is the indispensable guide to these expressions, identified the various and sometimes subtle ways in which Yiddish has curled up into the welcoming arms of English. Here are just some of them:

1.. The near repetition of a word with the addition of "sh" at the beginning of the repetition as a way to mock the idea as in "Fat, shmat, as long as he finishes his dinner."
2. Reversed syntax as in "Handsome, he's not."
3. A question phrased as a clear rejection, such as "I should pay for that meal?"
4. The use of questions to answer questions, often by simply nearly repeating the first question with a different inflection, such as "Did you call your mother?" answered by "Did *I* call my mother?"

Yiddish was rich in its special curses, its epigrammatic proverbs, and its revealing folk stories. The curses were neither subtle nor kind, but blunt.

May all your teeth fall out except one, and may that one always ache.
May you grow so rich that your widow's second husband never has to worry about making a living.

May you back into a pitchfork and grab a hot stove for support.
May you win a lottery and spend it all on doctors.

The proverbs were usually much gentler and wiser:

The face is the worst informer.
Weep before God—laugh before people.
The highest wisdom is kindness.
When trouble comes in the world, the Jewish people feel it first;
    when good fortune comes into the world the Jewish people feel
    it last.
Hope is a poor person's bread.
If you can't afford chicken, herring will do.
If we didn't have to eat, we'd all be rich.
All things grow with time except grief.
Better to suffer an injustice than to do an injustice.
If God lived on earth, people would break His windows.
Words should be weighed, not counted.
A joke is a half-truth.
For dying, you always have time.
Too good is unhealthy.
Which king is the best in the world? A dead one.

There were also numerous folk stories, many of which accentuated language (and wit) as a defense mechanism. For example, in one story a Jew was walking when he accidentally bumped into one of the czar's officers.

"Swine!" screamed the officer.

"Goldberg," replied the Jew with a deep bow.

In another folk tale, two Jews were walking in an area in Russia where a permit was needed. One of the Jews had a permit, but the other did not. A police officer suddenly appeared. The one without the permit begged the one with the permit to run, saying that when the officer stopped him he'd have the permit. Meanwhile, the one without the permit could get away.

Willing to help, the Jew with the permit broke into a run. The officer saw him and quickly gave chase. Before long, the police officer caught up with him.

"So," the police officer said, "you have no permit."

"Why would you think that?" the Jew said. "I have a permit."

The puzzled officer asked, "Why did you run if you have a permit?"

"My doctor told me I needed to run for my health."

"But didn't you see that I was running after you?"

The Jew shrugged. "Sure I did. But I thought your doctor had given you the same advice."

These and many other examples of Yiddish stories and expressions were extraordinary in presenting a wide variety of character types:

1. A *schlemiel* (rhymes with reveal) is a pitiful, unlucky, or socially maladjusted person. There is pity toward such a loser.

2. A *nebbish* is a helpless, ineffective person, a first cousin to a schlemiel. The usual distinction is that "a schlemiel keeps knocking objects off the table. The nebbish always has to pick them up."

3. A *schlimazel* is someone for whom fate provides one unlucky circumstance after another. One Yiddish folk saying is that "When a schlimazel starts to sell umbrellas, the sun comes out." In a famous comparison, the schlemiel pours soup on the schlimazel.

4. A *schlump* is someone who depresses all those who are around.

5. A *nudnick* is a pest.
6. A *schmendrick* is a weak, vacillating person, someone Rosten calls "an apprentice schlemiel."
7. A *schmegegge* (rhymes with "Peggy") is someone who is petty and not very admirable.
8. A *gonif* is a thief.
9. A *schadkhan* is a marriage broker.
10. A *schnorrer* is a beggar.
11. A *maven* is an expert on a subject.

These few of the many Yiddish types—some very similar when rendered into English but with more pronounced nuances in Yiddish—reflect the focus on human foibles and weaknesses, the self-mockery often accompanied by pity, that characterized the entire culture, including its humor. The fact that so many of the types were losers, and the fact, however much pity is included in the characterization, that these losers were mocked is also revealing. It shows a drive in the culture to escape such characterizations, that is, to succeed. Jews in their East European culture were unhappy and guilty as they accurately perceived their identity in the world as losers. Without the resources in their communities to succeed on a large scale, they built up a psychological reservoir of such needs that were unleashed with ferocity when they found a place that welcomed, nourished, and psychologically and financially rewarded that need to succeed. The Jewish whirlwind that blew across America was driven in part by such a psychological need.

In another sense, this kind of language shows an assertiveness, almost an angry, attacking nature. There was a sense of lashing out inherent in having so many terms to describe the weak. The power of words to hurt and to curse, combined with the Jews' skill with language, gave them a weapon. This weapon, so well honed but unable to be used in Eastern Europe, was unsheathed and brandished with great skill in America.

Finally, the innumerable number of words for different types of people illustrates the Jews' powers of observation. They were able to scrutinize their own society and satirize it, characterize its inhabitants (frequently by their weaknesses), and separate themselves from it emotionally. There are obvious heirs to such skills, from Lenny Bruce's scathing social criticisms to Jerry Seinfeld's precise and laserlike recognition of the minutiae of social life.

Of course, individual Yiddish words also made the journey in steerage across the Atlantic: *bobbe-myseh* (a silly tale), *fress* (to eat a lot in a gluttonous or quick manner), *kinder* (the children), *chutzpah* (having a lot of nerve), *shtick* (a technique of humor, a bit of clowning), *megillah* (a long story), *nosh* (to nibble on food), *nu* (often accompanied by a question mark, and with several shades of meaning such as "What's going on?"), *kvell* (to feel great pride, especially at the accomplishments of one's children), and dozens if not hundreds of other words have survived the trip and exist in America.

Individual Yiddish words that express important communal norms have also been important. The word *mishpoche* means an extended family and illustrates the centrality of family ties. In this sense the Jewish people was seen as a big family, with members being responsible for all other members of this family. The word *mensh*, meaning "a good person," carries with it an admirable assessment of someone who is kind and moral, who does good with no ulterior motive. To *kvetch* is to complain. *Oy* is harder to translate, for its pained expression conjures up a memory of thousands of years of pain. *Oy* is a cry from the depths of the Jewish soul, a feeling entirely missing in comparable English expressions. All these, and many other words, nurtured the Jewish comedians.

Yiddish also produced an important literature. The most famous writers—especially I. L. Peretz and Sholem Aleichem—illustrated simple Jews struggling against the society and the world. The poor schlemiels who were the heroes of those literary outputs were caught in a world they could not control or understand. Traditional Judaism did not provide adequate help. Aleichem deeply sympathized with his characters, giving them a human strength to triumph in the face of persecution, poverty, and the strains of communal and family life. Humor helped provide that strength; it was a powerful weapon in the psychological war to survive.

All the children of immigrants who grew up to be comedians had parents who spoke Yiddish, who used it to nourish their children's imaginations, who, whether they passed it on or not, had their minds and hearts molded by Yiddish, and so, whether the actual words were there or not, the sentiments and ideas certainly were. Their religion may have been stored away with the Jewish ritual objects they never used. Their attachment to Jewish communal life may have been weak, especially when they were young. Their grasp of Hebrew may have been nonexistent. Yet, they were Jewish at their center. As Sigmund Freud wrote in the preface to the Hebrew edition of his book *Totem and Taboo*, "What is still Jewish in you after you abandoned all those things common to your people?" Freud's answer about himself was: "Still very much, perhaps the main part of my personality." This personality, shaped by his mother and her *mama-loshen*, by the genetic and cultural inheritance he carried, was also very similar for the Jewish comedians. They may not have been as self-reflective as Freud, but their personalities were Jewish to the core, whatever they said, and however far they journeyed from Judaism.

Whereas Eastern European Jewish culture and the Yiddish language were instrumental in framing the comedic spirit of Jewish comedians, so, too, was that spirit nurtured by the forces that contributed generally to comedy in all humans.

There are many theories about humor. Indeed, such theories go at least back to the Greeks. Plato, for example, was concerned that humor could upset the social order by inciting violence. In contrast, Aristotle found in laughter a clear demarcation between humans and animals. Eventually, these ideas gave way to newer theories. Hobbes focused on the power that laughter could offer to those who could provide it. Kant suggested that humor results when events don't conform to our expectations.

Freud talked about humor, using many Jewish examples, in his book *Wit and Its Relation to the Unconscious*, published in 1905. He saw humor as a release of nervous energy that had been kept within. He believed also that humor allows humans to express deep sexual desires in a socially acceptable way. Finally, Freud saw Jewish humor as a source of self-ridicule.

Theodor Reik, a disciple of Freud, saw Jewish humor as reflective of a profound Jewish psychopathology. Reik identified the jokes as on a continuum with masochism at one end and a "paranoid superiority" at the other. The two ends of the spectrum are complementary in Reik's eyes, two halves of the same collective mind of the Jewish people. For Freud and Reik, a basic Jewish humor is present at all historical times. Such a view—that self-ridicule is the preeminent characteristic of Jewish humor—did not go unchallenged. Dan Ben-Amos, for example, argues that such self-mockery did not reflect any masochism but rather was an attempt by comics to separate themselves from the past as tradition understood it.

Other psychological theorists of humor have focused on such subjects as how humor provides a diversion from the pains and troubles of everyday life, how humor provides a game for the comic to play—with the audience participants seeing if they can grasp the wit of the comic and the comics seeing if they can gauge what their audiences will find funny—how humor mocks the unfair and the painful, and how comedy can provide consolation in times of loss and agony.

Sociologists have provided more sweeping and less specific theories. Henri Bergson, for example, in *Le rire* (1898) found in humor a socializing mechanism by which those who stepped outside acceptable social bounds could be effectively mocked and, if possible, brought back within the social consensus. Other sociologists have focused on other aspects, among others that humor eases communication among people, makes members of the same group aware that they are indeed part of a wider society, both provides illustrative examples and supports the values necessary for a social group to survive, protects a group against criticism from outsiders, and, crucially, provides a social glue to bond when other differences might separate people in a group.

But the comics who emerged from this Jewish background were not aware of psychological or sociological theories. As George Burns noted, they were not hungry for recognition; they were hungry for food. They did not question their humor but rather just recognized and used it. Nevertheless, the roles comedians played and most particularly the contributions of Eastern European Jewish culture shaped the personalities of these comedians and lay, either hidden or not, in their minds.

REFERENCES

An enormous number of books, articles, videos, records and CDs, Internet sites, archival and museum materials, personal experiences, and interviews were used in researching this book.

Some materials were used repeatedly throughout the book. In addition, comedians are not limited to a single chapter, and materials about them recur in various chapters. Therefore, I will first list general reference materials, then material about specific comedians, material used in various chapters, and finally materials pertinent to specific chapters.

There is an enormous amount of material on Jewish comedians, and it would take several volumes simply to list what is available. I will not be including here a listing of all of each comedian's record albums or CDs, television programs or appearances, or motion pictures because they are too numerous. Similarly, I have not listed all the biographical and autobiographical material in book form. Some of the record albums or CDs and some additional book materials are listed in individual chapters. A list of the key libraries, archives, and museums I used is included in the acknowledgment section as is a list of people interviewed. I do mention particular interviews when they were pertinent to a chapter, but almost all interviews wandered across a very wide range of ideas and were influential in many places.

References

These are the general references:

Allen, Steve. *Funny People*. New York: Stein & Day, 1981.
———. *More Funny People*. New York: Stein & Day, 1982.
Berger, Arthur Asa. *Jewish Jesters*. Cresskill, N.J.: Hampton Press, 2001.
Cahn, William. *The Great American Comedy Scene*. New York: Monarch, 1978. (This book is an update of the author's *Pictorial History of the Great Comedians* [New York: Grosset & Dunlop, 1970], which, in turn, was an update of *The Laugh Makers* [New York: G. P. Putnam's Sons, 1957]).
Cohen, Sarah Blecher, ed. *From Hester Street to Hollywood: The Jewish-American Stage and Screen*. Bloomington: Indiana University Press, 1983.
———. *Jewish Wry: Essays on Jewish Humor*. Bloomington: Indiana University Press, 1987.
Debenham, Warren. *Laughter on Record: A Comedy Discography*. Metuchen, N.J.: Scarecrow Press, 1988.
Franklin, Joe. *Joe Franklin's Encyclopedia of Comedians*. Secaucus, N.J.: Citadel Press, 1985.
Grace, Arthur. *Comedians*. Charlottesville, Va.: Eastman Kodak and Thomasson-Grant, 1991.
Janik, Vicki, ed. *Fools and Jesters in Literature, Art, and History*. Westport, Conn.: Greenwood Press, 1998.
Laugh. Conceived and produced by Andy Gould and Kathleen Bywater. Photos by William Claxton. New York: Morrow, 1999.
Lyman, Darryl. *The Jewish Comedy Catalog*. Middle Village, N.Y.: Jonathan David, 1989.
Romeyn, Esther, and Jack Kugelmass. *Let There Be Laughter! Jewish Humor in America*. Chicago: Spertus Press, 1997.
Smith, Ronald L. *Goldmine Comedy Record Price Guide*. Iola, Wis.: Krause, 1996.
———. *Stars of Stand-Up*. New York: Sure Sellers, 1995.
———. *The Stars of Stand-up Comedy: A Biographical Encyclopedia*. New York: Garland, 1986.
———. *Who's Who in Comedy: Comedians, Comics, and Clowns from Vaudeville to Today's Stand-Ups*. New York: Facts on File, 1992.
Whitfield, Stephen J. *In Search of American Jewish Culture*. Hanover, N.H.: University Press of New England, 1999.
Wilde, Larry. *The Great Comedians Talk about Comedy*. New York: Citadel, 1968.

Additional materials about individual comedians include:

Woody Allen

Allen, Woody. *Getting Even*. New York: Warner, 1971.

——— "Random Reflections of a Second-Rate Mind." *Tikkun* (Jan.–Feb. 1990): 13–15, 71–72.

———. *Without Feathers*. New York: Warner, 1975.

———. *Woody Allen on Woody Allen: In Conversation with Steg Bjorkman*. New York: Grove/Atlantic, 1995.

Baxter, John. *Woody Allen*. New York: Carroll & Graf, 2000.

Bleiweiss, Mark E. "Self-Deprecation and the Jewish Humor of Woody Allen." *Jewish Spectator* (winter 1989): 25–34.

Brode, Douglas. *Films of Woody Allen*. New York: Carol, 1991.

Hirsh, Foster. *Love, Sex, Death, and the Meaning of Life: The Films of Woody Allen*. New York: Limelight, 1990.

Lax, Eric. *On Being Funny: Woody Allen and Comedy*. New York: Charterhouse, 1975.

———. *Woody Allen: A Biography*. New York: Knopf, 1991.

Meade, Marion. *The Unruly Life of Woody Allen*. New York: Scribner, 2000.

Nichols, Mary P. *Reconstructing Woody: Art, Love, and Life in the Films of Woody Allen*. Lanham, Md.: Rowman and Littlefield, 1998.

Rich, Frank. "An Interview with Woody." *Time* (Apr. 30, 1979): 68–69.

Rosenbaum, Jonathan. "Notes toward the Depreciation of Woody Allen." *Tikkun* (May–June 1990): 33–39.

Rosenbloom, Ralph, and Robert Karin. *When the Shooting Stops, the Cutting Begins: A Film Editor's Story*. New York: Da Capo, 1986.

Zinsser, William K. "Woody Allen." *Saturday Evening Post* (Sept. 21, 1963): 26–27.

Richard Belzer

Belzer, Richard. *How to Be a Stand-up Comic*. Secaucus, N.J.: Citadel, 1992.

Jack Benny

Benny, Jack, and Joan Benny. *Sunday Nights at Seven: The Jack Benny Story*. New York: Warner, 1990.

Benny, Mary Livingstone. *Jack Benny*. Garden City, N.Y.: Doubleday, 1978.

Fein, Irving. *Jack Benny*. Boston: G. K. Hall, 1976.

Josefsberg, Milt. *The Jack Benny Show*. New Rochelle, N.Y.: Arlington House, 1977.

GERTRUDE BERG

Berg, Gertrude. "Let God Worry a Little Bit." In *Growing Up Jewish: An Anthology*, ed. Jay David, 55–59. New York: Morrow, 1996.

Berg, Gertrude, with Cherney Berg. *Molly and Me*. New York: McGraw-Hill, 1961.

Freedman, Morris. "The Real Molly Goldberg." *Commentary* (Apr. 1956): 359–64.

O'Dell, Cary. "Gertrude Berg Calls the Shots." *Television Quarterly* (summer 1996): 50–56.

Weber, Donald. "The Jewish-American World of Gertrude Berg: *The Goldbergs* on Radio and Television, 1930–1960." In *Talking Back*, ed. Joyce Antler, 85–99. Hanover, N.H.: Brandeis University Press, 1998.

———. "Memory and Repression in Early Ethnic Television: The Example of Gertrude Berg and *The Goldbergs*." In *The Other Fifties*, ed. Joel Foreman, 144–67. Urbana: University of Illinois Press, 1997.

———. "Taking Jewish American Popular Culture Seriously: The Yinglish Worlds of Gertrude Berg, Milton Berle, and Mickey Katz." *Jewish Social Studies* (fall 1998–winter 1999): 124–53.

MILTON BERLE

Berle, Milton. *B.S. I Love You: Sixty Funny Years with the Famous and the Infamous*. New York: McGraw-Hill, 1988.

———. Unpublished interview. American Jewish Committee.

Berle, Milton, with Haskel Frankel. *Milton Berle: An Autobiography*. New York: Delacorte, 1974.

Milton Berle: Mr. Television. New York: Museum of Television and Radio, 1985.

Wertheim, Arthur Frank. "The Rise and Fall of Milton Berle." In *American History, American Television: Interpreting the Video Past*, ed. John E. O'Connor, 55–78. New York: Ungar, 1983.

SANDRA BERNHARD

Bernhard, Sandra. *Confessions of a Pretty Lady*. New York: Harper & Row, 1988.

FANNY BRICE

Grossman, Barbara Wallace. *Funny Woman: The Life and Times of Fanny Brice*. Bloomington: Indiana University Press, 1991.

Katkov, Norman. *The Fabulous Fanny: The Story of Fanny Brice*. New York: Knopf, 1953.

MEL BROOKS

Adler, Bill, and Jeffrey Feinman. *Mel Brooks*. Chicago: Playboy Press, 1976.

Poretsky, H. Solomon. "Mel Brooks' Blazing Jewish Humor." *Jewish Spectator* (spring 1998): 47–49.

Smurthwaite, Nick, and Paul Gelder. *Mel Brooks and the Spoof Movie.* New York: Proteus, 1983.

Yacowar, Maurice. *Method in Madness: The Comic Art of Mel Brooks.* New York: St. Martin's Press, 1981.

LENNY BRUCE

Bruce, Lenny. *The Essential Lenny Bruce.* Ed. John Cohen. London: Macmillan, 1972.

———. *How to Talk Dirty and Influence People.* New York: Simon and Schuster, 1992.

Goldman, Albert. *Ladies and Gentlemen, Lenny Bruce!* New York: Ballantine, 1971.

Kofsky, Frank. *Lenny Bruce: Comedian as Social Critic and Secular Moralist.* New York: Monad Press, 1974.

Lenny Bruce: Swear to Tell the Truth [Video]. Produced by Robert B. Weide. Whyaduck Productions, 1998.

The Lenny Bruce Performance Film [Video]. Produced by John Magnuson. Stamford, Conn.: Vestron, 1982.

Lenny Bruce without Tears [Video]. Fred Barker Film and Video, 1975.

GEORGE BURNS

Burns, George. *All My Best Friends.* New York: Putnam, 1989.

———. *One Hundred Years, One Hundred Stories.* New York: Putnam, 1996.

———. Unpublished interview. American Jewish Committee.

George Burns File. New York Public Library, Billy Rose Collection.

Gottfried, Martin. *George Burns and the Hundred Yard Dash.* New York: Simon and Schuster, 1996.

www.geocities.com/Hollywood/Hills/1836/main.html George Burns and Gracie Allen

SID CAESAR

Caesar, Sid, with Bill Davidson. *Where Have I Been? An Autobiography.* New York: Crown, 1982.

EDDIE CANTOR

Cantor, Eddie, with Jane Kesner Ardmore. *Take My Life.* New York: Doubleday, 1957.

Eddie Cantor File. New York Public Library, Billy Rose Collection.

Goldman, Herbert G. *Banjo Eyes: Eddie Cantor and the Birth of Modern Stardom.* New York: Oxford University Press, 1997.

BILLY CRYSTAL
Crystal, Billy, with Dick Schaap. *Absolutely Mahvelous.* New York: Putnam, 1986.

FRAN DRESCHER
Drescher, Fran. *Enter Whining.* New York: Regan Books, 1996.

JUDY HOLLIDAY
Carey, Gary. *Judy Holliday: An Intimate Love Story.* New York: Seaview, 1982.
Holtzman, Will. *Judy Holliday.* New York: Putnam, 1982.

GEORGE JESSEL
Jessel, George. *So Help Me.* New York: Random House, 1943.

ANDY KAUFMAN
Zehme, Bill. *Lost in the Funhouse: The Life and Mind of Andy Kaufman.* New York: Delacorte, 1999.
Zmuda, Bob, with Matthew Scott Hansen. *Andy Kaufman Revealed!* Boston: Little, Brown, 1999.

DANNY KAYE
Freedland, Michael. *The Secret Life of Danny Kaye.* New York: St. Martin's Press, 1985.
Gottfried, Martin. *Nobody's Fool: The Lives of Danny Kaye.* New York: Simon and Schuster, 1994.

ALAN KING
King, Alan. *Name-Dropping: The Life and Lies of Alan King.* New York: Scribner, 1996.

BERT LAHR
Lahr, John. *Notes on a Cowardly Lion: The Biography of Bert Lahr.* Berkeley and Los Angeles: University of California Press, 2000.

SAM LEVENSON
Levenson, Sam. *Everything but Money.* New York: Watts, 1966.

JERRY LEWIS

Levy, Shawn. *King of Comedy: The Life and Art of Jerry Lewis*. New York: St. Martin's Press, 1996.

Lewis, Jerry, with Herb Gluck. *Jerry Lewis in Person*. New York: Atheneum, 1982.

Rapf, Joanna E. "Comic Theory from a Feminist Perspective: A Look at Jerry Lewis." *Journal of Popular Culture* (summer 1993): 101–203.

RICHARD LEWIS

Lewis, Richard. *The Other Great Depression*. New York: PublicAffairs, 2000.

THE MARX BROTHERS

Adamson, Joe *Groucho, Harpo, Chico, and Sometimes Zeppo*. New York: Simon and Schuster, 1973.

Anobile, Richard J. *Why a Duck?* New York: Darien House, 1971.

Arce, Hector. *Groucho*. New York: Perigee, 1980.

Barson, Michael, ed. *Flywheel, Shyster, and Flywheel: The Marx Brothers' Lost Radio Show*. New York: Pantheon, 1988.

Chandler, Charlotte. *Hello, I Must Be Going: Groucho and His Friends*. Garden City, N.Y.: Doubleday, 1978.

Crichton, Kyle. *The Marx Brothers*. Garden City, N.Y.: Doubleday, 1950.

Eyles, Allen. *The Marx Brothers: Their World of Comedy*. 2nd ed. New York: A. S. Barnes, 1969.

Gardner, Martin Allan. "The Marx Brothers: An Investigation of Their Films as Satirical Social Criticism." Ph.D. diss., New York University, 1970.

Gehring, Wes. *The Marx Brothers: A Bio-Bibliography*. New York: Greenwood Press, 1987.

Groucho Marx. Federal Bureau of Investigation File.

Jordan, Thomas H. *The Anatomy of Cinematic Humor: With an Essay on the Marx Brothers*. New York: Revisionist Press, 1975.

Kanfer, Stefan. *Groucho: The Life and Times of Julius Henry Marx*. New York: Knopf, 2000.

Louvish, Simon. *Monkey Business: The Lives and Legends of the Marx Brothers* New York: St. Martin's Press, 2000.

Marx, Arthur. *My Life with Groucho*. Boston: G. K. Hall, 1993.

Marx, Harpo, with Rowland Barber. *Harpo Speaks!* New York: Limelight, 1985.

Marx Brothers in a Nutshell [Video]. Produced by Robert B. Weide. Whyaduck Productions, 1982.

Mitchell, Glenn. *The Marx Brothers Encyclopedia*. London: B. T. Batsford, 1996.

Tiersma, Peter Meijes. *Language-Based Humor in the Marx Brothers Films.* Bloomington: Indiana University Linguistic Club, 1985.
The Unknown Marx Brothers [Video]. Troy, Mich.: Anchor Bay, 1996.

JACKIE MASON

Mason, Jackie, with Ira Berkow. *How to Talk Jewish.* New York: St. Martin's Press, 1992.
———. *The World according to Me.* New York: Simon and Schuster, 1987.
Mason, Jackie, with Ken Gross. *Jackie Oy! Jackie Mason from Birth to Rebirth.* Boston: Little, Brown, 1988.

ZERO MOSTEL

Sainer, Arthur. *Zero Dances: A Biography of Zero Mostel.* New York: Limelight, 1998.

GILDA RADNER

Gilda Live! [Video]. 1980.
Radner, Gilda. *It's Always Something.* New York: Avon, 1995.
Saltman, David. *Gilda: An Intimate Portrait.* Chicago: Contemporary, 1992.
Zweibel, Alan. *Bunny, Bunny: Gilda Radner.* New York: Villard, 1993.

JOAN RIVERS

Rivers, Joan. *Bouncing Back.* New York: HarperCollins, 1997.
———. *Don't Count the Candles, Just Keep the Fire Lit.* New York: Harper-Collins, 1999.
Rivers, Joan, with Richard Meryman. *Enter Talking.* New York: Delacorte, 1986.

ROSEANNE

Barr, Roseanne. *Roseanne: My Life as a Woman.* New York: Harper & Row, 1989.
Ehrenreich, Barbara. "The Wretched of the Hearth: The Undainty Feminism of Roseanne Barr." *New Republic* (Apr. 2, 1990): 28 ff.
Krohn, Katherine E. *Roseanne Arnold: Comedy's Queen Bee.* Minneapolis: Lerner Publishing, 1993.

MORT SAHL

Hungry i reunion. [Video]. Hungry i Productions, 1980.
Sahl, Mort. *Heartland.* Orlando: Harcourt, Brace, 1976.

JERRY SEINFELD

Gattuso, Greg. *The Seinfeld Universe: The Entire Domain.* Secaucus, N.J.: Carol, 1998.

Levine, Josh. *Jerry Seinfeld: Much Ado about Nothing.* Toronto: ECW Press, 1993.

Seinfeld, Jerry. *Sein Language.* New York: Bantam, 1993.

Tracy, Kathleen. *Jerry Seinfeld: The Entire Domain.* Secaucus, N.J.: Birch Lane, 1998.

Wild, David. *Seinfeld: Totally Unauthorized.* New York: Crown, 1998.

PHIL SILVERS

Silvers, Phil, with Robert Saffron. *The Laugh Is on Me: The Phil Silvers Story.* Englewood Cliffs, N.J.: Prentice-Hall, 1973.

HOWARD STERN

Colford, Paul D. *Howard Stern: King of All Media.* New York: St. Martin's Press, 1997.

Hoffman, Matthew. *The Completely Unauthorized Howard Stern.* Philadelphia: Courage Books, 1998.

Stern, Howard. *Miss America.* New York: Regan Books, 1995.

———. *Private Parts.* New York: Simon and Schuster, 1993.

BARBRA STREISAND

Edwards, Anne. *Streisand: A Biography.* Boston: Little, Brown, 1997.

THE THREE STOOGES

Fleming, Michael. *The Three Stooges.* New York: Doubleday, 1999.

Forrester, Jeffrey. *The Stooge Chronicles.* Chicago: Triumvirate, 1981.

Howard, Moe. *Moe Howard and the Three Stooges.* Secaucus, N.J.: Citadel, 1977.

Kurson, Robert. *The Official Three Stooges Encyclopedia.* Lincolnwood, Ill.: Contemporary Books, 1998.

SOPHIE TUCKER

Freedland, Michael. *Sophie: The Sophie Tucker Story.* London: Woburn Press, 1978.

Tucker, Sophie. *Some of These Days.* London: Hammond, 1948.

HENNY YOUNGMAN

Youngman, Henny, with Neal Karlen. *Take My Life Please.* New York: Morrow, 1991.

———. *Take My Wife, Please.* New York: Putnam, 1973.

Each chapter had its individual references as well as those above.

INTRODUCTION: THE WORLD OF JEWISH COMEDIANS

Interviews: Steve Allen, Leslie Fiedler, and Frank Rich.

"Analyzing Jewish Comics." *Time* (Oct. 2, 1978): 235.

Berger, Peter. *Redeeming Laughter: The Comic Dimension of Human Experience.* New York: Walter De Gruyter, 1997.

Boskin, Joseph. *Rebellious Laughter.* Syracuse: Syracuse University Press, 1997.

Chapman, Antony, and Hugh Foot, eds. *Humour and Applications.* London: Wiley, 1976.

Cowan, Lore, and Maurice Cowan. *The Wit of the Jews.* Nashville: Aurora, 1970.

Epstein, Lawrence J. *A Treasury of Jewish Anecdotes.* Northvale, N.J.: Jason Aronson, 1989.

Janus, Samuel S. "The Great Comedians: Personality and Other Factors." *American Journal of Psychoanalysis* (1975): 169–74.

Shechner, Mark. "Comics and Comedy." In *Jewish-American History and Culture: An Encyclopedia,* ed. Jack Fischel and Sandford Pinsker, 97–104. New York: Garland, 1992.

1. THE LAND OF HOPE AND TEARS

Interview: Brian Gari.

Cowan, Neil M. *Our Parents' Lives: Jewish Assimilation and Everyday Life.* New Brunswick, N.J.: Rutgers University Press, 1996.

Dawidowicz, Lucy S. "A Century of Jewish History, 1881–1981: The View from America." In *American Jewish Year Book 1982,* 3–98. New York and Philadelphia: American Jewish Committee and Jewish Publication Society, 1982.

Ellis Island [Video]. Produced and directed by Lisa Bourgoujian. New York: A&E Home Video, 1997.

Feingold, Henry L. *Let Memory Cease: Finding Meaning in the American Jewish Past.* Syracuse: Syracuse University Press, 1996.

———. *Zion in America.* New York: Twayne, 1974.

Gay, Ruth. *Unfinished People: Eastern European Jews Encounter America.* New York: Norton, 1996.

Gurock, Jeffrey S., ed. *East European Jews in America, 1880–1920: Immigration and Adaptation*. New York: Routledge, 1998.

Handlin, Oscar. *The Uprooted*. 2nd ed. Boston: Little, Brown, 1990.

Heinze, Andrew R. *Adapting to Abundance: Jewish Immigrants, Mass Consumption, and the Search for American Identity*. New York: Columbia University Press, 1990.

Hindus, Milton, ed. *The Jewish East Side, 1881–1924*. New Brunswick, N.J.: Transaction, 1996.

Howe, Irving, and Kenneth Libo, eds. *How We Lived*. New York: R. Marek, 1979.

———. *World of Our Fathers*. New York: Harcourt Brace Jovanovich, 1976.

Janus, Samuel S. "The Great Jewish-American Comedians' Identity Crisis." *American Journal of Psychoanalysis* (fall 1980): 259–65.

A Laugh, a Tear, a Mitzvah [Video]. Written by Sam Toperoff and produced and directed by Roman Brygider. Garden City, N.Y.: WLIW, 1997.

Meyerowitz, Rael. *Transferring to America: Jewish Interpretations of American Dreams*. Albany: State University of New York Press, 1995.

Sachar, Howard M. *A History of the Jews in America*. New York: Knopf, 1992.

Sanders, Ronald. *The Downtown Jews: Portraits of an Immigrant Generation*. New York: Harper & Row, 1969.

Seltzer, Robert, and Norman J. Cohen, eds. *Americanization of the Jews*. New York: New York University Press, 1995.

Weinberg, Sydney Stahl. *The World of Our Mothers: The Lives of Jewish Immigrant Women*. Chapel Hill: University of North Carolina Press, 1988.

2. CURTAIN UP AND CURTAIN DOWN

Allen, Ralph G. *The Best Burlesque Sketches*. New York: Applause, 1995.

Esposito, Tony. *Golden Era of Vaudeville*. Miami: Warner Bros., 1995.

Gilbert, Douglas. *American Vaudeville: Its Life and Times*. New York: Dover, 1963.

Jenkins, Henry. *What Made Pistachio Nuts?* New York: Columbia University Press, 1992.

Levenson, Sam. "The Dialect Comedian Should Vanish." *Commentary* (Aug. 1952): 168–70.

McLean, Albert F., Jr. *American Vaudeville as Ritual*. Lexington: University Press of Kentucky, 1965.

Rogin, Michael Paul. *Blackface, White Noise: Jewish Immigrants in the Hollywood Melting Pot*. Berkeley and Los Angeles: University of California Press, 1996.

Slide, Anthony. *The Encyclopedia of Vaudeville*. Westport, Conn.: Greenwood, 1994.

————, ed. *Selected Vaudeville Criticism*. Metuchen, N.J.: Scarecrow Press, 1988.

Sobel, Bernard. *A Pictorial History of Vaudeville*. New York: Citadel, 1961.

Vaudeville [Video]. American Masters, PBS, 1997.

www.briangari.com (Eddie Cantor's grandson).

www.eddiecantor.com.

www.theparamount.com (Sean McIntyre, "History of the Paramount Theatre").

www.vaudeville.org (American Vaudeville Museum).

Zeidman, Irving. *The American Burlesque Show*. New York: Hawthorn, 1967.

3. THEATER OF THE MIND

Brown, Robert J. *The Power of Broadcast Radio in Thirties America*. Jefferson, N.C.: McFarland, 1998.

The Danny Kaye Show. Audio File, n.d.

Dinnerstein, Leonard. *Antisemitism in America*. New York: Oxford, 1994.

Douglas, Susan J. *Listening In: Radio and the American Imagination*. New York: Times Books, 1999.

Dunning, John. *Tune in Yesterday: The Ultimate Encyclopedia of Old-Time Radio, 1925–1976*. Englewood Cliffs, N.J.: Prentice-Hall, 1976.

Eddie Cantor. Audio File, n.d.

Firestone, Ross, ed. *The Big Radio Comedy Program*. Chicago: Contemporary Books, 1978.

The Great Radio Comedians [Video]. Produced and directed by Perry Miller Adato. New York: McGraw-Hill Films, 1970.

Harmon, Jim. *Great Radio Comedians*. Garden City, N.Y.: Doubleday, 1970.

MacDonald, J. Fred. *Don't Touch That Dial! Radio Programming in American Life, 1920–1960*. Chicago: Nelson-Hall, 1979.

Maltin, Leonard. *The Great American Broadcast: A Celebration of Radio's Golden Age*. New York: Dutton, 1997.

The Marx Brothers Greatest Routines. Radio Spirits, 1995.

Speaking of Radio: An Audio-Biography of "The Jack Benny Program." 3 vols. Audio file, n.d.

Stanton, Frank N. "Psychological Research in the Field of Radio Listening." In *Educational Broadcasting*, 1–12. Chicago: University of Chicago Press, 1936.

Wertheim, Arthur Frank. *Radio Comedy*. New York: Oxford University Press, 1979.

www.old-time.com (Old Time Radio).
www.old-time.com/halper/index (Donna Halper's History of Radio).

4. Laughing in the Dark

Interviews: Annette Insdorf, Marvin Kitman, Leonard Maltin, Tom Tugend, and Elie Wiesel.

Birdwell, Michael E. *Celluloid Soldiers: The Warner Bros. Campaign against Nazism.* New York: New York University Press, 1999.
Brownlow, Kevin. *Behind the Mask of Innocence.* New York: Knopf, 1990.
Cavalcade of Comedy [Video]. Produced by Bret Wood. New York: Kino Video, 1998.
Cripps, Thomas. "The Movie Jew as an Image of Assimilationism, 1903–1927." *Journal of Popular Film,* no 3 (1975): 190–207.
Dickstein, Morris. "Urban Comedy and Modernity: From Chaplin to Woody Allen." *Partisan Review,* no. 3 (1985): 271–81.
Doneson, Judith E. *The Holocaust in American Film.* Philadelphia: Jewish Publication Society, 1987.
Edelson, Edward. *Funny Men of the Movies.* Garden City, N.Y.: Doubleday, 1976.
Erens, Patricia. *The Jew in American Cinema.* Bloomington: Indiana University Press, 1984.
Friedman, Lester D. *Hollywood's Image of the Jew.* New York: Ungar, 1982.
———. *The Jewish Image in American Film.* Secaucus, N.J.: Citadel, 1987.
Gabler, Neal. *An Empire of Their Own: How the Jews Invented Hollywood.* Anchor: New York, 1988.
MacCann, Richard Dyer. *The Silent Comedians.* Metuchen, N.J.: Scarecrow Press, 1993.
Maltin, Leonard. *The Great Movie Comedians.* New York: Harmony, 1982.
———. *Movie Comedy Teams.* New York: New American Library, 1985.
Manchel, Frank. *The Box-Office Clowns.* New York: Franklin Watts, 1979.
———. *The Talking Clowns.* New York: Franklin Watts, 1976.
McCaffrey, Donald W. *The Golden Age of Sound Comedy: Comic Films and Comedians of the Thirties.* South Brunswick, N.J.: A. S. Barnes, 1973.
Moore, Deborah Dash. *At Home in America: Second Generation New York Jews.* New York: Columbia University Press, 1981.
One Hundred Years of Comedy [Video]. Written and directed by Phillip Dye. North Hollywood: Passport Video, 1997.

Oster, Shai. "Shoah Business: Humor and the 'Second Generation.'" *Jewish Quarterly* (autumn 1998): 13–18.

Parish, James Robert. *The Funsters*. New Rochelle, N.Y.: Arlington House, 1979.

Sennett, Ted. *Laughing in the Dark: Movie Comedy from Groucho to Woody*. New York: St. Martin's Press, 1992.

Weinberg, David. "The 'Socially Acceptable' Immigrant Minority Group: The Image of the Jew in American Popular Films." *North Dakota Quarterly* (autumn 1972): 60–68.

Whitfield, Stephen J. "Laughter in the Dark." *Midstream* (Feb. 1978): 48–58.

———. "Movies in America as Paradigms of Accommodation." In *The Americanization of the Jews*, ed. Robert M. Seltzer and Norman J. Cohen, 79–94. New York: New York University Press, 1995.

Winokur, Mark. *American Laughter: Immigrants, Ethnicity, and 1930s Hollywood Film Comedy*. New York: St. Martin's Press, 1996.

www.whyaduck.com.

5. The Jewish Alps

Interviews: Phil Brown and Freddie Roman.

Adams, Joey, with Henry Tobias. *The Borscht Belt*. New York: Bobbs-Merrill, 1966.

Brown, Phil. *Catskill Culture: A Mountain Rat's Memories of the Great Jewish Resort Area*. Philadelphia: Temple University Press, 1998.

Catskills on Broadway. Dove Audio, 1994.

Frommer, Myrna Katz, and Harvey Frommer. *It Happened in the Catskills*. New York: Harcourt Brace, 1991.

Kanfer, Stefan. *A Summer World: The Attempt to Build a Jewish Eden in the Catskills from the Days of the Ghetto to the Rise and Decline of the Borscht Belt*. New York: Farrar, Straus, and Giroux, 1992.

Littenberg, Marcia B. "The Tummler: Carnivalian Laughter in the Catskills." *Jewish Folklore and Ethnology Review* (1997): 12–15.

The Rise and Fall of the Borscht Belt [Video]. New York: Arthur Cantor, 1987.

www.brown.edu/Research/Catskills_Institute (Phil Brown's Catskills Institute).

6. THE MAGIC BOX

Interviews: Steve Allen, Sid Caesar, Don Freeman, Marvin Kitman, Louis Nye, Soupy Sales, Ronald L. Smith, and Robert J. Thompson.

Adir, Karin. *Great Clowns of American Television.* Jefferson, N.C.: McFarland, 1988.
Caesar's Writers [Video]. Michael Hirsh Productions, 1996.
Gabler, Neal, Frank Rich, and Joyce Antler. *Television's Changing Image of American Jews.* New York: American Jewish Committee and the Norman Lear Center, 2000.
Marc, David, and David Bianculi. *Comic Visions: Television Comedy and American Culture.* 2nd ed. Malden, Ma.: Blackwell, 1997.
Milton Berle's Mad, Mad World of Comedy [Video]. Produced by Jack Haley Jr. Santa Monica, Calif.: Rhino Home Video, 1991.
Pearl, Jonathan, and Judith Pearl. *The Chosen Image: Television's Portrayal of Jewish Themes and Characters.* Jefferson, N.C.: McFarland, 1999.
Poole, Gary. *TV Comedians.* New York: Grosset & Dunlap, 1979.
Putterman, Barry. *On Television and Comedy.* Jefferson, N.C.: McFarland, 1995.
Shandler, Jeffrey. *While America Watches: Televising the Holocaust.* New York: Oxford, 1999.
Stand-up Comedians on Television. New York: Abrams/Museum of Television & Radio, 1996.
www.comedyorama.com/philsilvers/index.html.
www.mediahistory.com/teeveehtml.
Young, Jordan R. *The Laugh Crafters: Comedy Writing in Radio and TV's Golden Age.* Beverly Hills: Past Times Pub., 1999.

7. "IS THERE ANY GROUP I HAVEN'T OFFENDED?"

Interviews: Ed Asner, Shelley Berman, Dr. Irwin Corey, Avery Corman, Larry Coven, Shecky Greene, Buddy Hackett, Chana Halprin, Nat Hentoff, Victor Navasky, Norman Podhoretz, Stanley Ralph Ross, Avery Schreiber, and Tommy Smothers.

Letter: Tom Lehrer.

The Comedians: "Good Stuff!": Stand-up Debuts from "The Tonight Show" [Video]. Burbank, Ca.: Buena Vista, Carson Productions Group, 1994.

Goldman, Albert. "Boy-Man, Schlemiel: Jewish Humor." *Commonweal* (Sept. 29, 1967): 605–8.

Koziski, Stephanie. "The Stand-up Comedian as Anthropologist." *Journal of Popular Culture* (fall 1984): 57–76.

McCrohan, Donna. *The Second City*. New York: Perigee, 1987.

Mintz, Lawrence E. "Stand-up Comedy as Social and Cultural Mediation." *American Quarterly* (spring 1985): 71–80.

Raphael, Marc Lee. "From Marjorie to Tevya: The Image of the Jews in American Popular Literature, Theatre, and Comedy, 1955–1965." *American Jewish History* (Sept. 1984): 66–72.

Albums and CDs:

Woody Allen: The Nightclub Years. United Artists, 1972.

Woody Allen: Stand-up Comic. Rhino, 1999.

Barth, Belle. *If I Embarrass You Tell Your Friends*. After Hours, n.d.

The Edge of Shelley Berman, Verve, n.d.

Inside Shelley Berman, Verve, 1960.

Outside Shelley Berman, Verve, n.d.

Lenny Bruce in Concert. United Artists, n.d.

This Is Myron Cohen. RCA Victor, n.d.

Buddy Hackett. *The Original Chinese Waiter*. Dot, n.d.

Robert Klein. *Child of the '50s*. Buddah, 1973.

Jackie Mason, *I'm the Greatest Comedian in the World Only Nobody Knows It Yet*. Verve, n.d.

An Evening with Mike Nichols and Elaine May. Mercury, n.d.

Two Thousand Years with Carl Reiner and Mel Brooks. Rhino, 1994.

Mort Sahl at the Hungry i. Verve, n.d.

Sherman, Allan. *My Son, the Folk Singer*. Warner Brothers, 1962.

Warren, Rusty. *Songs for Sinners*. Crescendo, n.d.

8. "I Need the Eggs"

Interview: Frank Rich.

9. MASTERS OF THEIR DOMAIN

Interviews: Richard Belzer, David Brenner, Art Buchwald, Al Franken, Timothy
  Jay, Jonathan Katz, Milly Pulsinelli, and Abe Vigoda.

Berger, Phil. *The Last Laugh: The World of the Stand-up Comics.* New York: Ballantine, 1975.

Borns, Betsy. *Comic Lives: Inside the World of American Stand-up Comedy.* New
  York: Simon and Schuster, 1987.

Bushman, David. "The Stand-up Comedian on Television." In *Stand Up,* 19–49.
  New York: Abrams/Museum of Television and Radio, 1996.

Coupland, Douglas. "The Observationalist." In *Stand Up,* 109–19. New York:
  Abrams/Museum of Television and Radio, 1996.

Funny Is Money [Video]. Executive Producer, Norman Jewison. Touchstone,
  1999.

Gallo, Hank. Photographs by Ed Edahl. *Comedy Explosion.* New York: Thun-
  der's Mouth Press, 1991.

Gelbart, Larry. "Send Out the Clowns." In *Stand-Up Comedians on Television,*
  10–13. New York: Abrams/Museum of Television & Radio, 1996.

Hendra, Tony. *Going Too Far.* New York: Doubleday, 1987.

Postman, Neil. *Amusing Ourselves to Death: Public Discourse in the Age of Show
  Business.* New York: Viking, 1985.

Secret World of Sitcoms [Video]. Executive Producers Nancy Jacobs Miller and
  Michelle Van Kempen. Learning Channel, 1999.

Stebbins, Robert A. *The Laugh-Makers: Stand-up Comedy as Art, Business, and
  Life Style.* Montreal and Buffalo: McGill–Queen's University Press, 1990.

Stern, Dave. *Adam Sandler: An Unauthorized Biography.* Los Angeles: Renaissance Books, 2000.

Stone, Laurie. *Laughter in the Dark: A Decade of Subversive Comedy.* Hopewell,
  N.J.: Ecco Press, 1997.

Wilde, Larry. *How the Great Comedy Writers Create Laughter.* Chicago: Nelson-
  Hall, 1976.

Albums:

  Dangerfield, Rodney. *No Respect.* Casablanca, 1980.
  Rickles, Don. *Hello, Dummy.* Warner Brothers, n.d.
  Youngman, Henny. *Take My Album Please.* Waterhouse, n.d.

10. KOSHER AT LAST

Interviews: Karen Bergreen, Estelle Getty, and Riv-Ellen Prell.

Antler, Joyce, ed. *Talking Back: Images of Jewish Women in American Popular Culture*. Hanover, N.H.: Brandeis University Press, 1998.
Banks, Morwenna, and Amanda Swift. *Joke's on Us: Women in Comedy from Music Hall to the Present Day*. London: Pandora, 1987.
Horowitz, Susan. *Queens of Comedy*. Amsterdam: Gordon and Breach Science Publishers, 1997.
Martin, Linda. *Women in Comedy*. Secaucus, N.J.: Carol, 1986.
Prell, Riv-Ellen. *Fighting to Become Americans: Jews, Gender, and the Anxiety of Assimilation*. Boston: Beacon, 1999.
Silverman, Stephen M. *Funny Ladies*. New York: Abrams, 1999.
Unterbrink, Mary. *Funny Women*. Jefferson, N.C.: McFarland, 1987.
Warren, Rosalind, ed. *Revolutionary Laughter: The World of Women Comics*. Freedom, Calif.: Crossing Press, 1995.

Albums:
> *Totie Fields Live*. Mainstream, n.d.
> *The Next to Last Joan Rivers Album*. Buddah Records, n.d.
> ———. *What Becomes a Semi-Legend Most?* Geffen, 1984.

11. THE COST OF VICTORY

Interviews: Jeff Abraham, Joel Goodman, and Tim Jay.

Jerry Stiller Roast.

Dougherty, Barry. *New York Friars Club Book of Roasts*. New York: M. Evans, 2000.
Fisher, Seymour, and Rhoda Fisher. *Pretend the World Is Funny and Forever: A Psychological Analysis of Comedians, Clowns, and Actors*. Hillsdale, N.J.: Lawrence Erlbaum, 1981.
Herzl, Theodor. "The Solution of the Jewish Question." In *Zionist Writings*, 20–33. New York: Herzl Press, 1973.
Janus, Samuel S. "The Great Comedians: Personality and Other Factors." *American Journal of Psychoanalysis* (1975): 169–74.
———. "The Great Jewish-American Comedians' Identity Crisis." *American Journal of Psychoanalysis* (fall 1980): 259–65.

Janus, Samuel S., Barbara E. Bess, and Beth R. Janus. "The Great Comediennes: Personality and Other Factors." *American Journal of Psychoanalysis* (1978): 367–72.

Let Me In . . . I Hear Laughter: A Salute to the Friars [Video]. Produced by Dean Ward. Nostomania Productions, 1999.

McGhee, Paul, and Jeffrey Goldstein, eds. *Handbook of Humor Research*. New York: Spring, 1983.

Witty, Susan. "The Laugh Makers." *Psychology Today* (Aug. 1983): 22–29.

www.friarsclub.com.

12. Not the Last Laugh

Interviews: Suze Berger, Jeffrey Ross, and Jason Stuart.

Wendy Liebman [Video].

Appendix. Schlemiels and Nudnicks

Interview: Rabbi Bob Alper, Shelley Berman, Art Buchwald, Joseph Dorinson, Leslie Fiedler, Don Freeman, Joel Goodman, Rocky Kalish, Lawrence Mintz, William Novak, Soupy Sales, Richard Siegel, Rabbi Joseph Telushkin, Rabbi Moshe Waldoks, Stephen Whitfield, and Ruth Wisse.

Alter, Robert. "Jewish Humor and the Domestication of Myth." In *Veins of Humor*, ed. Harry Levin, 255–67. Cambridge: Harvard University Press, 1972.

Altman, Sig. *The Comic Image of the Jew*. Rutherford, N.J.: Farleigh Dickinson University Press, 1971.

Ausubel, Nathan. *A Treasury of Jewish Folklore*. New York: Crown, 1953.

Ben-Amos, Dan. "The 'Myth' of Jewish Humor." *Jewish Folklore* (1973): 112–31.

Berger, Arthur Asa. *The Genius of the Jewish Joke*. Northvale, N.J.: Jason Aronson, 1997.

Bergson, Henry. *Laughter*. St. Paul: Green Integer, 1999.

Bermant, Chaim. *What's the Joke: A Study of Jewish Humor through the Ages*. London: Weidenfeld and Nicolson, 1986.

Cousins, Norman. *Anatomy of an Illness*. New York: Norton, 1979.

Davis, Murray. *What's So Funny? The Comic Conception of Culture and Society*. Chicago: University of Chicago Press, 1993.

Dorinson, Joseph. "Jewish Humor: Mechanism for Defense, Weapon for Cultural Affirmation." *Journal of Psychohistory* (spring 1981): 447–64.

Eakin, Emily. "If It's Funny, You Laugh, but Why?" *New York Times,* Dec. 9, 2000, B7, B9.

Elbirt, Henry. *What Is a Jewish Joke? An Excursion into Jewish Humor.* Northvale, N.J.: Jason Aronson, 1991.

Frankl, Viktor. *Man's Search for Meaning.* Boston: Beacon, 1962.

Freud, Sigmund. *Jokes and Their Relation to the Unconscious.* New York: Moffat, Yard, 1916.

Grotjahn, Martin. "Jewish Jokes and Their Relation to Masochism." In *A Celebration of Laughter,* ed. Werner M. Mendel, 135–43. Los Angeles: Mara, 1970.

Howe, Irving. "The Nature of Jewish Laughter." *New American Mercury* (1951): 211–12.

Klein, Judith Weinstein. *Jewish Identity and Self-Esteem: Healing Wounds through Ethnotherapy.* New York: American Jewish Committee, 1980.

Kohn, J. P., and L. Davidsohn. "Jewish Wit and Humor." In *The Universal Jewish Encyclopedia,* 10:545–47. New York: Universal Jewish Encyclopedia, 1943.

Lewin, Kurt. *Resolving Social Conflict.* New York: Harper Bros., 1948.

Lewis, Paul. "Joke and Anti-Joke." *Journal of Popular Culture* (summer 1987): 63–73.

Lifschutz, E. "Merrymakers and Jesters among Jews (Materials for a Lexicon)." *YIVO Annual of Jewish Social Science* (1952): 43–83.

Mehlman, Jeffrey. "How to Read Freud on Jokes." *New Literary History* (winter, 1975): 439–61.

Mindess, Harvey. *The Chosen People?* Los Angeles: Nash, 1972.

Mintz, Lawrence E. "Jewish Humor." *American Humor* (spring, 1977): 4–6.

Novak, William, and Moshe Waldoks, eds. *The Big Book of Jewish Humor.* New York: Harper Perennial, 1981.

Oring, Elliott. *Jokes and Their Relations.* Lexington, Ky.: University Press of Kentucky, 1992.

Reik, Theodor. *Jewish Wit.* New York: Gamut Press, 1962.

Roback, A. A. "Sarcasm and Repartee in Yiddish Speech." *Jewish Frontier* (Apr. 1951): 19–25.

Rosenberg, Bernard, and Gilbert Shapiro. "Marginality and Jewish Humor." *Midstream* (spring 1958): 70–80.

Rosten, Leo. *The Joys of Yiddish.* New York: Pocket Books, 1970.

Rovit, Earl. "Jewish Humor and American Life." *American Scholar* (spring 1967): 237–45.

Saposnik, Irv. "Those Serious Jests: American Jews and Jewish Comedy." *Judaism* (summer 1998): 311–20.

Schlesinger, Kurt. "Jewish Humor as Jewish Identity." *International Review of Psycho-Analysis* (1979): 317–30.

Telushkin, Rabbi Joseph. *Jewish Humor: What the Best Jewish Jokes Say about the Jews.* New York: William Morrow, 1992.

Van Den Haag, Ernest. *The Jewish Mystique.* 2nd ed. New York: Stein & Day, 1977.

Whitfield, Stephen. "The Distinctiveness of American Jewish Humor." *Modern Judaism* (Oct. 1986): 245–60.

Ziv, Avner. "Jewish Humor." In *Encyclopaedia Judaica Year Book 1986/7*, 53–68. Jerusalem: Encyclopaedia Judaica, 1987.

———. *Personality and Sense of Humor.* New York: Springer, 1984.

———, ed. *Jewish Humor.* New Brunswick, N.J.: Transaction, 1998.

Ziv, Avner, and Anat Zajdman. *Semites and Stereotypes: Characteristics of Jewish Humor.* Westport, Conn.: Greenwood, 1993.

ACKNOWLEDGMENTS

It is a great pleasure to thank all of those who have made researching and writing this book endlessly fascinating.

My biggest concern in researching the book was reaching the comedians. Luckily, they were a wonderful group of people.

Soupy Sales was the first comedian I spoke with. My father's cousin Marian Dick and her husband, Fred, knew Soupy. It was a great thrill for me to speak with him because I can distinctly recall Soupy Sales making me laugh when I was young. I got to ask him about how he did some of the material on his show. When we later met, he was as gracious as possible.

Soupy also gave me a great lead. He told me that I had to contact Barry Dougherty at the Friars Club. I did. After all, this was probably the only time in my life that I'd be able to say, "Soupy Sales suggested I call you." I spoke with Barry, editor of the *Friars Epistle*, and then with Jean Pierre Trebot, the executive director, who invited me to see the club. While visiting and talking with them, I noticed on the wall a large checklist indicating preparations for a roast of Jerry Stiller. Two weeks later, Jean Pierre had tickets to the event forwarded to me. Still later, Barry was extremely kind in providing a photograph for the book.

At the roast, I met, among others, Richard Belzer, who agreed to an interview, and Jeff Ross, who would turn out to be enormously kind in many ways. When I interviewed him, Jeff told me about a new documentary on the Friars made by a young filmmaker named Dean Ward. The documentary was to be shown at the HBO Theater in New York. Jeff suggested I contact Dean. I called Dean Ward, and he was extremely cordial. At the filming, I spoke with Freddie Roman, Abe Vigoda, and Dr. Irwin Corey. All were exceptionally kind. Abe Vigoda called me over as he was speaking with Art Buchwald so I could join the conversation. Jeff Ross, ever helpful, then agreed to let me go backstage with him when he appeared at Caroline's on Broadway, the comedy club; I did go to see him there. Jeff also put me in contact with others.

Don Freeman, critic at the *San Diego Union-Tribune*, put me in touch with Steve Allen, who, although not Jewish, knew everyone in show business. He was characteristically gracious and kind and gave me wonderful advice. His warmth and laughter gave me much-needed confidence. I spoke with him about a year before he died, and I was among the millions of his fans who felt his loss.

It was Bill Novak who put me in touch with Jonathan Katz. Jonathan provided interesting information on the origin of his show.

Shelley Berman was one comedian I very much wanted to reach. I was a bit too young to have fully understood the genius of his work, although I vividly remember his presence. After my research I became convinced that he was perhaps the most underappreciated of all the comedians, and I wanted to correct that in the book. I simply wrote him a letter, and he called. It is impossible to express my full appreciation to Shelley Berman. He started with a wonderful interview, but that contribution soon broadened to include much more. Shelley became my coach. He was the one who convinced me I could really enter the comedy world and write about it. He answered question after question. He prodded me to make the calls when I was reluctant. I e-mailed him with updates.

I called when I needed advice. My wife suggested I adopt him as my uncle. I thought that was a good idea. After Shelley Berman I knew I could write this book.

I began interviewing other comedians. Sid Caesar was kind enough to spend an hour discussing his groundbreaking career. Norm Crosby was warm, witty, and kind. The problem was that he was so funny that I laughed through most of the interview. Louis Nye reminisced about routines he had done decades ago. Shecky Greene started doing imitations as we spoke and asked me to name someone I wanted him to imitate. I asked him if he could do Shelley Berman, whose voice I now knew so well. Shecky did a perfect imitation. He was uncommonly open and perceptive about his life and career. Al Franken kindly took me through a contemporary view of Jewish comedy. Buddy Hackett made my wife laugh for two minutes before she'd let me talk to him. He was honest and direct and very helpful. Ed Asner and I spoke for a long while, especially about his days in Chicago. His incredible memory and intelligence were very helpful to me in understanding the era. I caught up with David Brenner backstage at a synagogue. He had just gotten married live on television and had some wonderful stories about that. It took me a while to figure out that I should call Tommy Smothers. Leonard Maltin had suggested to me that many of Jack Benny's listeners hadn't realized he was Jewish. I tried to think of a Gentile comedian who relied on timing and whom Benny might have influenced. Eventually, Tommy's name came to mind. He was absolutely wonderful. He confirmed Maltin's idea and told me some interesting stories.

I wanted to talk with some gay Jewish comedians, and Suze Berger and Jason Stuart were kind enough to agree. I spoke at great length with both of them, getting insights that went far beyond laughter.

Speaking with Suze reminded me of my biggest disappointment in interviewing comedians. There are relatively few Jewish women comedians, and I could not interview enough of them. I did speak with Estelle Getty, who is as charming and warm as a viewer might expect, and Karen Bergreen, who is just starting on her comedy career.

I interviewed many other people in preparing the book. For a Jewish background, I started with Rabbi Bob Alper, who is a full-time comedian. Bob had many interesting insights As the coeditor of *The Big Book of Jewish Humor*, Rabbi Moshe Waldoks knows a lot and has thought a lot about the subject. His intelligence and far-ranging knowledge were valuable guides. Bill Novak was his coeditor and the author of many other books. Bill not only gave me guidance about comedy, though. We also spent time talking about writing strategies and the publishing world, and Bill gave me much-needed advice. Richard Siegel, executive director of the National Foundation for Jewish Culture, invited me in to see him and then provided advice and materials. Rabbi Joseph Telushkin, author of many crucial books on Jewish life, including the invaluable *Jewish Humor: What the Best Jewish Jokes Say about the Jews*, directed me to some useful materials. Rabbi Jonathan Pearl, an expert on the portrayal of Jews on television, answered some important questions. Elie Wiesel's kind support of my writing is deeply appreciated. He called one day to talk about this book.

I also spoke about Jewish comedians and Jewish humor with many extraordinary professors. They included Joseph Dorinson, Leslie Fiedler, Annette Insdorf, Lawrence Mintz, Robert J. Thompson (who directs the Center for the Study of Popular Television at Syracuse), Steve Whitfield, and Ruth Wisse. Tim Jay was wonderfully helpful in talking about obscene language in comedy. His quick mind, though, led us in all sorts of useful directions. Riv-Ellen Prell deserves special mention. Her original and bold insights about how male Jewish comedians dealt with Jewish women helped shape a substantial part of the chapter about Jewish women comedians.

Others I interviewed included Brian Gari (Eddie Cantor's grandson, who also provided the great photograph of the comedian); Larry Coven, a comedy teacher and former member of Second City; Charna Halpern, the director of OlympicImprov and an important part of Second City's history; Stanley Ralph Ross, the creator of many television shows; comedy writer Rocky Kalish; Avery Corman, the novelist; Joel Goodman of the HUMOR Project; Jeff Abraham, who guided me through the world of public relations; and Milly Pulsinelli, who had worked for Jerry Seinfeld's father.

Ronald L. Smith is a one-man treasure trove of knowledge. Ron's pioneering work in the field of comedy saved me enormous amounts of time. In his work, Ron has collected crucial data on all the comedians, their records and CDs, their routines, and their biographies. It's impossible to do work in this field without standing on his shoulders. I highly recommend his work. Ron was also very kind in talking about the different comedians with me. His tremendous help with the selection of photographs was invaluable and deeply appreciated.

Several important intellectuals and journalists were very helpful. Leonard Maltin gave me a whole series of valuable suggestions and intriguing ideas. Victor Navasky of the *Nation* took me on a political tour in a most entertaining way. Nat Hentoff was extremely provocative on the subject of Lenny Bruce and much else. Norman Podhoretz also gave me some extremely valuable ideas about Bruce and other subjects. Marvin Kitman, syndicated television critic at *Newsday*, didn't just provide extraordinarily interesting insights about Jewish comedy and television but also took an active interest in the book's progress. Frank Rich of the *New York Times* provided one valuable idea after another. His knowledge of culture and Jewish life, and his willingness to listen and react, helped me gain deeper insights about some important aspects of the book.

Besides interviews, I also got materials and suggestions from a variety of people. Tom Lehrer sent me a most interesting letter. Joey Bishop called just to say hello. Donna Halper, an expert on radio, was enormously helpful in providing advice and guiding me through a new area. Michael Terry, head of the Jewish Division at the New York Public Library, personally helped guide me to get materials I needed, most especially unpublished interviews with comedians conducted by the American Jewish Committee. Andrew M. Ingall, coordinator of the National Jewish Archive of Broadcasting at the Jewish Museum, was kind enough to give me a tour and set up some viewings. My good friend Dr. Carl Rheins, executive director of YIVO, was, as always, supportive.

Others who helped included Dan Sharon, librarian at the Asher Library at the Spertus Institute of Jewish Studies; Mark Dawidziak, television critic at the *Cleveland Plain Dealer* and an expert on vaudeville; Don L. F. Nilsen, executive secretary of the International Society for Humor Studies; John Keene of the Research Department at the National Comedy Hall of Fame Museum and Library; Rabbi Steve Moscowitz and Steve Siegel at the 92nd Street Y; David E. E. Sloane, executive director of the American Humor Studies Association; Rabbi Bradley Shavit Artson, dean of the University of Judaism's Ziegler School of Rabbinic Studies; Ed Dunkelblau, past president of the American Association for Therapeutic Humor; Tom Tugend of the *Los Angeles Jewish Journal*; Vincent Nastri of Barry Katz Management; Mrs. M. Amsterdam; Jeff Scheckner, research consultant for United Jewish Communities; Ronald Grele, director of the Oral History Research Office at Columbia University; Michelle Sampson of the American Jewish Historical Society; George Abbott, a librarian at Syracuse University; Stewart Ain of the *Jewish Week*; Rabbi Steven Carr Reuben; Rosemary Hanes of the Motion Picture Broadcasting and Recorded Sound Division of the Library of Congress; Harvey Mindess; Elliott Oring; Arthur Asa Berger; Paul Lewis; Joseph Boskin; Phil Brown of the Catskills Institute, who was also helpful with photos; Susan J. Douglas; Aaron Kornblum, research archivist at the U.S. Holocaust Memorial Museum; Nancy Saul Simon of the Wiesenthal Center; Jackie "the Jokeman" Martling; Sherry Gutes; David Pfeffer of the National Archives and Records Administration; Judy Weiss; Myrna Katz Frommer, coauthor of *It Happened in the Catskills*; Velvel Pasternak; Kristine Krueger of the National Film Information Service at the Margaret Herrick Library; Zoe Burman, the outreach and reference coordinator at UCLA's Film and Television Archives; Shira Dicker of the National Foundation for Jewish Culture; Steve Everitt of the British Phil Silvers Appreciation Society; Paul G. Wesolowski, publisher of the *Freedonia Gazette* and an expert on the Marx Brothers; Arnold Dashefsky; and Steve Pinker, the cognitive scientist and author of *How the Mind Works*. Finally, I want to thank the entire courteous and helpful staffs at the Museum of Television and Radio and the Library of the Performing Arts of the New York Public Library.

Another concern I had when writing the book was finding old comedy albums. Ron Smith made some suggestions. I also got many albums through eBay. After a long search I was still missing seven albums. I had bought some albums from David Stein on eBay, and I turned to him with my dilemma because I knew he had an enormous collection of Jewish comedy albums. David not only had every album I was missing, but also volunteered to make them available to me.

It was quite a task getting the books, articles, and videos necessary to research this book. The librarians and library staff at Suffolk County Community College were nothing less than heroic in their efforts. I explained my book to Luisa Reichardt, the campus head librarian, and she enthusiastically provided support. I also appreciate the help of Hedi BenAicha, associate head librarian, whose enthusiasm was always encouraging.

Susan Rubenstein DeMasi, the media librarian, became almost a director of research at the beginning of this project. She was relentless in finding materials and making suggestions. Her own knowledge of vaudeville was an additional source of help. Sue's enthusiasm was critical. MaryAnn Romano and Irene Rose at the Media Resources Center were always helpful. David Baruch provided information and advice.

The members of the Circulation Department who helped me get books through interlibrary loans were simply extraordinary. Marilyn Ventiere and Bonnie Plaue called or e-mailed, making sure I knew when the next batch of books or articles arrived. They cheerfully followed this book's progress. I also want to thank others in the Circulation Department: Margaret Blackmore, Linda DeFeo, and Anna Forte.

Many of my friends were helpful. My rabbi, Howard Hoffman, has always been extremely supportive of my writing. His wife, Elaine, a librarian, guided me at a very early stage, as I was considering writing this book. Rabbi Howard Buechler, a wonderful friend, provided direct and much appreciated help with this book. His class of adult learners was the first to hear a lecture on the subject, and their enthusiasm was very valuable. Rabbi Stanley Greenstein was a constant source of kind words. Rabbi Adam Fisher always is terrific to speak with and has always provided intellectual nourishment. Debbie Friedman was characteristically kind and helpful.

The administrators and staff at Suffolk County Community College have been extremely helpful. Bob Arrigon, Phil Christensen, Bill Connors, and Steve Schrier are among those who have been especially supportive. Gerry O'Connor, Ed Joyce, and Steve Klipstein were respectively the chair and assistant chairs of the English Department for most of the research and writing of the book. More recently, Ed Joyce became chair and Michele Aquino assistant chair. Their help was very much needed, and it was always given.

The members of the English Department at the college are nothing less than an extended family. I literally should thank all of them, for they all have made teaching there a valuable experience. There are some people who played a particular role in my writing this book. Don Gilzinger enthusiastically provided materials. Tony Martone arranged for some interviews and was always a good sounding board. Tony DiFranco offered valuable insights. Jeff Coven was helpful in arranging an interview as was Michelle Aquino. Among those I spoke with about the book are Molly Altizer, David Axelrod, Lloyd Becker, Mark Bourdeau, Carol Cavallo, Maury Dean, Marilyn Levine, Sam Ligon, Jim Mattimore, and Sandra Sprows. Other faculty at the college who provided help include Alan Bernstein, Richard Britton, Alice Goode-Elman, Lowell Kleiman, David Miller, and Valerie Parks.

The departmental and divisional secretaries and student aides I have worked with over the years were always particularly helpful. They include: Ellen Bolier, Arnita Mason, Kathy Morrisette, Kathryn Seher, and Sharon Weeks.

Many students expressed interest in the book. One student, however, deserves special mention. Shane McConnell gathered materials, including material he found on his own, read through articles and made notes, and, in general, was consistently valuable, often volunteering for tasks before they were requested. I expect one day he will be teaching and writing on his own.

Barbara Shair has helped free me up to work on the book by

taking on some tasks for me. She is deeply dedicated to Jewish life, and her support is profoundly appreciated.

Susan Lustig has worked with me in Jewish life for many years in a variety of ways. Her intelligence, curiosity, and help have made it easier to write this book.

Doug Rathgeb has been a close and deeply valued friend for almost forty years. He's a mystery writer and librarian in California and, of course, passed on bibliographical advice and other important pieces of information.

Mike Fitzpatrick has my vote for sainthood. He has schlepped with me as I gave speeches in such places as New York, Boston, Philadelphia, St. Louis, and elsewhere. In the name of research, we've systematically explored Jewish delicatessens all over the place. After eating, though, we've gone to bookstores and hunted for needed materials. Mike provides constant and invaluable help on a variety of levels. I can only imagine how much poorer my life would be without his incredible friendship. His brother, John, is also a good friend and was particularly enthusiastic about this book.

Geoff Shandler, then senior editor at PublicAffairs, acquired the book and helped me shape it by making many crucial and insightful suggestions. Geoff's uncanny editorial eye, psychological acuity, and never less than brilliant mind were vital to my work. I deeply appreciate his faith in this book and in me.

When Geoff left, I was incredibly fortunate that Paul Golob was his replacement. Paul's own brilliance, exemplified by a series of extraordinary perceptions and valuable editorial suggestions, made completing work on the book both intellectually stimulating and pleasurable.

Peter Osnos is the publisher at PublicAffairs. Peter's enthusiasm and support were palpable. No author could ask more from a publisher. He has built a publishing house that is extraordinary, and I have been lucky enough to be associated with it.

Gene Taft, the director of publicity, took an active interest in the book from the very beginning. David Patterson's incredibly efficient help is deeply appreciated. I'd also like to thank Robert Kimzey and all the other wonderful people I worked with at PublicAffairs.

It was my agent, Don Gastwirth, who started the process. He called and asked if I had some thoughts about writing a Jewish-related book. The basic idea for this book appeared full-blown in my mind two minutes after speaking with Don. A minute later, without trying to think of one, the title mentally arrived. I don't turn down such gifts. I immediately recontacted Don. He was very enthusiastic, and that enthusiasm never wavered. Don guided me through the uncertain waters of the publishing world with great knowledge, care, concern, and skill. I had heard tales of agents who didn't return calls, but there was never a single time that happened. Don patiently answered all my questions in an amazingly helpful manner. His passion for the book and his sensitivity to finding it the right home were crucial.

Don's brother, Dr. Joseph L. Gastwirth, has always provided valuable support and kind words.

My cousins Toby Everett and Dr. Sheldon Scheinert have always been enthusiastic about my writing. Throughout our lives, they have both been great friends as well as relatives, and I'm sure their influence can be seen in these pages.

My in-laws, Harvey and Marsha Selib and Judy Marshall, have always been most helpful and kind.

I also want to thank the other members of my extended family.

My late father, Fred Epstein, was always enthusiastic about my writing, and he would have especially liked this book. The book's dedication to my mother, Lillian Scheinert Epstein, is only a very small attempt to thank her. The lessons she taught me, the example she set, the love she gave, and the wisdom she imparted fundamentally shaped my life. My mother was a source of support for my writing and much else in my life.

My brother, Richard, was the first reader of the text. His intelligence and great wit made him a perfect reader. In addition, despite the fact that Richard is two years younger than I am, he seems to recall far better than I do every routine we heard from every comedian. His interest in the subject was infectious; his constant support was vital. He expressed belief that I could write this book before I believed I could, and I credit that faith in me with making it possible to both start and finish the book. His wife, Perla, and children, Adam and Sondra, listened to tales of the book with interest.

Finally, my family makes all that I do possible. My wife, Sharon, has always been an incredible partner. She seems to know exactly what to say. Her advice is constantly grounded in good sense. She has been irreplaceably central in my life. Our children, Michael, Elana, Rachel, and Lisa, have filled our lives with wonder and joy and more than a few laughs.

INDEX

ABC (American Broadcasting Company), 149
Academy Awards, 203
Academy of Dramatic Arts, 223
Actor's Equity strike, 38
Adams, Joey, 113
Adler, Hermann, 287
Admiral Broadway Revue (television show), 140, 141
African Americans, 19, 39, 62; and the civil rights movement, 198; and segregation, 109; after World War II, 157–158
Albee, Edward F., 28, 32
Albee, Reed, 28
Aleichem, Sholem, 305
Alexander, Jason, 244, 270
Algonquin Club Roundtable, 45
All about Eve (film), 115
All in the Family (television show), 250, 264
Allen, Gracie, xx, 23–27, 69, 74–75, 261
Allen, Marty, 163–164
Allen, Steve, 151, 173, 176, 178, 183, 185–186, 227
Allen, Woody, x, xv–xvi, 195–208, 228, 295; and anti-Semitism, 190, 204;
and Brooks, 208, 211, 214, 216; and Catskill resorts, 125; and Dangerfield, 221–222; early career of, 187–191; on God, existence of, 299; and Mason, 177; and Richard Lewis, 229; and Rudner, 262; and Sahl, 167; and Seinfeld, 246; and Shandling, 229; and Steinberg, 226; and television, 141, 152
Alsace, 5
Alta Vista, 280–281
Alvarez, Marie, 180
America First Committee, 107
American Federation of Labor, 38
American Jewish Committee, 18
American Psychological Association, xxi
Anderson, Eddie, 62
Animal Crackers (play), xvi, 87, 92
Annie Hall (film), 202–204, 208
Anti-Semitism, 32, 49–51, 60, 63, 134, 227; and the Baby Snooks character, 70; and Caesar, 139; and Catskill resorts, 124; decline of, 122, 137–138; and film, 100, 103; and Klein, 225; and Lewis, 123;

Anti-Semitism (*cont.*)
  and Nazism, 77–78; and Stern,
  238; and television, 146, 148–149;
  and Woody Allen, 190, 204; and
  World War II, 106–109
Appel, Don, 141
Arnaz, Desi, 274
Arthur, Bea, 264
Aspen Festival, 281
Auschwitz, 123. *See also* Holocaust

Baby Snooks character, 70–71, 88
Back to School (film), 222
Back from the Front (film), 101
Bailey, Pearl, 129
Baker, Josephine, 205
Baldwin, James, 40
Ball, Lucille, 274
Bananas (film), 199, 201
Banducci, Enrico, 169
Bar mitzvah, 17–18, 43
Barr, Roseanne. *See* Roseanne
Barrison Theater, 46
Barth, Belle, 180
Beatty, Warren, 203
Beerkill Lodge, 114
Belkin,Gary, 141
Bellboy, The (film), 119–120
Belzer, George, 57
Belzer, Richard, 236–237, 240
Ben-Amos, Dan, 306
Benigni, Roberto, 123
Benny, Jack, x, xvii, xix, 14, 23, 37, 148,
  138, 162, 238; and anti-Semitism,
  51, 60, 63; childhood of, 15, 17, 46;
  in film, 57–58, 81, 84, 85, 89,
  101–102; and the Friars Club, 274;
  musical acts of, 46–47; and
  Nazism, 77–78, 101–102; and

radio, 55–62, 65, 66–67, 69, 74–76;
  and Seinfeld, 245; special genius
  of, 57; and television, 153–154; and
  Woody Allen, 188
Benson (television show), 242
Berg, Gertrude, 70–72, 144, 146
Berg, Lew, 72
Bergman, Andrew, 212
Bergman, Ingmar, 190, 229
Bergreen, Karen, 281
Bergson, Henri, 307
Berle, Milton, x, xxi, 14–18, 132–133, 146;
  and anti-Semitism, 51; childhood
  of, 15, 17, 274; and Fay, 49; and
  film, 81; and the Friars Club, 275;
  and jokes that mocked Jews, 32;
  and Nazi sympathizers, 77; and
  radio, 68, 69; and television,
  48–49, 129–131, 134, 138–139
Berlin, Irving, 48, 274
Berle, Roz, 132
Berle, Sadie, xx, xix, 19, 49
Berman, Shelley, 182–187, 228; and
  Brooks, 214; and Woody Allen,
  188
Bernhard, Sandra, 262–263
Bernie, Herman, 72
Bible, 291, 298
Billy Madison (film), 251
Binghamton University, 261
Biograph Studios, 49
Birds, The (film), 214–215
Birdwell, Michael, 99
Birnbaum, Louis, 4, 18
Birnbaum, Nathan, 21
Bishop, Joey, 111
Blackface tradition, 39–40
Blacks. *See* African Americans
Blanc, Mel, 77

Blazing Saddles (film), 140, 211–213

Blue Angel (club), 187

Bluth, Dorothy, 4

Bogart, Humphrey, 170

Boosler, Elayne, 260–261

Born Yesterday (play), 115

"Borscht Belt" (Catskill Mountains), 104–128, 140, 159, 164, 221, 229, 262, 290

Brenner, David, 229, 241–242

Brice, Fanny, x, xix, 14, 17; Baby Snooks character of, 70–71, 88; and the blackface tradition, 40; entry of, into vaudeville, 47–48; and film, 81; and radio, 70–71; and Woody Allen, 205

Broadway Romeo, A (film), 57–58

Brookman, Kitty, 13

Brooks, Albert, 216–218

Brooks, Mel, 13, 121, 185–187, 208–216, 263; and Caesar, 139–140, 142–143, 187; and Nazism, 283–284; and Reiner, 186; and television, 150; and Woody Allen, 208, 211, 214, 216

Brown's Hotel, 118

Bruce, Lenny, xxi, xvii, 134, 155–156, 170–174, 180, 237, 304; and Berman, 184; death of, 175; famous routines of, 171–172; and Sahl, 167, 169

Bureau of Motion Pictures, 103

Burns, George, x, xix–xxi, 14–16, 56–57, 284–285, 307; and anti-Semitism, 51; and the blackface tradition, 40; childhood of, 4, 11, 16, 18, 21–22, 35; early career of, 22–27; and film, 81, 84, 85; and the Friars Club, 274; introduction of, to

Gracie Allen, 23–24; on Hitler, 76–77; and Jessel, 36–37; marriage of, 95; and radio, 65, 69; and television, 152, 154; and Rudner, 261

Burns Brothers, 22

Burrows, Abe, 273

Buttons, Red, 114, 132

Caddyshack (film), 222

Caeser, Sid, xxi, 139–143, 186; and Brooks, 139–140, 142–143, 187; and Catskill resorts, 113; and television, 131–143, 146

Caesar's Hour (television show), 141

Cagney, James, 170

Cannon Street Theater, 22

Cantor, Eddie, 11–14, 74–76; and Berle, 274; childhood of, 16, 36, 38; close relationship of, with his audience, 40–41; and Coughlin, 63, 105; and film, 94–96, 98; first job of, 38–39; and isolationism, 78; and Israel, 63–64; and radio, 65–66, 69, 74–75; speech given by, at the New York World's Fair, 63; and television, 152–153

Capitalism, 171

Carlyle, Thomas, 287

Carnegie Hall, 184, 233

Carson, Johnny, 224

Carter, Jack, 162

Castle Garden, 4

Catcher in the Rye (Salinger), 157

Catholicism, 171, 173–176. *See also* Christianity

Catskill Mountains ("Borscht Belt"), 104–128, 140, 159, 164, 221, 229, 262, 290

Cavett, Dick, 195

CBS (Columbia Broadcasting System), 72, 144, 147, 179, 226–227, 268

Celebrity (film), 207

Celluloid Soldiers: The Warner Bros. Campaign against Nazism (Birdwell), 99–100

Censorship rules, 66

Chaplin, Charlie, xix, 80–81, 100, 119, 133

Chelm (town), 38

Chicken Soup (television show), 223

Christianity, xxi, 22, 106–107, 138, 197, 239, 291. *See also* Catholicism; Protestantism

Civil rights movement, 198

Civil War, 8, 39

Class, socio-economic, 19, 89

Coca, Imogene, 141

Cocoanuts (film), 81–82

Cohan, George M., 47

Cohen, Jacob, 220–221

Cohen, Myron, 158–160, 177

Cohen, Sammy, 80

Cohens and the Kellys (film), 80

Collins, Hal, 130

Comden, Betty, 115

Comic Strip (club), 261

Commedia dell'arte, 180–181

Commentary, 146

Communism, 168, 171

Confessions of a Nazi Spy (film), 100

Consciousness, double, 51

Cosell, Howard, 201

Cossacks, 3

Coughlin, Charles L., 63, 105–107

Crimes and Misdemeanors (film), 199, 206

Crom, Rick, 279

Crosby, John, 58

Crosby, Norm, 224–225

Crystal, Billy, 141, 218–219, 250

Cuckoo on the Choo Choo (film), 96

Czar Alexander II, 6

Czechoslovakia, 290. *See also* Eastern Europe

Daily Show, The (television show), 249, 250

Dale. *See* Marks, Charlie ("Dale")

D'Amato, Skinny, 118

Dana, Bill, 151

Dangerfield, Rodney, xvii, 222–223, 221, 251, 280, 285

David, Larry, 243–244

Davidson, Max, 80

Davis, Bette, 115

Davis, Sammy, Jr., 149, 162

Day the Clown Cried, The (film), 123

Dearborn Independent, 50

Deconstructing Harry (film), 196, 206–207

Defending Your Life (film), 217

Democratic Party, 108, 293

Desegregation, 62

"De-Semitization" process, 94

Diamond, Selma, 141, 150

Diary of Anne Frank, The, 137

Dick Van Dyke Show (television show), 141, 150

Diller, Phyllis, 274

Discrimination. *See* Anti-Semitism

Douglas, Susan J., 59–60

Drescher, Fran, 264, 268–269

Dr. Katz, Professional Comedian (animation), 230–231

Duck Soup (film), xvi, 68, 86, 90–92, 235

Dumb Dora acts, 24

Dumont, Margaret, xvi

Dylan, Bob, 185

Eastern Europe, xviii–xix, 4–6, 8, 13, 110, 290–295, 303, 307
Easy Money (film), 222
Edison, Thomas, 37
Ed Sullivan Show (television show), 55, 162, 179–180, 223, 265
Edwards, Gus, 35, 43, 49
Eichman, Adolf, 137
Einstein, Harry, 216, 274, 275
Eisenhower, Dwight D., 76, 147
Elijah, 288
Ellis Island, 4, 9–10
Erens, Patricia Brett, 98
Ex-Lax Corporation, 5

Fabray, Nanette, 141
Farley, Lewis, 22
Farley Theater, 22–23
Fay, Frank, 49–50
Fenneman, George, 153
Fields, Lew, 33–34, 50, 80
Fields, Totie, 256, 257
Films (listed by name)
    All about Eve, 115
    Annie Hall, 202–204, 208
    Back to School, 222
    Back from the Front, 101
    Bananas, 199, 201
    The Bellboy, 119–120
    Billy Madison, 251
    The Birds, 214–215
    Blazing Saddles, 140, 211–213
    A Broadway Romeo, 57–58
    Caddyshack, 222
    Celebrity, 207
    Cocoanuts, 81–82
    Confessions of a Nazi Spy, 100
    Cohens and the Kellys, 80
    Crimes and Misdemeanors, 199, 206

    Cuckoo on the Choo Choo, 96
    Day the Clown Cried, The, 123
    Deconstructing Harry, 196, 206–207
    Defending Your Life, 217
    Duck Soup, xvi, 68, 86, 90–92, 235
    Easy Money, 222
    Funny Girl, 263
    Getting a Ticket, 94
    Great Dictator, 100
    The Groove Tube, 236
    Hannah and Her Sisters, 206
    High Anxiety, 214
    History of the World, Part I, 215
    Hokus Pokus, 96
    Horse Feathers, 86–88, 90
    I'll Never Heil Again, 100
    In Hollywood with Potash and Perl-mutter, 80
    It Might Be Worse, 81
    Kid Millions, 95
    The King of Comedy, 262
    Life is Beautiful, 123
    Life Stinks, 216
    Lost in America, 217
    Love and Death, 202
    Malice in the Palace, 96
    Man on the Moon, 232
    Manhattan, 203–204, 208
    Me and the Colonel, 103
    Modern Romance, 217
    Monkey Business, 87, 90
    Mother, 217
    Mr. Saturday Night, 218–219
    The Muse, 217–218
    My Friend Irma, 119
    Night at the Opera, 87, 92–94
    A Night in Casablanca, 88, 102–103
    Nutty Professor, 119, 121–122, 235
    Paper Moon, 263

Films (*cont.*)
   Partners Again, with Potash and Perl-mutter, 80
   Play It Again Sam, xvi
   The Producers, 209–211, 283–284
   Real Life, 217
   Room Service, 87–88
   Schindler's List, 247
   Silent Movie, 214
   Sleeper, 201–202
   Small-Time Crooks, 208
   Springtime for Hitler, 209
   Sunset Boulevard, 115
   The Sunshine Boys, 33
   Sweet and Lowdown, 207
   Take the Money and Run, 185, 200–201
   Taxi Driver, 217
   To Be or Not to Be, 101, 102, 215–216
   The Twelve Chairs, 210–211
   Up in Arms, 97–98
   The Waterboy, 251
   What Price Pants?, 81
   What's Up, Doc?, 263
   Whoopee!, 94, 97
   You Nazty Spy, 100
   Young Frankenstein, 213–214
   You're Never Too Young, 120
   Zelig, 204–205
Fine, Larry, 41. *See also* Three Stooges
Fine, Sylvia, 97
Fisher, Art, 44
Fisher, Rhoda, 273
Fisher, Seymour, 273
Fitzgerald, F. Scott, 24, 92, 205
Fleishmann's (resort), 72
Flynn, Errol, 100
Ford, Henry, 50, 107
Forverts (Jewish Daily Forward), 14
Foster, Phil, 116, 162

Four Nightingales, 43
France, 28
Frank, Anne, 137
Frank, John, 115
Franken, Al, 231–232, 237
Frankl, Viktor, 294
Freedman, Morris, 146
French Revolution, 291
Freud, Sigmund, 275, 305, 306
Friars Club, 270, 274–275, 280, 285
Funny Girl (film), 263

Gelbart, Larry, 141
Gentile culture, xix, xxi, 61, 199–200; and intermarriage, 95; and television, 127
George Burns and Gracie Allen Show (television show), 152
Germany, 5
Gestapo, 101, 102. *See also* Nazism
Gestapo (play), 101
Getting a Ticket (film), 94
Getty, Estelle, 264
Gilbert, John, 140
Glass Hat (club), 118
Glazier, Sidney, 209
Godfrey, Arthur, 170
Goldberg, Molly, 72
Goldbergs, The (radio show), 71–72, 144–145
Golden Girls, The (television show), 264
Goldthwait, Bob, 230
Goldwyn, Samuel, 80, 94, 97
Gompers, Samuel, 38
Gonif, 303
Gordon, Mark, 183
Gornick, Vivian, 190
Gosfield, Maurice, 147
Gottfried, Gilbert, 230
Gould, Jack, 131

Great Dictator (film), 100
Green, Adolph, 115
Greene, Shecky, 165, 167, 222
Green Mill, 161
Greenwich Village (film), 115
Groove Tube, The (film), 236
Grossinger's, 124

Hackett, Buddy, 116–117, 147, 164–165, 169
Hal Roach Studios, 80
Hammer, Alvin, 115
Hammerstein, William, 31
Hannah and Her Sisters (film), 206
Hanukkah, 124
Hardy, Oliver, 90
Harlowe, Honey, 170
Harvard University, 49
Hasidic Jews, 289
Haskalah, 291
Hawn, Goldie, 263
Hays Code, 99
Hays Office, 99
HBO (Home Box Office), 242, 280, 281
Healy, Ted, 41
Hearst, William Randolph, 99, 258
Hebrew. *See also* Yiddish
    Bible, 291, 298
    school, 17
Hepburn, Katharine, 170
Herman, Pee-Wee, 230–231
Herzl, Theodor, 277
High Anxiety (film), 214
Hiken, Nat, 147
History of the World, Part I (film), 215
Hitler, Adolf, 50, 62, 123–124, 283–284;
    Burns on, 76–77; and film,
    100–102. *See also* Gestapo; Holo-
    caust; Nazism
Hobbes, Thomas, 306

Hokus Pokus (film), 96
Holliday, Judy, 115–116, 131–132
Holocaust, 52, 77, 102–103, 123, 137, 291.
    See also Hitler, Adolf; Nazism
Homicide (television show), 236
Hope, Bob, 223–224
Horse Feathers (film), 86–88, 90
Horwitz, Jerome, 41. *See also* Three
    Stooges
Horwitz, Moe, 41, 100. *See also* Three
    Stooges
Horwitz, Samuel, 41. *See also* Three
    Stooges
Hotel Gradus, 116
Howe, Irving, 94
HUAC (House Un-American Activi-
    ties Committee), 168

I'll Say She Is! (play), 45
I'll Never Heil Again (film), 100
Imperial Theater, 35
Improv, 229
Industrial Revolution, 8
In Hollywood with Potash and Perlmutter
    (film), 80
Inside Shelley Berman (album), 184
International Ladies Garment Workers
    Union, 15
International Military Tribunal at
    Nuremberg, 137
Internet, 280–281
IRC (Internet Relay Chat) channels, 281
Irish Americans, 19, 27, 64
Isolationism, 78
Israel, 63, 76, 122, 137–138, 267
It Might Be Worse (film), 81
It's Garry Shandling's Show (television
    show), 229
I've Got a Secret (television show), 176

Jack Benny Program (television show), 153–154

Janus, Samuel, xxi, 19, 271–273

Japanese Americans, 109

Jay, Timothy, 271

Jazz Singer, The (play), 36

Jessel, Edward Aaron, 5

Jessel, George, 5, 14, 123, 181, 298; and Berman, 183; and the blackface tradition, 40; childhood of, 15, 17, 35, 36; and film, 81; and the Friars Club, 274; "mama" routine of, 36; and radio, 67–68; routines, sale of, 113; serious work of, 36–37

Johnstone, Tim, 45

Johnstone, Will B., 45

Jolson, Al, 40

Joyce, James, 210

Joys of Yiddish, The (Rosten), 300

Kafka, Franz, 184, 185

Kahn, Madeline, 263

Kamen, Milt, 141

Kant, Immanuel, 306

Kantrowitz, Esther, 11

Kaplan, Abie, 22

Kaufman, Andy, 232–238, 252, 263

Kaufman, George S., 92

Kaye, Danny, 97–98, 103, 114–115

Keaton, Buster, 80–81

Keeney's Theater, 47

Keillor, Garrison, 33

Keith, B. F., 28, 32

Kelley, Mary, 23

Kellog's Cafeteria, 113

Kennedy, John F., 185, 227

Kennedy, Robert F., 227

Kid Millions (film), 95

King, Alan, 165, 270, 276

King, Martin Luther, Jr., 227

King, Rodney, 237

King of Comedy, The (film), 262

Kinsey Report, 255

Kiss Them For Me (play), 115

Kitman, Marvin, 223

Klein, Robert, 225, 226

Ku Klux Klan, 50

Kubelsky, Meyer, 3–4, 5, 17, 102

Lady in the Dark (play), 97

Lahr, Bert, xix, 16, 19, 41–42, 81

Landsmanschaften, 13, 122

Larry Sanders (television show), 229–230, 249–250

Laugh-In (television show), 263

Laurel, Stan, 90

Laverne and Shirley (television show), 162

Law and Order: Special Victims Unit (television show), 236

Lawford, Peter, 162

Lee, Pinky, 150

Leeds, Thelma, 216

Lehrer, Tom, 175–176

Leifer, Carol, 261

Lembeck, Harvey, 147

Leno, Jay, 279, 280

Leonard, Jack E., 161–162, 223

Le rire (Bergson), 307

Letterman, David, 279, 280

Levenson, Sam, xxi, 158–160, 177

Levy, Lou, 42

Lewis, Danny, 118

Lewis, Jack, 37

Lewis, Jerry, 118–123, 131, 235, 238, 285; and Brooks, 187, 215; and Sherman, 176

Lewis, Joe E., 161

Lewin, Kurt, 295–296
Lewis, Richard, 228–229, 260
Liebman, Max, 140
Liebman, Wendy, 280–281, 285
Life is Beautiful (film), 123
Life Stinks (film), 216
Lindbergh, Charles, 40, 107
Linkletter, Art, 275
Liszt.com, 281
Littlefield, Warren, 243–244
Loeb, Philip, 146
Lombard, Carole, 102
Lopez, Trini, 149
Lost in America (film), 217
Louis-Dreyfus, Julia, 245
Love and Death (film), 202
Lowell, A. Lawrence, 49
Lubitsch, Ernst, 101, 215
Ludwin, Rick, 244
Lunch with Soupy Sales (television
    show), 149
Lusitania (ship), 83

McCarey, Leo, 90–91
McCarthy, Joseph R., 157, 166
McFadden, George, 221
McGhee, Paul, 271
McGraw, John, 35
Malice in the Palace (film), 96
Maltin, Leonard, 80
Mama-loshen, 298, 305
Man on the Moon (film), 232
Manchuria, 7
Manhattan (film), 203–204, 208
Marie, Rose, 150
Marks, Charlie ("Dale"), 33–34, 50, 130
Marr, Sally, 169–170
Marriage: of Benny, 63; inter-, 27,
    94–95, 228; at a young age, 4

Martin, Dean, 118–120, 131, 162
Martin, Nora, 152
Marx, Chico, 68–69, 81–98. *See also*
    Marx Brothers
Marx, Groucho, xvi, xx, 57; autobiogra-
    phy of, 298; childhood of, 16, 17;
    entry of, into vaudeville, 42–46;
    and film, 81–98; and radio, 68–69;
    and television, 152–154. *See also*
    Marx Brothers
Marx, Gummo, 42–44. *See also* Marx
    Brothers
Marx, Harpo, xvi; autobiography of,
    297; childhood of, 17; entry of,
    into vaudeville, 42–46. *See also*
    Marx Brothers
Marx, Minnie, xx, 19, 42, 43. *See also*
    Marx Brothers
Marx, Sam, 5, 18. *See also* Marx Broth-
    ers
Marx, Zeppo, 44–45, 81–83. *See also*
    Marx Brothers
Marx Brothers, x, xvi–xvii, 15, 235; and
    anti-Semitism, 51; and Bruce, 175;
    entry of, into vaudeville, 42–46;
    and film, 81–98, 98, 102–103; and
    Kaye, 97; and Nazism, 102–103;
    and radio, 68–69; and Rudner,
    262
Mason, Jackie, xvii–xviii, xxi, 116,
    177–180, 221, 223, 269, 285
Mason, James, 37
Maude (television show), 264
Maven, 303
May, Elaine, 181–82
Mayer, Louis B., 99
May Laws, 7
Me and the Colonel (film), 103
Meara, Anne, 182, 250

Meir, Golda, 63–64
Mercury Theater, 115
Merrymakers, role of, 289–290
MGM, 92, 99
Michaels, Felicia, 279
Michaels, Lorne, 217, 264
Midler, Bette, 263
Mills Hotel, 11
Miner's Bowery Theater, 38
Minnelli, Liza, 274
Minstrel show, 39
Modern Romance (film), 217
Monkey Business (film), 87, 90
Mooney, Edward (cardinal), 106
Moreno, Wences (Señor Wences), 129
Morris, Howie, 141
Morris, William, 32
Mother (film), 217
Mount Zion, 18
Mr. Saturday Night (film), 218–219
MTV (Music Television Network), 249
Murray, Jan, 162
Muse, The (film), 217–218
Mutual aid societies (*Landsmanshaften*), 13, 122
My Friend Irma (film), 119

NAACP (National Association for the Advancement of Colored People), 168
Nanny, The (television show), 268–269
National Foundation for Jewish Culture, 276
National Jewish Population Survey, 228
Native Americans, 94–95, 254
Naughty Marionette, 201
Nazis, 63, 99–103, 108, 123, 137, 225; and anti-Semitism, 77–78; and Benny, 77–78, 101–102; and Brooks, 216,

283–284. *See also* Gestapo; Hitler, Adolf; Holocaust
NBC (National Broadcasting Corporation), 130, 144, 151, 243
Nebbish, 302
Network Allocation Plan, 74
New Deal, 106, 181
Newsweek, 133
New York Athletic Club, xv
New Yorker, The, 279
New York Evening Post, The, 7
New York Giants, 35
New York Times, The, xiv, 152
New York Tribune, The, 15
New York World's Fair, 63
Nichols, Mike, 181–182
Nietzche, Friedrich, 275
Night at the Opera (film), 87, 92–94
Night in Casablanca, A (film), 88, 102–103
Nixon, Richard, 168
Nudnick, 303
Nuremberg tribunal, 137
Nutty Professor (film), 119, 121–122, 235
Nye, Louis, 151

O'Brien, Pat, 46
O'Donnell, Mabel, 42
Office of War Information, 75, 103
Outside Shelley Berman (album), 184

Palace (vaudeville house), 28
Palace Cafeteria, 113
Palmer House, 139
Paper Moon (film), 263
Paramount Pictures, 92
Paramount Theater, 28–29
Partners Again, with Potash and Perlmutter (film), 80

Passover, 146

Pastor, Tony, 27

PBS (Public Broadcasting System), 217

Pearl Harbor, 76

Peewee Quartet, 22

Pelley, William Dudley, 106

Perelman, S. J., 92

Peretz, I. L., 305

Picon, Molly, 48

Pioneer Hotel, 116

Plato, 306

Play It Again Sam (film), xvi

Playboy, 255, 267

Playwrights Theater Club, 181

Pobedonostev, Konstantin, 6

Podhoretz, Norman, 169, 174

Poland, 4, 5, 76, 101. *See also* Eastern Europe

Presley, Elvis, 131

Press Agents Association, 274

Private Parts (Stern), 238

Producers, The (film), 209–211, 283–284

Producers, The (play), 210, 283–284

Protestants, 107, 291. *See also* Christianity

Protocols of the Elders Zion, 50

Purim, 289

Purimshpiels, 289–290

Queen Esther, 289

Rabbinical Court, 289

Rabbis, 18, 289

Race. *See* African Americans

Radner, Gilda, 264

Rainey, Bill, 72

Reagan, Ronald, 228, 239

Real Life (film), 217

Red Channels, 146

Red Cross, 75

Reik, Theodor, 306

Reilly, Larry, 23

Reiner, Carl, 146–147, 150, 186, 208, 244, 250

Reiner, Rob, 250

Reiser, Paul, 240, 247–248

Renan, Ernest, 287

Reuben, Aaron, 141

Rich, Frank, xiv

Richards, Michael, 245

Rickles, Don, 162, 223, 224, 236

Rivers, Joan, x, 117–118, 182, 221, 253–260, 262, 285

Rivers, Tony, 253

Rogers, Will, xii, 169

Rogin, Michael, 39–40

Room Service (film), 87–88

Roosevelt, Franklin D., 106, 108

Roseanne, 264–268

Rosenberg, Ethel, 157

Rosenberg, Julius, 157

Rosh Hashanah, 18, 124

Ross, Jeffrey, 278–281, 285

Ross, Stanley Ralph, 186

Rosten, Leo, 300

Roth, Philip, 182, 191

Rubin, Benny, 98

Rudner, Rita, 261–262

Rudy Vallee Show, 78

Russia, 4–8

Russian Orthodoxy, 6

Russo-Japanese War, 7

Sabbath, 12–13, 110

Sagansky, Jeff, 268

Sahl, Mort, xvii, 166–169, 171, 180, 221; and Berman, 184–185; and Brooks, 187; and Woody Allen, 188–189

Sales, Soupy, 149, 150
Salinger, J. D., 157
Salisbury, Cora, 46
Sandler, Adam, 250–252
Saturday Night Live (television show),
    217, 231–233, 250, 252, 264
Sayer, Leo, 216
Schadkhan, 303
Schindler's List (film), 247
Schlemiel, 302
Schlimazel, 203
Schlump, 303
Schmegagge, 303
Schmendrick, 303
Schnorrer, 303
Schoenberg, Minnie, 5
Schreiber, Avery, 182
Second City, 257–258
Secularization, 292–293, 297
Segregation, 109
Seinfeld, Jerry, ix–x, xvii, xxii, 227, 240,
    285, 304; early career of, 242–243;
    and television, 242–248, 270
Seinfeld (television show), 245–248, 270
Señor Wences, 129
Sephardic Jews, 5
Seven Frolics, 41–42
Shandling, Garry, 229–230
Shawn, Dick, 179
Shepherd, David, 181
Sherman, Allan, 176–177
Sidney, George, 80
Silent Movie (film), 214
Sills, Paul, 181, 182
Silver Legion, 106
Silvers, Phil, 15, 147, 148; childhood of, 16,
    17, 35; and television, 130, 134–135
Silver Shirts, 106
Simon, Neil, 33, 141, 202

Sinatra, Frank, 131, 149, 162
Sleeper (film), 201–202
Smalley, Stuart, 231
Small-Time Crooks (film), 208
Smith. *See* Sulzer, Joe ("Smith")
Smothers, Tommy, 61, 226
Smothers Brothers, 226
Songs of Tom Lehrer, The (album),
    175–176
Soupy's Soda Shop (television show), 149
Southern Methodist University, 62
Spanish Inquisition, 215
Spellman, Cardinal, 173–174
Spolin, Viola, 181
Springtime for Hitler (film), 209. *See also*
    The Producers (film)
State Department (United States), 99
Staten Island Ferry, 22
Steamship companies, 8–9
Stein, Joe, 141
Steinberg, David, 182, 226
Stereotypes, 31–32, 39, 57, 60, 148–149
Stern, Howard, 237–240, 244
Stewart, Jon, 249–250
Stiller, Ben, 250
Stiller, Jerry, 182, 250, 270–271
Storch, Larry, 162
Straw Hat Revue (play), 97
Streisand, Barbra, 263
Strikes, 15, 38
Stuart, Jason, 282
Sullivan, Ed, 55, 162, 179–180, 223, 265
Sulzer, Joe ("Smith"), 33–34, 50, 130
Sunset Boulevard (film), 115
Sunshine Boys, The (film), 33
Surprise Lake Camp, 38
Swan Lake Inn, 117
Sweet and Lowdown (film), 207
Synagogues, 17–18

Tags, development of, xix
Take the Money and Run (film), 185, 200–201
Talent agencies, 31
Talent Scouts (television show), 170
Talmud, xvii, 288, 289, 298
Taxi (television show), 234
Taxi Driver (film), 217
Taylor, Elizabeth, 257
Television (publication), 146
Television shows (listed by name)
    Admiral Broadway Revue, 140, 141
    All in the Family, 250, 264
    Benson, 242
    Caesar's Hour, 141
    Chicken Soup, 223
    The Daily Show, 249, 250
    Dick Van Dyke Show, 141, 150
    George Burns and Gracie Allen Show, 152
    The Golden Girls, 264
    Homicide, 236
    It's Garry Shandling's Show, 229
    I've Got a Secret, 176
    Jack Benny Program, 153–154
    Larry Sanders, 229–230, 249–250
    Laugh-In, 263
    Law and Order: Special Victims Unit, 236
    Lunch with Soupy Sales, 149
    Maude, 264
    The Nanny, 268–269
    Seinfeld, 245–248, 270
    Soupy's Soda Shop, 149
    Talent Scouts, 170
    Taxi, 234
    The Tonight Show, 224, 260
    You Bet Your Life, 152–153
    Your Show of Shows, 139, 140, 141

Temple, Shirley, 90
Texaco Star Theater, 129, 130
Thalberg, Irving, 92
Theatrical Drugstore, 113
Three Stooges, 35, 41; and film, 96–97, 100–101; and Nazism, 100–101
Three Nightingales, 42
Time magazine, x, 169, 184
To Be or Not to Be (film), 101, 102, 215–216
Tolkin, Mel, 141
Tonight Show, The (television show), 224, 260
Tony Awards, 210, 284
Torah, 298
Totem and Taboo (Freud), 305
Totem Lodge, 124
Tucker, Sophie, xix, 48, 274; and the blackface tradition, 40; childhood of, 4, 15
Tugend, Tom, 98
Tummler, 111
Twain, Marx, xii
Twelve Chairs, The (film), 210–211
2000-Year-Old Man, The (album), 186

Ulysses (Joyce), 210
Unions, 15. *See also* Strikes
United Nations, 225
University of Chicago, 181, 183
Up in Arms (film), 97–98
Usenet groups, 281
USO (United Service Organizations), 75, 76

Valentino, Rudolph, 170
Van Dyke, Dick, 141, 147, 150–151
Variety, 49–50, 76, 146
Vaudeville, 14, 20, 21–54, 56, 80

Victoria Theater, 31
Vietnam War, xii, 227
Village Vanguard, 115
Village Voice, 190
Vitagram Studio, 41

Waldheim, Kurt, 225
Waldoks, Moshe, 290
Wanger, Walter, 82
War Advertising Council, 74
War crimes, 137
Warner, Harry, 99–100
Warner Brothers, 99–100, 176, 212
War of Independence, 63
Warren, Rusty, 180
Washington, George, 132
Waterboy, The (film), 251
Weber, Joseph, 33–34, 50, 80
Weddings, rituals at, 289–290
Welch, Joe, 33, 50
Welles, Orson, 115
Wertheim, Arthur, 134
What Price Pants? (film), 81
What's Up, Doc? (film), 263
White Roe Lake, 114–115
Whoopee! (film), 94, 97
Wilder, Gene, 212, 213–214
William Morris Agency, 178
Williams, Robin, 234
Wilson, Don, 75
Winchell, Walter, 35
Wit and Its Relation to the Unconscious (Freud), 306
Wolff, David, 46
Woollcott, Alexander, 45
Works Progress Administration (WPA), 181
World According To Me, The (play), 179
World Series, xvii

World War I, 14, 50, 51, 104, 109–110, 170
World War II, xii, 62, 74, 97, 105, 107–108, 124; economic growth after, 156; image of Jewish women after, 254–255; and intermarriage rates, 228; Rickles during, 223; sense of responsibility after, in the American body politic, 199
Wynn, Ed, xvii, xx, 37, 65, 151; childhood of, 15; and film, 81, 84; and radio, 67; stage character of, 37–38

Yiddish, xiii, 12, 14, 22, 96–97; accent, deliberate use of, xix–x, 72–73; folklore, 38; newspapers, 14, 122; prevalence of, surveys on, 105; special status of, in the creation of the comedic spirit, xvii, 298–307
Yiddishkeit, 47
Yom Kippur, 17, 63, 124, 146
You Bet Your Life (television show), 152–153
You Nazty Spy (film), 100
Young and Rubicam, 63
Young Frankenstein (film), 213–214
Youngman, Henny, xx, 11, 17, 117, 150, 162–163, 167
You're Never Too Young (film), 120
Your Show of Shows (television show), 139, 140, 141

Zelig (film), 204–205
Ziegfeld, Florenz, 39
Ziegfeld's Follies, 37, 48
Zionism, 146, 277
Ziv, Avner, 296
Zmuda, Bob, 232

PUBLICAFFAIRS is a new nonfiction publishing house and a tribute to the standards, values, and flair of three persons who have served as mentors to countless reporters, writers, editors, and book people of all kinds, including me.

I. F. STONE, proprietor of *I. F. Stone's Weekly*, combined a commitment to the First Amendment with entrepreneurial zeal and reporting skill and became one of the great independent journalists in American history. At the age of eighty, Izzy published *The Trial of Socrates*, which was a national bestseller. He wrote the book after he taught himself ancient Greek.

BENJAMIN C. BRADLEE was for nearly thirty years the charismatic editorial leader of *The Washington Post*. It was Ben who gave the *Post* the range and courage to pursue such historic issues as Watergate. He supported his reporters with a tenacity that made them fearless, and it is no accident that so many became authors of influential, best-selling books.

ROBERT L. BERNSTEIN, the chief executive of Random House for more than a quarter century, guided one of the nation's premier publishing houses. Bob was personally responsible for many books of political dissent and argument that challenged tyranny around the globe. He is also the founder and was the longtime chair of Human Rights Watch, one of the most respected human rights organizations in the world.

. . .

For fifty years, the banner of Public Affairs Press was carried by its owner Morris B. Schnapper, who published Gandhi, Nasser, Toynbee, Truman, and about 1,500 other authors. In 1983 Schnapper was described by *The Washington Post* as "a redoubtable gadfly." His legacy will endure in the books to come.

Peter Osnos, *Publisher*